D... *...ights seeking Christ*

The Knights of Columbus
Colorado Knights of Columbus Charities Fund, Inc. • USA

IMPRIMI POTEST
Richard J. Baumann, S.J.

NIHIL OBSTAT
William C. Beckman
Censor Librorum

IMPRIMATUR
+ Most Reverend Charles J. Chaput, O.F.M. Cap.
Archbishop of Denver
February 25, 2004

The *Nihil Obstat* and Imprimatur are official declarations that the work contains nothing contrary to Faith and Morals. It is not implied thereby that those granting Nihil Obstat and Imprimatur agree with the contents, statements, or opinions expressed.

ACKNOWLEDGEMENT
Additional meditation materials may obtained from Fr. Mark Link's Vision 2000 series of scripture devotions (Action 2000, Mission 2000, Vision 2000) which follow the 3-year Lectionary cycle.

Direct inquiries to the Colorado Knights of Columbus:
  K2C@KofC-Colorado.org   toll free: 1-800-796-4166
  For ordering information visit: http://kofc-colorado.org/K2C/index.html

Printed in Canada

ISBN 0-9707008-1-4

Contents

Charles J. Chaput, O.F.M. Cap.

People have rightly written and said a great deal over the last 40 years about the importance of the lay apostolate. No vocation in the Church has a monopoly on holiness, and many a priest struggling with doubt or fatigue has recovered his own strength by drawing on the witness of good lay men and women.

In my own priesthood, the steadiest, most fruitful lay witness I've encountered has always come from the Knights of Columbus. Week in and week out, the Knights are always there to serve the Church, and no bishop ever forgets how vital they are to his own ministry and to the needs of his people.

But even the most devoted workers in the vineyard need to rest in the Lord and refresh their faith. "Knights to Christ" is a wonderful source of spiritual nourishment and a great way for every Knight to anchor himself in the roots of his apostolate.

May God grant everyone who opens and reads this little book the joy of His presence and the zeal to serve the Gospel in a way that brings Jesus Christ to the whole world, and the whole world to Jesus Christ.

+Charles J. Chaput, O.F.M. Cap.
Archbishop of Denver
Colorado State Chaplain
Knights of Columbus 1999-2001

My fellow Knights,

    Welcome our "Knights to Christ" meditation book based on the work of Fr. Mark Link, S.J., renowned author, lecturer and retreat master.

    I was introduced to Fr. Link's work when challenged by Fr. Ken Leone, Pastor of St. Frances of Cabrini Parish and Chaplain of Council 9349 in Littleton, Colorado, on offering spirituality to the Knights of Columbus. Fr. Leone

Robert G. "Jerry" O'Connor

informed me that men of all ages were starving for spirituality yet it is offered by few Catholic organizations.

    Upon reading Fr. Link's daily meditation books, I was hooked on spirituality! It was then, as District Deputy that I had the vision for "Knights to Christ". In time I realized the power in Fr. Link's books when two of my brothers returned to their Catholic faith after adopting his daily meditation. May you enjoy the power of "the Word of God" each day to strengthen your Catholic Faith while living more fully principles of the Knights of Columbus.

    I want to thank my wife Trudy for her support, Steve Hesprich, my assistant, and his team from Our Lady of Loreto council number 12336, headed by Mark Flores, Editor, for their sacrifice and efforts in making "Knights to Christ" a reality.

"...for the greater honor and glory of God".

Fraternally,

Jerry O'Connor
State Deputy, 1999-2001

As iron sharpens iron, so man sharpens his fellow man.
~ Proverbs 27:17

Most men desire to build, to create, and to be successful. Some succeed greatly. Some fail miserably. But even among those who have lived a life of accomplishment, often there are some regrets. The admiration of our colleagues and all the money in the world will never make up for a child that hungers for a father, a wife that desires intimacy, or a parish that is lacking in leadership.

This is where our fraternity comes in. Together, we can bring true meaning to our Faith. We can be strong fathers and attentive husbands. We can build solid friendships among our brethren. We can excel at our professions, and we can be practical Catholic gentlemen.

Today, more than ever, our society needs solid, responsible and confident men who will lead out of love, compassion and respect for others. God is calling us to play a noble role that no one else can. If we heed that call and "sharpen" one another's understanding of what it means to be a Knight, then our greatest source of manhood will be revealed to us – Jesus Christ.

I am not a professional writer; and, although all errors of fact and judgment are exclusively my own, I would like to acknowledge with sincere gratitude those who assisted me in the preparation of this volume.

I owe a special debt of gratitude to an outstanding institution, the public library system of Arapahoe County in Colorado. Throughout my months of research, the library fulfilled all of my requests for material with amazing promptness and courtesy.

The *Knights to Christ* project, code-named *"K2C"*, is the culmination of the vision of Sir Knight Jerry O'Connor, the State Deputy of Colorado. I met with Jerry one Sunday evening and his passion for K2C has fueled my journey all the way to the summit of this project. Thanks, Jerry, for the opportunity to reach out to our brothers across our great state.

I would not be involved with this special project were it not for Sir Knight Steve Hesprich. Steve brought me on board and essentially turned me loose on it. Thank you, Steve, for entrusting me with K2C, and your continued friendship.

I would be remiss if I did not acknowledge Mark Link, S.J., who contributed the bulk of the meditations contained herein. I highly recommend any of Fr. Link's other works for Knights seeking a higher plane of spirituality.

I would like to acknowledge the research efforts of Sir Knight Joe McAleer, who coordinated initial efforts to categorize Fr. Link's works under the four principles of Knighthood. Joe was ably assisted by Brother Knights Mike Mullen and Ron Gerber. Their work saved countless hours of research and provided a solid foundation to build upon. Mr. John Sprague made important contributions to the selection of Saints entries for inclusion in the book. The editorial suggestions, understanding cooperation, and constant encouragement from Brother Knight Jeremiah Joiner inspired me to finish this book.

Special thanks to my brothers at Our Lady of Loreto, my home parish. Brother Knight Terry Zugates gave our cover design the professional look it so richly deserves. Sir Knight John Russo and Brother Knight George Brown reviewed the initial draft and delighted in bringing precision to the Scriptures and offering editorial commentary. Sir Knight Terry Retzke teamed with Kathy Schneider and assisted materially in the preparation of many of the

Unity entries from the second quarter onward. Terry has been steadfast in promoting spirituality in our council and I have always admired the manner in which he lives the Good News. Sir Knight Duane "Skip" Munger inspired all references to Fr. Vincent R. Capodanno, a great Catholic American. When Skip presented me with a St. Christopher medal earlier this year, little did I know he was continuing the legacy of Fr. Vincent. Thanks, Skip, for your counsel and fellowship which I cannot ever adequately acknowledge.

As with everything else in my life, this volume would not have been possible without the encouragement, assistance and criticisms offered from the very beginning by my wife, Melissa, whose help during these bewildering months will now have to be repaid.

To our three boys – Christian, Douglas & Zev – and our newborn daughter, Demeris Hope: Yes, the book for the Knights is done – we can play now!

Vivat Jesu,

Mark D. Flores, Editor-in-Chief
Our Lady of Loreto Council 12336
Fr. Vincent R. Capodanno Assembly 2617
Foxfield, Colorado

September 1, 2000

We few, we happy few, we band of brothers;
For he today that sheds his blood with me shall be my brother;
be he ne'er so vile, this day shall gentle his condition.
~ Shakespeare, Henry V

THE SPIRIT OF FATHER MCGIVNEY:
PRIEST AND APOSTLE

Descriptions are never easy. Memory is imperfect and it is hard to find exactly the right words to capture the skin tones, the shape of the nose, the highlights of the hair. Television police dramas are filled with the proof of the fallibility of the ability to remember. Paradoxically, one does not have the same difficulties capturing the spirit of the person, their inner values and attitudes. These leave an impression deeper than physical characteristics. It is this inner profile, the contours of his spirituality, that we seek of Father Michael J. McGivney, who died more than a century ago. Retrieving his spirit and spirituality from the scant records of the past is not easy nor is the task anywhere yet complete. It is an important exercise, however, because this little book, "*Knights to Christ*," is based upon the spiritual vision of our founder. Drawing together texts from Sacred Scripture, the Fathers of the Church and other spiritual writers, it is intended to lead each Knight more deeply into the spirituality that flows from the heart of Father McGivney, priest and apostle. May all who use this little book come to know Father McGivney through imitation of his example of heroic charity.

Michael J. McGivney was a man of his times: son of Irish immigrant parents in a part of the country charged with anti-Catholic sentiment, he knew the meaning of deprivation and poverty. The effects of alcoholism and domestic violence in the immigrant community were inescapable and the young McGivney knew first hand the disastrous consequences of poor working conditions and unfair labor practices for the family. Such cultural conditions produced in him a heart sensitive to the sufferings and misery of others. As a youngster in a good Catholic home he discovered that his strength came from the bonds of faith and love which knit his family together, prepared each of them for life in the world and kept them close to the Church of Christ. Early in his teens the desire to spend himself for others and draw them to Christ became a vocation to the priesthood. Though never physically robust, his sensitive nature and priestly heart led him to pour himself out, often beyond the limits of his health, in providing for the spiritual and material needs of those committed to his care.

Though he carried out all of his sacramental and pastoral duties with care, and identified with his parishioners in their sufferings and struggles, it was betterment of young Catholics that so preoccupied Father McGivney throughout his entire life.

The founding of the Knights of Columbus when he was but 29 years old is the great monument to his pastoral vision and concern. He was determined to form a brotherhood for young Catholic working and professional men which would support them in their faith, provide for the care of their families, especially those left behind by sudden or untimely death, and channel the charity of their time and service to the needs of the less fortunate and the works of the Church. The phenomenal success and growth of the Knights of Columbus did not come without the price of exhausting research and preparations, delicate relationships between officers and members, skillful molding of the spirit and organization of the earliest members of the Order and constancy in the face of the opposition and criticism which came from other priests.

Father McGivney *the priest,* Father McGivney *the apostle to the young* – these were expressions of his deep attachment to the eternal high priest, Jesus Christ. To speak of him as priestly, even in the most adverse of situations, is to say that he was always Christlike. He signs one of his few surviving letters, "In the Sacred Heart." The source of his patience, his endurance, and his inexhaustible charity was the Sacred Heart of Jesus. Nineteenth century Catholic piety was centered on the Sacred Heart and the McGivney family would have been no exception. All of the priestliness and charity of Michael McGivney found its source in Christ and was an attempt to draw others into that circle of love which exists between Christ and his Church. Michael McGivney was in love with Jesus Christ and his Church and spent his short life on earth finding new ways to express that love and to share it with others.

The few photographs we have of him suggest that Father McGivney was somewhat retiring in disposition. Some have seen in him a certain severity. But the record is clear that McGivney, God's servant and priest, was friendly and open, had a delightful sense of humor and drew the young of the parish to himself with
unfailing magnetism. It was his work with the young, however, that was charismatic and unusual. As any priest, he wanted the men and women of his parish to be good Catholics, but he wanted them to enjoy life at the same time. He celebrated Mass for them and preached his sermons. He heard their confessions and lent a willing ear to their difficulties and struggles. He outdid himself, however, in preparing entertainment, plays, fairs, any wholesome fun which would bring joy and a bit of diversion in a world where there was little leisure and even less money to provide an easier life.

One of the most famous of Father McGivney's spiritual friends was Chip Smith, an Irish lad condemned to death for the drunken murder of a policeman. The young curate at St. Mary's devoted himself to the spiritual welfare of young Smith, visiting him daily in the New Haven jail, arranging a High Mass to be celebrated there before his death, complete with choir to provide the music, and walked with him to the gallows. The priest and the condemned man embraced. Smith expressed his gratitude for the priestly guidance and support which made it possible for him to face death with courage and tranquility. In the end it was the devoted priest who carried away the burden of sorrow which he lifted from the young man's shoulders. He was long afterwards affected by that encounter.

It was from these two characteristics of his spirituality, as *priest* and *apostle to the young* that Father McGivney came to be an *apostle for Christian family life*. His convictions about the sanctity of family life and its importance for Church and society came from his own experience of what the loss of a parent can mean or the chaos which results when Christian ideals do not reign in the home. His program for the formation of strong Christian families can be found in the fraternal order of the Knights of Columbus. A knight is a man of courage, duty and honor. A Knight of Columbus is a Catholic, a man of faith, who accepts the responsibilities of his vocation with courage and honor. He depends upon God and his brother Knights to fulfill the duties of his state in life. He is called to be a better husband and father because he is a Knight of Columbus. For Father McGivney the Knights of Columbus were as much a program for spiritual formation as a benevolent society which cares for the widow and orphan. Membership in the Knights of Columbus is not meant to take a man from his home, but to prepare him to go to his family strengthened in his relationship with Jesus Christ and renewed in his resolve to spend himself for others as Christ did.

Father McGivney was *priest and apostle* and we pray that one day we will be able to add one more title … canonized saint.

Rev. Gabriel B. O'Donnell, O.P.
Postulator, The Father McGivney Guild
One Columbus Plaza; New Haven, CT 06410

CHARITY _____

Love the Lord your God with all your heart, with all your soul, and with all your strength, and with all your mind; and love your neighbor as yourself.
~ Luke 10:27

There are three theological virtues: faith, hope and CHARITY. These virtues are gifts from God, given to us in Baptism. CHARITY is the greatest of the three (1 Corinthians 13:13).

CHARITY empowers us to love God and one another as Jesus loved us. Why do we often refer to it as CHARITY, and not simply love?

The Greek language (the New Testament was written in Greek) uses three words to designate love: *eros*, *philia*, and *agape*. *Eros* referred to sexual love. *Philia* refers to friendship love. *Agape* is Christian love. It was translated as CHARITY to stress its uniqueness. It begins in time and reaches perfection in eternity. Paul wrote:

What no one ever saw or heard, what no one thought could happen, is the very thing God prepared for those who love him.
~ 1 Corinthians 2:9

UNITY

Father!... May they be one, so that the world will believe that you sent me.
~ John 17:21

One Sunday morning, an old African chief was present at the celebration of the Eucharist. Tears flooded his eyes as he watched members of the Ngoni, Senga, and Tumbuka tribes worshipping side by side. Suddenly, his mind flashed back to his boyhood, when he used to watch Ngoni warriors, after a day's fighting, wash Senga and Tumbuka blood from their spears and bodies. The contrast between what he had seen then and what he saw now was the difference between night and day.

That morning, the wise, old chief understood as never before, the meaning of Christianity. It is about God calling all people to join hands and hearts in and through Christ, and live together in UNITY.

As Knights, we have heard that call and dedicate ourselves to live and promote that UNITY in our councils, our families, and our nation.

Give me faith, LORD,
and let me help others find it.
~ Leo Tolstoy

FRATERNITY

How wonderful it is, how pleasant, for God's people to live together in harmony! ~ Psalm 133:1

Edward R. Murrow was one of the first news commentators to use the media with power and skill. Morrow made this provocative statement: "Someday, we'll be able to talk to our audience any place in the world, almost any time we want. When that day comes, what will we say?"

By the time of Murrow's death in 1965, that prediction had already come true. But we still haven't decided what to say. Someone suggested giving serious consideration to the words of Dr. Martin Luther King, Jr.:

"We must learn to live together as brothers or perish together as fools."

As Knights, we commit ourselves to live as brothers not only in our council, but also in our family and our world.

A friend loves at all times, and a brother is born for adversity. ~ Proverbs 17:17

PATRIOTISM _____

Blessed is the nation whose God is the LORD, the people chosen as His very own. ~ Psalm 33:12

Governor Adlai Stevenson delivered a memorable address to the American Legion convention in New York City. About the meaning of PATRIOTISM, he said:

I venture to suggest that what we mean is a sense of national responsibility which will enable America to remain master of her power – to walk with it in serenity and wisdom, with self-respect and the respect of all mankind; a patriotism which is not short, frenzied outbursts of emotion, but the tranquil and steady dedication of a lifetime.

These are words that are easy to utter, but this is a mighty assignment. For it is often easier to fight for principles than to live up to them.

The Knights are willing to fight for those principles. Through our leadership, the words "under God" were inserted in the Pledge of Allegiance. We are committed to continued unselfish service to our nation.

A man's country is not just a certain area of land. It is a principle, and patriotism is loyalty to that principle.
~ Walter Scott

This booklet is composed of 366 daily meditations on the Knightly values of CHARITY, UNITY, FRATERNITY, and PATRIOTISM. Notable fixed dates throughout the calendar year are referenced and a corresponding meditation is catered to that date as appropriate.

We begin each meditation by reciting the following prayer reverently:

Almighty God,
Look upon our assembly of Knights
And fill us with the spirit of your wisdom.
May we always act in accordance with your will,
And may our bonds as brothers deepen as we journey toward you in faith.
Just as you led the wise men by the light of a star to your infant Son,
Ennoble us with the resolve to become shining stars for our nation
And for your greater honor and glory.
AMEN!

After reciting this introductory prayer, we follow these four steps:

❑ We *read* the meditation prayerfully. When we finish, we return to any part of it that struck us in a special way.

(Spend about one minute on this step)

❑ We *think* about the part that struck us. Why were you drawn to it?

(Spend about four minutes on this step)

❑ We *speak* to God about our thoughts, speaking to him as we would to a close and trusted friend.

(Spend about one minute on this step)

❑ We *listen* to God's response. We simply rest in God's presence with an open mind and an open heart.

(Spend about four minutes on this step)

End each daily meditation by praying the *Our Father* or the *Hail Mary* slowly and reverently.

Some practical considerations _____

Prayer Time – When something becomes important to us, we don't leave it to chance. We schedule it right into our daily lives.

In other words, just as a physical fitness program requires a time commitment, so does a spiritual fitness program. In his book, *Hungry for God*, Ralph Martin wrote:

A real estate man I know gets up early in the morning to pray; an aerospace engineer prays and reads Scripture on his lunch hour; a production manager for a computing firm prays after the children are in bed.

And so the first step in a meditation program is to build into our daily schedule a ten-minute period for raising our minds and hearts to God.

Three meditation periods that some people have tried and found helpful are:

     ❏ After showering in the morning

     ❏ During your noon lunch break

     ❏ Just before retiring

Prayer Place – The *Little Brothers* is a religious order whose vocation is to live among the poor, praying for them and sharing their lot.

The first thing a Little Brother does when he moves into a poor area is to set up a place where he can pray. Often a mat on the floor, before a crucifix on a wall, is sufficient. A second-century writer, Origen, wrote:

Any place can be a suitable place for prayer. But, we would do well, if possible, to find a place in our own home, where we won't be disturbed, and pray there.

Many people find that a "prayer chair", located in a bedroom or side room of the house, makes a good prayer place.

Next to the chair, it helps to have a table with a Bible, a crucifix, your *K2C* book or some other meditation book, a writing pad for jotting down your thoughts, and a pen or pencil.

Prayer Posture – Author Warren Young asks: "How much would we give for a formula that guaranteed to make us look younger, brighter, more attractive – and feel that way, too?"

He goes on to explain that the formula is built right into our body. Maintain a good posture (Try straightening your back as you read this, and see what he means). Posture plays an important role in prayer as well. Here are three points to check, when it comes to prayer posture:

❏ *Are you comfortable?* Many people find sitting in a comfortable chair is a good posture for praying. They also find that it helps to keep the back fairly straight. Believe it or not, a straight back helps to cut down on distractions.

❏ *Are your eyes at rest?* It sometimes helps to fix them on something, like a picture of Jesus on a wall. Sometimes closing your eyes helps. Just experiment.

❏ *Is your breathing smooth and relaxed?* Don't strain, but try to set up a slow, rhythmic pattern of inhaling and exhaling (Close your eyes and try this now to see how it induces a certain peace).

Prayer Expectancy – Feeling the presence of God is a rare gift. When and if God gives it to us, we simply rest in his presence with a grateful heart. Any effort on our part, however, to try to *feel* the presence of God is usually always wrong.

In his book, *The Taste of New Wine*, Keith Miller says that when he began a meditation program, he was concerned because he did not *feel* God's presence.

One day, he shared his concern with a friend. Then, it suddenly dawned on him that *feeling* is not the point of *praying*. This gave him a new insight into himself and his problem. He wrote:

"I had always wanted to feel God's presence in my prayers and I became depressed when I didn't... so I tried praying... whether I felt spiritual or not and found for the first time in my life that we can live on raw faith. Moreover, I found that often the very act of praying this way brings later a closer sense of God's presence."

Miller's final point is an important one. The *grace of prayer* often comes not during the time of prayer, but outside it – later on. In other words, seeds planted during prayer often take time to germinate.

Miller was also disturbed by distractions that he experienced during prayer. His mind would flit from a phone call he should make to a letter he should write.

A friend suggested he keep a notepad next to his 'prayer chair'. When such thoughts came to mind, he could just jot them down and continue praying. He did this, and to his surprise he found that a number of distractions were things he should do. He discovered that God can even speak to us through our distractions.

Saint Francis de Sales puts a similar spin on distractions. He writes that if distractions are handled properly, they can enhance prayer. When they occur, he says:

Bring your wayward heart back home quietly. If you did nothing else during prayer but return your heart continually and patiently to the Master's side, your time of prayer would be well spent.

Prayer Journal – A journal is simply a brief record of thoughts, distractions, feelings or ideas that occurred during our mediation.

Some find it helpful to address these notations directly to God. For example:

LORD,
Thank you for the peace you put into my heart during prayer this morning. Help me maintain this peace during this day, because I have some difficult conferences scheduled.

Notations need not be long. This much is certain. Journaling is a proven way to get in touch with our deeper self. You become tuned to the wordless conversation going on in the depths of our being between God and ourselves. It also facilitates our faith sharing in small groups with Brother Knights.

That brings us to a final, important point. Many find it to be one of the highlights and surprises of a meditation commitment.

Faith Sharing – It is strongly recommended that every Knight join a faith sharing group of brothers who meet regularly, preferably weekly.

These meetings can take place at the office before work, during the noon lunch break, at the home of a host, or in a parish room after Saturday morning Mass. The purpose of the meetings is support and sharing. Meetings should last 30-40 minutes unless the group decides otherwise.

Beginning Meetings _____

Meetings start with a *Call to Prayer*. A member lights a candle and the following prayer is said reverently:

FIRST READER
Jesus said, "I am the light of the world…
Whoever follows me will have the light of life
And will never walk in darkness." ~ John 8:12

SECOND READER
Lord Jesus,
You also said that where two or three come together in your name,
You are there with them.
The light of this candle symbolizes your presence among us.

THIRD READER
And, Lord Jesus,
Where you are,
There too are the Father and the Spirit.
And so we begin our meeting in the presence and name
Of the Father,
The Son,
And the Holy Spirit.

The meeting proper begins with the leader responding briefly to these two questions:

How faithful was I to my commitment to reflect daily on the Bible reading?
Which daily meditation hit home for me and why?

*Closing Meetings*_____

All meetings end with a *Call to Mission*: a charge to witness to
Jesus in daily life. It consists in reverently praying the following:

FIRST READER
We conclude our meeting by listening to Jesus say to us
What he said to his disciples in his Sermon on the Mount:

SECOND READER
"You are like light for the whole world. A city built on a hill cannot
be hid...

No one lights a lamp and puts it under a bowl;
Instead, it is put on a lamp stand,
Where it gives light for everyone in the house.

In the same way
Your light must shine before people,
So that they will see the good things you do
And praise your Father in heaven. ~ Matthew 5:14-16

At this point, a member of the group extinguishes the candle that
was lit at the beginning of the meeting. Then the final reader
continues:

FINAL READER
The light of this candle is now extinguished.
But the light of Christ in each of us must continue to shine in our
lives.
Toward this end, we pray together the LORD's Prayer:
"Our Father..."

(N.B.: For handy reference, the above Meeting Format is printed on page 375 of this book.)

We conclude our meditation program by asking God's blessing on our effort, and with this thought to motivate us:

To fall in love with God
Is the greatest of all romances;
To seek God,
The greatest adventure;
To find God,
The greatest human achievement.

January 1

CHARITY is renewing our commitment to the Church

Be transformed by the renewing of your mind. ~ Romans 12:2

At the dawn of the new millennium, Pope John Paul II invited the faithful to recommit to the Gospel by taking a pledge to work for peace and justice. It reads as follows:

As disciples of Jesus in the new millennium, I [we] pledge to –
- ❏ Pray regularly for greater justice and peace
- ❏ Learn more about Catholic social teaching and its call to protect human life, stand with the poor, and care for creation.
- ❏ Reach across boundaries of religion, race, ethnicity, gender, and disabling conditions.
- ❏ Live justly in family life, school, work, the marketplace, and the political arena.
- ❏ Serve those who are poor and vulnerable, sharing more time and talent.
- ❏ Give more generously to those in need at home and abroad.
- ❏ Advocate for public policies that protect human life, promote human dignity, preserve God's creation, and build peace.
- ❏ Encourage others to work for greater charity, justice, and peace.

The Jubilee Pledge is the Holy Father's call to action. How can we as Knights serve the poor and work for justice in each of the areas noted in the pledge?

Every day we ought to renew our purpose.
~ Thomas á Kempis

January 2

UNITY is lending your strength to our council

I am the vine, and you are the branches. Those who remain in me and I in them, will bear much fruit. ~ John 15:5

A popular tradition concerns a Greek slave, named Aesop. Like Jesus, he used stories to teach people, especially small children. One of his stories is about a man who had several sons who were always fighting among themselves. One day he called them together and set in front of them a bundle of branches. Then he invited each son to try to break the bundle in half.
Of course, none of them could break the bundle. But when the father untied the bundle and gave the branches – one by one – to the sons to break, they broke them with ease. The father then made his point:
"My sons, if you remain united, you will be able to withstand any enemy. If you do not remain united, any enemy will be able to defeat you." ~ Mark Link, S.J.

How am I contributing to the unity of our council?

If one part of the body suffers, all the other parts suffer with it.
~ 1 Corinthians 12:26

January 3

FRATERNITY is a spirit of collective pride

How wonderful it is, how pleasant, for God's people to live together in harmony! ~ Psalm 133:1

Jerry Kramer was a star member of the legendary Green Bay Packers. In his best-selling book, *Instant Replay*, he describes his feelings after a big win. We rushed to the locker room… shouting and absolutely floating. "Magnificent," Coach Lombardi said… He couldn't finish the sentence… Tears started trickling down his cheek. He just knelt down crying, and led us in the *Our Father*… The guys walked around the room, hugging each other… I felt so good. I felt so proud, proud of myself and proud of my teammates and proud of my coaches… It sent a beautiful shiver up my back.
~ Mark Link, S.J.

What was the closest you ever came to this same feeling of fellowship and fraternity with your Brother Knights?

In Christ there is no East or West,
In Him no South or North,
But one great fellowship of love
Throughout the whole wide earth.
~ Old hymn

PATRIOTISM is having the courage to dream

Jesus said, "What is humanly impossible is possible for God."
~ Luke 18:27

Robert E. Sherwood was a speechwriter for President Franklin Roosevelt. He also won the Pulitzer Prize in drama three times.
On one occasion – mustering all the drama at his command – he
said we must dedicate ourselves to two objectives: the achievement
of world peace and the affirmation of the right of every person to
live as the image of God. He added, "To those who say that these
unlimited objectives are unthinkable, impossible, let us reply that it
is the alternative to them which is unthinkable, impossible."
He concluded by calling upon America to dedicate itself to the
achievement of these unlimited objectives as boldly and as
confidently as our forefathers, "who proved that… nothing
undertaken by free men and free women is impossible."
~ Mark Link, S.J.

We Knights have remained true to our heritage of faith, fellowship
and philanthropy. What dream do you have for the Knights that
would continue to build on this proud heritage for future
generations?
Sir Knights, what were your aspirations when you attained the
Fourth Degree?

*When you dream alone, it remains a dream, but when you dream
with others, it can become a reality.*
~ Kahlil Gibran

January 5

CHARITY is stumbling into warm hands

My son, your sins are forgiven. ~ Mark 2:5

Harold Hughes described himself as "a drunk, a liar, and a cheat."
He was so convinced he'd never change that he decided to end it all.
At that moment, however, he remembered enough from the Bible to
realize that to take one's life was wrong. So he knelt down sobbing
and explained to God why he was going to end it all. Suddenly,
something happened that he never experienced before in his life. He
wrote later:
"God was reaching down and touching me. Like a stricken child
lost in a storm, I suddenly stumbled into the warm hands of my
Father. Joy filled me, so intense it seemed to burst my breast…"
Ten years later, Harold Hughes was elected governor of Iowa.
~ Mark Link, S.J.

Have you ever turned down or avoided participation in a Knights
activity? Would the Father's warm touch have helped you see it
through?

I have swept away your sins like a cloud.
Comeback to me; I am the one who saves you.
~ Isaiah 44:22

January 6

UNITY is paying back a sacrifice

Happy is the person who remains faithful under trials.
~ James 1:12

It was the first year for canoe racing in the 1924 Olympics. Bill
Havens was on the four-man team to represent the U.S. in Paris.
But as the time for departure neared, it was clear that his wife would
give birth to their first child while he was away. Bill hesitated. His
wife insisted that he go. But the more Bill thought about it, the
more he felt his priorities lay with his wife and their first child. An
alternate member took Bill's place.
The team went to Paris and won the gold. Meanwhile, Bill's wife
was late in giving birth to a boy, whom they would name Frank.
Bill never mentioned his disappointment in missing out on the
Olympics.
In 1952, Bill got a cable from Helsinki, where the Olympics were
going on. It read:

I'm bringing home
the gold medal you lost
while waiting for me to be born. ~ *Frank*
~ Mark Link, S.J.

What was the biggest sacrifice you've made for your family? What
was the biggest sacrifice you've made for your council?

If you want the rainbow, you gotta put up with the rain.
~ D. Parton

January 7

FRATERNITY is service to Church, country and council

Do not those who plot evil go astray? But those who plan what is good find love and faithfulness. ~ Proverbs 14:22 NIV

In corporate America, it's sometimes difficult to climb the ladder of so-called "success" without sacrificing the ideals of living as a Catholic gentleman. The long hours at the expense of your family, the political back-stabbing among colleagues, the cutthroat competitive environment, and today's me-oriented, material culture all run contrary to Catholic teaching. ~ A Sir Knight

Ideally, we, as Knights, never plot evil. But do we unwittingly forget to do what is right and just in our everyday lives?

Goodness is the only investment that never fails.
~ Henry David Thoreau

January 8

CHARITY is digging even when all hope is lost

God is love... Perfect love drives out all fear. ~ 1 John 4:16, 18

In 1988 a terrible earthquake in Armenia killed 30,000 people. Minutes after it hit, a father ran to his son's school building and found it completely flattened.
Remembering that his son's classroom was in the back right corner of the building, he went there and began digging furiously. They told him it was hopeless, but he kept digging. In the 38th hour of digging, he heard his son's voice calling, "Dad!"
Incredibly, a tiny wedge shape had formed, leaving just enough space for his son and thirteen other boys to survive.
The son said to his dad, "I told the others not to worry. I knew you'd come for me and then they would be saved too."
That beautiful story is a kind of parable of how we should trust our heavenly Father, whose love for us exceeds all imagining.
~ Mark Link, S.J.

What gives some people so much trust? As Knights, are we prepared to trust in God even in the gravest situations?

I will never forget you!
I have written your name on the palms of my hands.
~ Isaiah 49:16

January 9

UNITY is lighting up the darkness together

*Your light must shine before people... so that they will praise your
Father .* ~ Matthew 5:16

Some villages in India are totally without electricity. People use
tiny oil lamps, much like those used in Jesus' time, to light their
homes.
The temple in one of these rural villages has a large frame hanging
from its ceiling. Cut into the frame are a hundred slots into which
tiny oil lamps can be placed.
When the people go there after dark, they carry their oil lamps from
their homes to guide them through the darkness. Upon arriving in
the temple, they place their lamp in one of the slots. By the time the
last villager arrives, the darkness has been dispelled and in its place
is a glorious sea of light.
~ Mark Link, S.J.

What keeps you from becoming the spark of light that we Knights
have pledged to create to dispel the darkness in our world?

Every believer in this world must become a spark of light.
~ Pope John XXIII

January 10

FRATERNITY is kneeling next to a brother

Those who declare publicly that they belong to me, I will do the same for them before my Father in heaven. ~ Matthew 10:32

One Sunday morning, not long after the Civil War, a freed slave wandered into a fashionable church in Richmond, Virginia.
When the time for Communion came, to the consternation of many present, the ex-slave walked up to receive.
Sensing the mood of these people, a prominent, respected man walked down the aisle and knelt next to his black brother. That man's courageous witness set an example that day that no one forgot.
The man was Robert E. Lee, former general of the Confederate army. ~ Story told by Billy Graham

What are some of the things that keep me from witnessing to brotherhood in my life?

Shine through me and be so in me that every soul I come in contact with may feel your presence in my spirit.
~ John Henry Newman

January 11

PATRIOTISM is serving the LORD and your people

The Son of Man did not come to be served; he came to serve.
~ Matthew 20:28

On Thursday evening, April 12th, 1945, radio stations interrupted all broadcasts to announce President Roosevelt's death. It was critical, because World War II was at a crucial point.
Harry Truman was sworn in as president. Later, Truman addressed Congress. His final words were dramatic.
He lifted his face upward, raised his arms to heaven and said:
"I humbly pray Almighty God, in the words of King Solomon: Give me... an understanding heart to judge Thy people, that I may discern between good and bad... I ask only to be a good and faithful servant of my LORD and my people (1 Kings 3:9)."
~ Mark Link, S.J.

What is one way you and your Brother Knights might better serve our nation? Sir Knights, what patriotic project has your assembly tackled this year?

Do a little more than you're paid to do;
Give a little more than you have to;
Try a little harder than you want to;
Aim a little higher than you think possible.
~ Art Linkletter

January 12

CHARITY is a heart full of love

If we love others, we live in the light... But if we hate others, we are still in the darkness; we walk in it and do not know where we are going, because the darkness has made us blind.
~ 1 John 2:10-11

In Feodor Dostoevski's novel, *The Brothers Karamazov*, a distraught woman comes to Father Zosima for help. She says that if he cannot help her, she thinks she will end her own life.
Her problem is that she no longer believes in God. She came to this point bit by bit without realizing it. Now her life is meaningless. All ashes!
Father Zosima tells her she must go home and, without fail – and in a practical way, every day – love the people around her.
If she does this, he promises, bit-by-bit she will come to the point where she'll find it impossible *not* to believe in God.
~ Mark Link, S.J.

What is Father Zosima's point; and why do/ don't you tend to agree with it?

The world is full of beauty when your heart is full of love.
~ Author unknown

UNITY is a journey with unsung heroes

Love binds all things together in perfect unity. ~ Colossians 3:14

Seminarian Mark Bosco was touched by a remark from Mother
Teresa: "The AIDS patient is the newest face of the suffering
Christ." He then decided to join 1,000 cyclists preparing for a 600-
mile trip from San Francisco to Los Angeles, to raise money for
AIDS research.

The night of the fifth day, he wrote:

"Tonight in camp I needed help for my sore neck and back. A
chiropractor named Christine told me that she and about 60 other
chiropractors were volunteering to keep us in good form. She said
that this would probably be her only vacation time this year, but that
she wouldn't have missed the trip for the world. There are many
unsung heroes on this ride, including 50 or so UPS drivers who
devoted their vacation to following us in trucks with our tents, gear,
and food." ~ Mark Link, S.J.

Do you recall a Knights project that moved you as deeply?

*There's no limit to how much good you can do, if you don't care
who gets the credit.* ~ Author unknown

FRATERNITY is giving of yourself always and everywhere

I tell you the truth... I am not trying to do what I want, but only what he who sent me wants. ~ John 5:30

A plaque in London contains these words:

To the memory of Charles Gordon
Who at all times and everywhere gave
His Strength to the Weak
His Substance to the Suffering
His Heart to God.

Whether the plaque's author knew it or not, he was describing the heart of Jesus. No finer tribute could be paid to a person.
~ Mark Link, S.J.

Can you recall some recent occasion when you went out of your way to help – someone weaker than yourself, someone poorer than yourself, and someone suffering more than yourself?
How have we supported, spiritually and financially, the widows and children of brothers who have passed away?

I am only one, but still I am one.
I cannot do everything, but I can do something;
And because I cannot do everything,
Let me not refuse the something that I can do.
~ Edward Everett Hale

PATRIOTISM is sitting together at the table of brotherhood

They said to one another, "Here comes that dreamer... Let's kill him... Then we will see what becomes of his dreams.
~ Genesis 37:19-20

It was a summer day in Washington when Martin Luther King, Jr., spoke these memorable words to a huge crowd:
"I have a dream that one day this nation will rise up and live out the true meaning of its creed: 'We hold these truths to be self-evident; that all men are created equal.' I have a dream that one day on the red hills of Georgia the sons of former slaves and the sons of former slave owners will be able to sit down together at the table of brotherhood... This is our hope. This is the faith that I go back to the South with. With this faith, we will be able to hew out of the mountain of despair a stone of hope." ~ Mark Link, S.J.

Sadly, the Scripture from Genesis above proved to be prophetic. Dr. King would later be slain out of sheer hatred. What has become of his dreams and are they worth keeping alive?

It isn't a calamity to die with dreams unfulfilled, but it is a calamity not to dream. ~ Benjamin E. Mays

January 16

UNITY is building the city of God together

Go then, to all peoples everywhere, and make them my disciples.
~ Matthew 28:18

I watched them tear a building down;
A gang of men in a busy town.
With a mighty heave and lusty yell,
They swung a beam and a sidewall fell.
I said to the foreman,
"Are these men as skilled
As the men you'd have here if you had to build?"
He laughed and said, "No indeed!
Just a common laborer is all I need.
And I can wreck in a day or two
What it took the builder a year to do."
And I thought to myself as I went my way,
"Which of these roles have I tried to play?
Am I a builder who works with care
Measuring life by the rule and square,
Or am I a wrecker as I walk the town
Content with the labor of tearing down?" ~ Mark Link, S.J.

What evidence suggests I am a builder and not a wrecker? How would my Brother Knights classify me?

What great thing would you attempt if you knew you would not fail?
~ Robert H. Schuller

January 17

FRATERNITY is few words but many deeds

God will reward each of us according to what we have done.
~ Romans 2:6

Jan Gies and his wife Miep were members of the Dutch underground. They achieved fame through 14-year-old Anne Frank's diary. It described in moving detail what it was like for the Frank family and four other Jews to be hiding out in a warehouse from the Nazis.

After two years, the Franks were caught. During that period, Jan Gies risked his life daily, smuggling ration coupons to buy food and then smuggling the food to the Franks and to the four others in hiding.

Someone said of Gies, "Jan was not a person to stand in the lime-light… He was throughout his life a man of few words, but many deeds." ~ Mark Link, S.J.

What are your feelings about publicizing the good works of our council?

The world will little note nor long remember what we say here, but it can never forget what they did here. ~ Abraham Lincoln

PATRIOTISM is reverence for all life

*I was sick and you took care of me, in prison and you visited me…
whenever you did this for one of the least important of these
followers of mine, you did it for me!"* ~ Matthew 25:26, 40

Tip O'Neil was a member of Congress for 34 years. He was
speaker of the House for ten years, the longest consecutive term for
any speaker in the history of Congress.
On the wall of his office hung these words from the last speech that
Hubert Humphrey ever gave. Tip said they summed up his own
philosophy and values.
"The moral test of government is how it treats those who are in the
dawn of life, the children… in the twilight of life, the aged… in the
shadows of life, the sick, the needy, and the handicapped."
~ Mark Link, S.J.

How might our assembly witness to our special concern for the sick,
the needy, the handicapped and our nation's homeless veterans?

*By having reverence for life, we enter into a spiritual relationship
with the world.* ~ Albert Schweitzer

January 19

CHARITY is laying claim to your power and glory

If I have no love, I am nothing. ~ 1 Corinthians 13:2

Talk-show hostess, Oprah Winfrey, has a wonderful way with her guests. Her honesty relaxes them, and it's not rare for her to cry with them right on the show. Her great compassion comes from the fact that she suffered greatly in her early life.
To the graduation class of Spelman College, she said from the heart: "Stop wasting time being mundane... We are daughters of God – here to teach the world how to love... It doesn't matter what you've been through, where you come from, who your parents are... What matters is how you choose to love, how you choose to express that love through... what you have to give to the world. Be a queen. Own your power and your glory!" ~ Mark Link, S.J.

What is your power and your glory? What tends to keep you from claiming it – and expressing it lovingly?

Love is a fabric which never fades, no matter how often it is washed in the water of adversity and grief. ~ E.C. McKenzie

January 20

UNITY is an endeavor to light the world

*For freedom, Christ set us free; so stand firm and do no submit
again to the yoke of slavery.* ~ Galatians 5:1

On this date in 1961, President John F. Kennedy, himself a Knight
of the Fourth Degree, delivered this inaugural address:
*In the long history of the world, only a few generations have been
granted the role of defending freedom in its hour of maximum
danger. I do not shrink from this responsibility – I welcome it...
The energy, the faith, the devotion which we bring to this endeavor
will light our country and all who serve it – and the glow from that
fire can truly light the world...*
Most Americans are familiar with his famous phrase: "And so, my
fellow Americans: ask not what your country can do for you – ask
what you can do for your country." But the long forgotten conclusion of his address was this:
*My fellow citizens of the world: ask not what America will do for
you, but what together we can do for the freedom of man.*
~ A Sir Knight

Sir Knight Kennedy's words are still moving, even today. How can
our Brother Knight's words be applied as a call to action for our
council?

*Let every nation know, whether it wishes us well or ill, that we shall
pay any price, bear any burden, meet any hardship, support any
friend, oppose any foe, in order to assure the survival and the
success of liberty.* ~ Sir Knight John F. Kennedy

FRATERNITY is love in work clothes

When, LORD, did we ever see you… a stranger and welcome you in our homes, or naked and clothe you?… The King will reply, "I tell you, whenever you did this for one of the least important of these… you did it for me. ~ Matthew 25:37, 40

In 1952, Mother Teresa saw an abandoned woman in the street, literally, being eaten by bugs. She carried the unfortunate victim to a hospital, but it wouldn't accept her.
Next, Mother Teresa carried the woman to city officials, demanding she be helped. When this didn't work, she demanded a shelter where she could care for the woman and other victims like her.
Glad to be rid of the problem, they led her to an abandoned shelter, once used by Hindu pilgrims. Thus began Mother Teresa's first home for the destitute and the dying. ~ Mark Link, S.J.

How are we as Knights becoming more involved in helping people who cannot help themselves?

Service is nothing but love in work clothes.
~ E.C. McKenzie

CHARITY is helping others, not eliminating them

Be self-controlled and alert. Your enemy the devil prowls around like a roaring lion looking for someone to devour. ~ 1 Peter 5:8

On this date in 1973, the Supreme Court ruled on the matter of *Roe v. Wade*. But the madness began years earlier with the mother of the sexual revolution and Planned Parenthood, Margaret Sanger. In an effort to sterilize the Black population, she wrote: "(we propose to) hire three or four colored ministers… with engaging personalities. The most successful educational approach to the Negro is through a religious appeal… We do not want word to go out that we want to exterminate the Negro population… (Margaret Sanger, letter to Clarence Gamble, October 1939)." She advocated limiting the immigration of "Slavs, Hebrews, and Latins (Margaret Sanger, "Racial Quotas in Immigration", *Birth Control Review*, August 1920)," because of their lower intelligence. She championed the sterilization of those who are ill-suited to propagate the race, using as her motto: "More (children) from the fit, less from the unfit (Margaret Sanger, *The Pivot of Civilization*)."

This is the undercurrent of the abortion movement. What would you say to someone who still believes abortion is a compassionate alternative to childbirth?

As we celebrate the 100th birthday of Margaret Sanger, our courageous leader, we should be very proud of what we are and what our mission is. It is a very grand mission; abortion is only the tip of the iceberg. ~ Faye Wattleton, Planned Parenthood speech, February 1979

UNITY is celebrating our oneness

Do your best to preserve the unity which the Spirit gives.
~ Ephesians 3:3-5

In early 1984, the Olympic flame was flown from its home in
Olympia, Greece, to New York City. Runners then carried it to Los
Angeles.
As it went from city to city, something beautiful began to happen.
Towns greeted the runners ringing church bells and blowing fire
sirens. Tears flowed down people's cheeks and spontaneous singing
broke out.
One elderly lady spoke for many when she said to a runner, "Thank
you, son, for making me feel like this again."
When the torch reached the Coliseum, 93,000 people stood and
cheered wildly. It climaxed an experience of unity that few
Americans will ever forget. ~ Mark Link, S.J.

What can I personally do to nourish unity in our council?

*The strength of the Pack is the Wolf, and the strength of the Wolf is
the Pack.* ~ Rudyard Kipling, *The Second Jungle Book*

January 24

FRATERNITY is bringing tears to the Duke's eyes

When you have done all you have been told to do, say, 'We are ordinary servants; we have only done our duty.' ~ Luke 17:9-10

Everett Alvarez Jr. made John Wayne cry when they met at a White House dinner. Alvarez was the first American pilot shot down over North Vietnam. For many Americans he symbolized the suffering of all who served in Vietnam. Alvarez spent 8 years as a POW. He was fed dead birds, rice crawling with roaches, and sewer-water soup to make him sick and weak. In a small yard outside his cell, he scratched the outline of a cross in the painted stucco. Later he would add the words, "LORD, I am not worthy, but only say the word and my soul shall be healed." To stay focused on survival, Alvarez re-enacted daily all that he could recall of the Mass as an altar boy. When he was put with other POWs, Alvarez found strength in teamwork. The very few Americans who chose not to be part of the group were more interested in themselves and ultimately collaborated with the enemy. On Christmas Day 1971, his captors let him read a letter from his mother that said his wife had left him. Still, Alvarez emerged from captivity with a new spirit. He remarried soon after his release in 1973, earned a law degree, and served in the Reagan administration.
~ Everett Alvarez, Jr., adapted from *Chained Eagle*

What lessons about fraternity can we glean from Alvarez's POW nightmare?

We're not afraid of storms, for we're learning to sail our ship.
~ L.M. Alcott

January 25

PATRIOTISM is malice toward none and charity for all

To be controlled by the Spirit results in life and peace.
~ Romans 8:6

The vast crowd in Washington broke into a thunderous applause
when Lincoln arrived for his second inaugural. It stunned him,
because he'd gotten so used to boos. No president in history had
been hated so bitterly as he had been, because of the war and his
stand on slavery.
The crowd grew deathly silent when he began his address. It was an
amazing speech, ending with these words:

"With malice toward none; with charity for all; with firmness in the
right, as God gives us to see the right, let us strive on to finish the
work we are in; to bind up the nation's wounds; to care for him who
shall have borne the battle, and for his widow and his orphan – to do
all which may achieve and cherish a just and lasting peace among
ourselves and with all nations." ~ Mark Link, S.J.

Lincoln's sentiments have withstood the test of time. How has our
assembly served our community and nation as instruments of peace?

LORD, make me an instrument of your peace.
Where there is hatred, let me sow love.
~ Saint Francis of Assisi

January 26

CHARITY is giving your son to the nation in military service

My love for you will never end… so says the LORD who loves you.
~ Isaiah 54:10

Dr. Jonas Salk won fame for developing a polio vaccine in 1953.
His brother, Dr. Lee Salk, wrote a popular book, called *My Father,
My Son*.
He began the book by describing a touching scene between his
father and himself. He wrote:
"One blustery winter afternoon in 1944, my father waited with me
in Penn Station for the train that would take me away to the army
center where I would begin my World War II military service. He
looked at me with tears clouding his eyes, hugged me tightly, kissed
me on the cheek and told me good-bye in a choked voice. Then,
wanting to give me something… he took off his watch and gave it to
me."
~ Mark Link, S.J.

When have you felt the love of a parent or child as deeply as Dr.
Salk and his father felt for each other? How did you express it?

*Two people who love each other are in a place more holy than the
interior of a church.* ~ William Lyon Phelps

UNITY is working together in pouring rain

We are one body in union with Christ. ~ Romans 12:5

John XXIII's *Journal of a Soul* has this entry dated November 1939: "Every evening from my window I see an assemblage of fishing boats… They come around in tens and hundreds… One can hear the cheerful voices of the fishermen. I find the sight very moving. The other night, towards one o'clock, it was pouring with rain but the fishermen were still there, undeterred from their heavy toil… What an inspiring example to us, who are fishermen of Jesus Christ. We must do as they do – work day and night with our torches lit, each in his own little boat – yet working as a team for the spread of God's Kingdom on earth." ~ Mark Link, S.J.

What kind of new leadership initiatives might the Knights undertake nationally to spread God's Kingdom on earth?

Our chief want in life is somebody who shall make us do what we can. ~ Ralph Waldo Emerson

January 28

FRATERNITY is remembering the best and brightest

In the day of my trouble I shall call upon thee, for thou wilt answer me. ~ Psalm 86:7 KJV

On this date in 1985, seven brave Americans died as they reached for the stars aboard the space shuttle *Challenger*. As our nation mourned, our faith compelled us to consider the contradictions –

… that a flowering plant might sprout from volcanic ash,
… that days after a devastating earthquake we might discover the survival of helpless infants,
… that the violence of conflict might yield to the peace of reconciliation,
… and that in the horror of so vividly seeing seven human lives instantaneously obliterated, we might remember the Easter mystery of the Resurrection.

For the crew of the *Challenger* – Gregory Jarvis, Christa McAuliffe, Ronald McNair, Ellison Onizuka, Judith Resnik, Dick Scobee and Michael Smith… they were escaping the bounds of earth, looking towards the heavens, and while exulting in their journey, were delivered into the hands of God.
~ *St. Ignatius Newsletter of Boston College*, adapted

The measure of a man is the way he bears up under misfortune. In time of grief, are you able to feel God's embrace or do you turn to Him in anger?

The souls of the just are in the hands of God, and no torment shall touch them. ~ Book of Wisdom

January 29

CHARITY is hugging a wayward father

If you forgive… your Father in heaven will also forgive you.
~ Matthew 6:14

A young man, whose father had abandoned his family, was on retreat.
At one point, he imagined himself kneeling before Jesus as he hung on the cross. He wrote:
"An enormous guilt was upon me. I wept for forgiveness.
As I wept, God forgave me… He loved me in all my filth…
I took the next day off from work to think and pray. While I was reading the Bible, I began to think of my father… That night I went to his apartment and asked his forgiveness for hating him… We hugged and kissed one another…
I took a cab most of the way home that night, but I wanted to walk the last couple of blocks. Joy overflowed in me…
With arms outstretched, I screamed, "I love you, God!"
He blessed me greatly that night. ~ Letter to Mark Link, S.J.

What keeps me from forgiving others?

We are like beasts when we kill. We are like men when we judge.
We are like God when we forgive. ~ E.C. McKenzie

UNITY is keeping the faith even in the face of adversity

John the Baptist came, and he fasted and drank no wine, and you said, 'He has a demon in him!' The Son of Man came, and he ate and drank, and you said... 'He is a glutton and a wine-drinker.'
~ Luke 7:33-34

Robert Fulton pioneered the first American steamship, the *Clermont*.
A crowd lined New York's Hudson River to watch its attempt at a first voyage.
A critic in the crowd shouted, "They'll never get it started!"
But it did start! It picked up speed! Faster and Faster! Smoke poured from its funnel. The crowd on the bank cheered wildly.
The critic, who said, "They'll never get it started," now laughed and shouted, "They'll never get it stopped!" ~ Mark Link, S.J.

How do I handle stupid, unfair criticism?

Don't let criticism disquiet you. If it's stupid, smile at it. If it's unfair, tolerate it. If it's justified, learn from it.
~ Anonymous

FRATERNITY is being big brothers to little brothers

Let the children come to me and do not stop them, because the Kingdom of God belongs to such as these. ~ Matthew 19:14

Babe Ruth was born in Baltimore, Maryland in 1895. He died 53 years later of cancer in a New York hospital.
Babe loved kids; and they loved him. During the 1926 World Series, he promised a very sick John Sylvestri, that he'd hit a home run for him – and did.
Part of Babe's love for children stemmed from his own turbulent childhood. He lived above the family saloon, played hooky, stole, and drank. His parents finally committed him to St. Mary's Industrial School.
There, Catholic brothers shaped him up and gave him his love for baseball. ~ Mark Link, S.J.

What are some of the things Knights do for 'little brothers', especially in a Church setting? Are you involved in our Columbian Squires Circle?

Whoever you are, there is some younger person who thinks you are perfect… There is someone who would miss you if you were gone. There is a place that you alone can fill.
~ Jacob M. Braude

February 1

PATRIOTISM is putting our trust in God

This is impossible for man, but for God everything is possible.
~ Matthew 19:26

After being elected president, Abraham Lincoln stayed in
Springfield, Illinois, until it was time for his inauguration.
Times were bad: states were seceding, and the South was readying
for war. Lincoln walked to the rear platform and spoke his farewell
to the crowd: "Here I lived a quarter of a century, and have passed
from a young to an old man. Here my children have been born, and
one buried. I now leave, not knowing when or whether ever I may
return, with a task before me greater than that which rested upon
Washington." ~ Mark Link, S.J.

When have you said farewell to a happy past and set out to face an
uncertain future? When was the last time our assembly ventured
into a seemingly insurmountable task?

*Without the assistance of the Divine Being... that attended George
Washington, I cannot succeed. With that assistance, I cannot fail.*
~ Abraham Lincoln

February 2

CHARITY is a father's deep compassion for his son

Give me... an understanding heart. ~ 1 Kings 3:9

Walter Petrvage grew up in a small town in Pennsylvania. Among his fond memories is his father's deep compassion.
On the night of the senior prom he took his father's car without permission. In his rush to get away without deception, he left the driver's door slightly open to check clearance as he backed out of the narrow garage. It hit the garage, springing the hinges. He laid awake most of the night worrying. When he came downstairs about noon, his dad said, "I took the Chevy to the body shop. They'll have it fixed tomorrow. We can decide who'll pay for it then." He paused and then said, "Did you have a good time at the prom?" ~ *Catholic Digest*

How compassionate are you – as Jesus was to His people and the father to his son?

You may call God love, you may call God goodness. But the best name for God is compassion. ~ Meister Eckhart

February 3

UNITY is loyalty to Christ even in times of trial

Do not be surprised at the painful test you are suffering... Rather be glad that you are sharing Christ's sufferings, so that you may rejoice when his glory is revealed. ~ 1 Peter 4:12-13

A Belgium doctor invited nurse Edith Cavell to set up a medical clinic in Brussels. When war came in 1914, she secretly treated and helped 200 Allied soldiers to escape. The Germans were outraged and sentenced her to death.
A chaplain describes her last moments:
"We partook of Holy Communion together. At the close of the little service, I began to repeat the words, 'Abide with me,' and she joined...
Then I said good-bye... She smiled and said, 'We shall meet again.'"
When the British ship *Stella* was sinking with 105 victims still on it, a woman stood on the bridge and sang "Abide with Me." Immediately the others joined in, remaining faithful to the LORD to the end. ~ Mark Link, S.J.

How is rejoicing in suffering different from just enduring suffering? What should be the Knights' attitude toward scorn and ridicule of our faith (see 1 Peter 4:16-17)?

Just over the hill is a beautiful valley, but you must climb the hill to see it. ~ E. C. McKenzie

February 4

FRATERNITY is putting another life ahead of your own

There is no greater love than this: to lay down one's life for one's friends. ~ John 15:13

As a child, Maximilian Kolbe (1894-1941) had a deep devotion to Our Lady. On one occasion he had a vision in which Mary offered him either a white garment, symbolizing purity, or a red one, symbolizing martyrdom. "I choose both," the boy replied. Following the German conquest of Poland in 1939, he was arrested, but soon released. Fr. Kolbe devoted himself to helping Jewish refugees; when the Nazis discovered this, he was again arrested and sent to the death camp Auschwitz in 1941. There he tried to set an example of faith and hope for the other prisoners. When a prisoner escaped from camp, the Germans chose ten men at random and sentenced them to death by starvation; one of them was a Polish sergeant, Franciszek Gajowniczek. Fr. Kolbe left his place in the ranks and asked permission from the commandant to take Gajowniczek's place. The shocked German officer agreed, and Kolbe and nine others were taken away to die. Maximilian helped the others prepare for death; he was the last to succumb, dying on the eve of the Assumption of the Blessed Virgin Mary in 1941.
~ J.M. Guerin

Fr. Kolbe teaches us that sometimes being a Knight requires us to work against an evil system, even to the point of disobeying immoral or unjust laws. Do any circumstances exist today where Knights may have to emulate Fr. Kolbe?

The bird a nest, the spider a web, man friendship.
~ William Blake

February 5

CHARITY is the grace of God

Your constant love reaches the heavens;
your faithfulness extends to the skies…
Your justice is like the depths of the sea…
You are the source of all life,
and because of your light we see the light. ~ Psalm 36:5-7, 9

In his play *Long Day's Journey into Night*, Eugene O'Neill has
Edmund describe a mystical experience.
Actually, it was one that O'Neill himself had one night on a square-
rigger bound for Buenos Aires. He wrote:
"For a moment, I lost myself… I became the white sails and flying
spray, became the beauty and the rhythm, became the moonlight and
the ship and the dim-starred sky! I belonged… within something
greater than my own life… To God if you want." ~ Mark Link, S.J.

What is the closest thing I have ever had to an experience similar to
O'Neill's?

I was snatched up to the highest heaven…
I heard things which cannot be put into words.
~ 2 Corinthians 12:2-4

February 6

UNITY is sharing our lives and our dreams

The apostles gathered frequently to pray as a group, together with Mary the mother of Jesus and with his brothers. ~ Acts 1:14

A Chicago businessman wrote about his years of sharing his faith in a group with seven other businessmen:
"I am in a faith-sharing group that meets every Saturday morning at seven. We have never yet missed a meeting.
We share our insights and reflections from our daily meditations of the past week. As we grew together, we developed a lot of love, a lot of compassion. We have shared with each other more than our faith. We have shared our joys, our pains and worries, our dreams and our hopes. We have shared our lives…
There is nothing I would not do for the members of our group. I feel very blessed." ~ Mark Link, S.J.

Describe a similar unity you have experienced with your Brother Knights. If you cannot recall any such experiences, why not?

No machine can replace the human spark: compassion, love and understanding. ~ Louis V. Gerstner, Jr.

February 7

FRATERNITY is being a brother even to those who reject you

There was no room for them to stay in the inn. Luke 2:7

Dr. Charles Drew was an African-American graduate of prestigious Amherst University.
A surgical consultant for the U.S. Army, he developed the process for preserving blood and using it for transfusion. Incredibly, he was not allowed to donate his blood to the Red Cross Blood Bank because he was black. More incredibly and more tragically, after a car accident in 1950, he was refused his own discovery, at a North Carolina hospital.
He died during the long drive to find a hospital that would treat black patients. ~ Mark Link, S.J.

What are Knights doing to combat prejudice in the nation we love? What more might we do?

There may be times when we are powerless to prevent injustice, but there must never be a time when we fail to protest it.
~ Elie Wiesel

February 8

PATRIOTISM is serving God and nation nobly

Praise God with trumpets… Praise God with drums and dancing.
~ Psalm 150:3-4

Julia Ward Howe was an American poet and activist. She worked
for the abolition of slavery, the vote for women, prison reform, and
world peace. She penned the stirring lyrics of "The Battle Hymn of
the Republic" to provide more suitable words for the melody "John
Brown's Body."
The hymn went on to become the marching song of the North, just
as 'Dixie' became the marching song of the South.
~ Mark Link, S.J.

What unique set of talents do we Knights possess and how might we
better use them to greater service of God and nation?

God sent His singers upon earth
with songs of sadness and mirth,
That they might touch the hearts of men
and bring them back to heaven again.
~ Henry Wordsworth Longfellow

February 9

CHARITY is giving a bolt to a competitor

Jesus said, "Love your enemies." ~ Matthew 5:44

The Italian team of Monti and Siorpraes was heavily favored to win
the Olympic bobsled event in 1964 in Germany.
They had great first and second runs; but a little-regarded British
team of Nash and Dixon had an even greater first run. Their axle
broke, however, just before their scheduled second run. They were
crushed.
To the amazement of everyone, Monti removed the bolt from his
Italian sled and gave it to the British team.
Nash and Dixon went on to win the gold in a tremendous upset
victory, while Monti and Siorpraes settled for the bronze.
In a bit of poetic justice, Monti would lead the Italian two-and-four
man sleds to gold medals four years later. ~ Mark Link, S.J.

The sportsmanship of the Italian team is a beautiful image of the
kind of love Jesus invites us to show our enemies in our daily lives.
How well do we as Knights demonstrate true sportsmanship?

For when the One Great Scorer comes
To write against your name,
He marks – not that you won or lost –
But how you played the game.
~ Grantland Rice

February 10

UNITY is discerning and doing God's will

Those who declare publicly that they belong to me, I will do the same for them before my Father in heaven. ~ Matthew 10:32

The preacher at F.W. de Klerk's inauguration made a disturbing point.
He said that the South African president had the awesome responsibility of discerning God's will and acting on it.
This planted a seed in de Klerk's mind that grew and grew. Slowly, it led him to pursue the dismantling of the dehumanizing apartheid system and granting citizenship to 35 million blacks.
de Klerk said later that he knew that in pursuing this unpopular policy he would be rejected by his own people, but this did not deter him. ~ Mark Link, S.J.

In what areas can the Knights display the same political bravery?

Silently and imperceptibly, as we wake or sleep, we grow strong or weak, and at last some crisis shows us what we have become.
~ Bishop Westcott

February 11 *Lourdes (1858)*
Song of Bernadette

The Spirit... will lead you into all the truth. ~ John 16:13

In 1858, a girl named Bernadette reported apparitions of Mary at a hillside in Lourdes, France.
Sick people visited the site and were cured. Over 1,300 cures are well documented.

In the 1930s, Alexis Carrel, a skeptical New York surgeon and Nobel prize winner, went to Lourdes to investigate the claims. While there, he witnessed a girl being cured. He stood in silence, totally stunned. That night, he went for a long walk. Ending up in a church, he prayed:
"I still doubt... Beneath... intellectual pride a smothered dream persists... the dream of believing."

He returned to his hotel and recorded his observations. In *The Voyage to Lourdes*, he describes what then happened:
"A new coolness penetrated the open window. I felt the serenity of nature enter my soul with gentle calm. All intellectual doubts had vanished." ~ Mark Link, S.J.

How do you understand such miracles?

For those who believe, no explanation is necessary. For those who do not believe, no explanation is possible.
~ Fran Werfel, *Song of Bernadette*

February 12 *Abraham Lincoln's Birthday (1809)*

PATRIOTISM is national restoration

*If my people, who are called by my name, will humble themselves
and pray and seek my face and turn from their wicked ways, then
will I hear from heaven and will forgive their sin and will heal their
land.* ~ 2 Chronicles 7:14

We have been the recipients of the choicest bounties of Heaven.
We have been preserved these many years in peace and prosperity.
We have grown in numbers, wealth and power as no other nation
has ever grown.
But we have forgotten God.
We have forgotten the gracious Hand which preserved us in peace,
and multiplied and enriched and strengthened us; and we have
vainly imagined, in the deceitfulness of our hearts, that all these
blessings were produced by some superior wisdom and virtue of our
own.
Intoxicated with unbroken success, we have become too self-
sufficient to feel the necessity of redeeming and preserving grace,
too proud to pray to the God that made us!
It behooves us then to humble ourselves before the offended Power,
to confess our national sins and to pray for clemency and
forgiveness. ~ Abraham Lincoln

What might God say if he appeared to our nation's leader tonight as
he did to Solomon (2 Chronicles 7:12)? What is our assembly
planning this fraternal year in service to God and country?

*Democracy is a device that insures we shall be governed no better
than we deserve.* ~ George Bernard Shaw

February 13

UNITY is witnessing proudly to our identity

These are shadows of things to come; but the substance belongs to Christ. ~ Colossians 2:17

Tip O'Neill was a member of the House of Representatives for 34 years.
In the memoirs of his political life, Tip says that he'll never forget a day in Missouri in 1960 when he was with Jack Kennedy in a campaign parade. He wrote:
"Somebody mentioned that in the neighborhood we were driving through there was a good deal of concern over the Catholic issue.
Then we passed a Catholic school, with all the nuns standing outside, holding their Kennedy signs. 'Stop the car,' said Jack.
He got out and shook hands with all the sisters, and I loved him for it." ~ Mark Link, S.J.

How ready am I to witness to the goals of the Knights even if it means risking my own popularity?

He who sells principles for popularity is soon bankrupt.
~ E.C. McKenzie

February 14 *St. Valentine*

LOVE is a man and his maiden

There are three things that are too amazing for me, four that I do not understand: the way of an eagle in the sky, the way of a snake on a rock, the way of a ship on the high seas, and the way of a man with a maiden. ~ Proverbs 30:18-19

How was it with you when you first fell in love with the girl you married? Or (if you feel that you never were in love) look at her now through another man's eyes. Think about those things that are attractive in her. Love her with a sensitive appreciation and watch her become beautiful as she reflects and radiates the love you have poured out to her...
As Christians we can be sure that romantic love is as old as Time itself, for it came into being in the Garden when the first man and woman gazed on each other. We must recognize that it was our Creator who gifted us with the capacity for the intense and passionate emotions required to fall in love. Clearly, God intended for our emotional potential to be fully developed in marriage and to find its fulfillment in oneness with our beloved.
~ Ed Wheat, excerpted from *Love-Life for Every Married Couple*

Knights, make time for your Ladies today, and every day.

To love another person is to see the face of God.
~ Victor Hugo, *Les Miserables*

February 15

PATRIOTISM is honesty, loyalty and courage

Do not ask me to abandon or forsake you! For wherever you go I will go, wherever you lodge I will lodge, your people shall be my people, and your God my God. ~ Ruth 1:16

Once there was a war between the birds and beasts. The Bat was on the birds' side. When he saw defeat was imminent, he crept away and hid under a log until the fight was over. When the victorious beasts were going home, Bat slipped in among them. The beasts noticed him and said, "Didn't you fight against us?"
Bat replied, "Oh no! I'm one of you. What kind of bird has fangs like this? I'm a beast."
They said nothing more, and let Bat stay with them. Another battle ensued, but this time the birds prevailed. As soon as Bat saw his side was beaten, he attempted to switch allegiances once again. And so it was, Bat went back and forth throughout the war. Eventually, peace reigned. The two sides reconciled and realized the Bat's duplicity. They cast him out saying, "Hereafter, you will fly alone at night, and will never have any friends, among either those that fly, or those that walk." So until this day, the Bat sneaks around in the dark, and no one cares what kind of creature he is.
~ adapted from Aesop's fables

Along our journey to eternal life, each Knight will have to take a stand, or risk the fate of the Bat. What does this tale teach us about honesty, loyalty and courage? Sir Knights, how do you practice responsible citizenship?

Be true to your work, your word, and your friend. ~ Thoreau

CHARITY is choosing the best man

You have heard it said, "Love your friends, hate your enemies."
But now I tell you, "Love your enemies." ~ Matthew 5:43

Abraham Lincoln succeeded James Buchanan as president in 1861.
Ed Stanton, a member of Buchanan's cabinet, disdained and
ridiculed Lincoln.
A year into the presidency, Lincoln had to replace his Secretary of
War. He chose Stanton, explaining, "I know the terrible things he
said about me. But he's the best man for the job."
Shortly thereafter, Lee surrendered to Grant, and Lincoln was
assassinated. One of the first public officials to reach Lincoln's side
was Stanton. When Lincoln breathed his last, Stanton said with
heartfelt sincerity, "There lays the world's greatest ruler. Now he
belongs to the ages." ~ Mark Link, S.J.

How do you respond to ridicule? What keeps you from responding
as Lincoln did? Have you ever witnessed the Knights of Columbus
being ridiculed for their beliefs and practices? How did you react?

Without love and compassion for others, our own apparent love for
Christ is fiction. ~ Thomas Merton

February 17

UNITY is taking the risk to do something you believe in

*Any country that divides itself into groups which fight each other
will not last very long; a family divided against itself falls apart.*
~ Luke 11:17

Abraham Lincoln delivered his famous "Divided House Speech" at
the Illinois State Convention in Springfield in 1858.
Before doing so, he read it to several friends. One said it was ahead
of its time. Another called it a fool utterance. A third predicted that
it would drive away as many voters who had just come over to the
Republican party. A fourth did not agree fully with it, but said,
"Deliver that speech as read and it will make you President."
Lincoln did and the rest is history. ~ Mark Link, S.J.

Can you recall a time when you risked a great deal because of your
convictions? Are the Knights called to take a stand on certain
issues?

*If I had to... erase my whole life... and I had one choice allowed me
that I might save from the wreck, I would choose that speech and
leave it to the world just as it is.*
~ Lincoln on his Divided House Speech

February 18

FRATERNITY is recognizing that all of us are brothers

Forgive your brother from the heart. ~ Matthew 18:35

In the film, *All Quiet on the Western Front*, a German soldier is in a foxhole, taking cover from artillery fire.
Suddenly, an enemy French soldier leaps into the same hole to take cover as well. The German leaps on him and stabs him. But the Frenchman doesn't die immediately.
The German – hardly more than a boy – studies the French soldier's dying eyes. Moved to pity, he makes him comfortable and gives him drink.
When he dies, the German soldier feels great remorse. He speaks to the dead Frenchman, saying:
"When you jumped in here, you were my enemy – and I was afraid… But you're just a man like me… If we threw away these rifles and these uniforms, you could be my brother… You have to forgive me." ~ Mark Link, S.J.

How can we help our brothers discover the kind of fraternity we have *before* it's too late?

Forgiveness is the fragrance a violet sheds on the heel that has crushed it. ~ Mark Twain

February 19

CHARITY is believing in Jesus

God loved the world so much that he gave his only Son, so that everyone who believes in him may not die but have eternal life.
~ John 3:16

A boy was born with an eye defect. He could see clearly only nearby objects. When the school told his parents that he needed glasses, they ignored it, saying "We didn't need glasses when we were kids. Why should he?"
When the boy grew up, he went to a doctor. After fitting him with glasses, the doctor told him to look outside.
"Wow!" the boy gasped. "It's so beautiful!"
Later, he told Father John Powell about the episode saying:
"That was the second most beautiful experience of my whole life."
Naturally, Father Powell asked him: "What was the most beautiful experience?"
He said, "When I came to believe in Jesus and saw that God is truly my Father... and felt the warmth of His love.
~ *A Reason to Live! A Reason to Die*, excerpted

How aware are you of God's love for you? How can our council further promote this awareness?

The measure of our love for God depends upon how deeply aware we are of God's love for us. ~ Diodochus

50

February 20

UNITY is keeping love alive with little surprises

Every husband must love his wife as himself. ~ Ephesians 5:33

Andy was married to a girl named Kim, and things weren't going well.
He consulted a lawyer who had known him since he was a boy.
After explaining the problem, he asked the lawyer to prepare separation papers. The lawyer peered over his glasses at Andy, whom he knew better than Andy thought.
He advised Andy to wait six months. In the meantime, he should call her from work on occasion, bring home small gifts, and take her to dinner on special days. *Then* go through with the separation. That'll show her what a mistake she made. Reluctantly, Andy agreed.
Six months later, the lawyer ran into Andy on the street and said, "Your papers are ready."
Andy replied, "I intended to call you. I've decided not to separate from Kim. You wouldn't believe how she has changed since I last saw you." ~ Mark Link, S.J.

Guess who changed – the Knight or the Lady? How might this story apply to your life?

A wedding is an event, but marriage is an achievement.
~ Anonymous

February 21

FRATERNITY is valuing fatherhood over self

Parents,
do not treat your children in such a way as to make them angry.
Instead raise them with Christian discipline and instruction.
~ Ephesians 6:4

General Douglas MacArthur led the Allies to victory over Japan in World War II.
He once said, "By profession I am a soldier and I take pride in that fact. But I am prouder – infinitely prouder – to be a father. A soldier destroys in order to build; the father only builds, never destroys. The one has the potentiality of death; the other embodies creation and life… It is my hope that my son, when I am gone, will remember me not from the battle but in the home repeating with him our simple daily prayer, "Our Father…"
~ Courtney Whitney, *MacArthur: Rendezvous With History*

How can I carry the spirit behind Knightly fraternity into my family relationships?

My father didn't tell me how to live; he lived, and let me watch him do it. ~ Clarence Budington Killand

February 22 *George Washington's Birthday (1789)*

PATRIOTISM is affection for brethren who have served

Humble yourselves before the LORD, and he will lift you up.
~ James 4:10

General Washington carried with him, in his field notebook, twenty-four pages of personal prayers he had handwritten. The following is his prayer for the United States of America:

Almighty God, we make our earnest prayer that Thou wilt keep the United States in Thy Holy protection; and Thou wilt incline the hearts of the citizens to cultivate a spirit of brotherly affection and love for one another, particularly for their brethren who have served in the field. And finally that Thou wilt most graciously be pleased to dispose us all to do justice, to love mercy, and to demean ourselves with that charity, humility, and pacific temper of mind which were the characteristics of the Divine Author of our blessed religion, and without a humble imitation of whose example in these things we can never hope to be a happy nation. Grant our supplication, we beseech Thee, through Jesus Christ our LORD. Amen.

In our nation today, it is easy to forget that this great American was at the core an extremely devout man. How can we as Knights, especially Sir Knights, answer Washington's prayer?

Give me peace to hear the calling on me in Thy word, that it may be wisdom, righteousness, reconciliation and peace to the saving of my soul. ~ George Washington

February 23

CHARITY comes in a plain brown envelope

*When you help a needy person, do it in such a way that even your
closest friend will not know about it.* ~ Matthew 6:3-4

The New York *Times* ran an amazing story. St. Jude's Children's
Research Hospital in Memphis, Tennessee, get hundreds of
donations – large and small – daily.
One day they received a plain envelope with no return address.
Inside was a McDonald's Monopoly Sweepstake's ticket for a $1
million "Instant Winner."
St. Jude's called McDonald's. Officials came with a representative
of the Arthur Andersen accounting firm. After checking the board
with a jeweler's eyepiece, he declared it a winner.
McDonald's and St. Jude officials agreed to respect the donor's
apparent desire to remain anonymous. They made no effort to find
out who it was. ~ Mark Link, S.J.

Is your participation in worthy Knights causes influenced by
whether or not you receive recognition?

*It is possible to give without loving, but it is impossible to love with-
out giving.* ~ Richard Broundstein

February 24

UNITY is Knights gathered as one

You are like light for the whole world... Your light must shine before people ~ Matthew 5:14, 16

A teacher asked her students, "What if an incredible explosion destroyed all life on earth except for those of us in this classroom? Where would the Church be?"
They thought a minute. Then a boy said, "It would be in this room. We would be the Church."
This story makes an important point. The Church is not a place where people gather. It is the people who gather. To have Church we must gather. It's like the bread that we use for the Eucharist. Hundreds of grains of wheat must be gathered to make it. In a similar way, only by gathering do we make the risen Christ visible in today's world.
Jesus assured us, "Where two or three come together in my name, I am there with them." ~ Mark Link, S.J.

What can we as Knights do to unify our parish and the Catholic Church?

If you find a perfect church, by all means join it! Then it will no longer be perfect. ~ Billy Graham

February 25

FRATERNITY is seeing a brother safely through

Pray always that you will have the strength to go safely through and… stand before the Son of Man. ~ Luke 21:36

A very young man in a military hospital had lost a leg and was sinking rapidly. Abraham Lincoln happened by, saw him, and offered to write a letter to his mother. When the boy finished dictating it, Lincoln added this postscript: "This letter was written by A. Lincoln."
When the boy read the letter, he gazed at Lincoln and asked, "Are you our President?"
The President nodded. Then Lincoln added, "Is there anything else I can do for you?"
He said feebly: "I guess you might hold my hand and see me through." ~ Mark Link, S.J.

Lincoln was given a rare opportunity to comfort a fellow human being and seized it. Recall a time when you squandered an opportunity to display kindness.

I shall pass through this world but once. Any good therefore that I can do, or any kindness that I can show to any human being, let me do it now. Let me not defer it or neglect it, for I shall not pass this way again. ~ attributed to Stephen Grellet

CHARITY is a dream realized

*Love the LORD your God with all your heart, with all your soul,
and with all your mind.* ~ Mark 12:30-31

Fifteen year-old Therese Martin entered the Carmelite convent in
France. From the day she entered, she dreamed of doing "great"
things for God. The years passed without her dream being even
remotely realized. Naturally, she was disappointed.
Then one day she was reading Saint Paul, where he says the 'best'
way to holiness is not doing 'great' things for God, but 'loving'
things [1 Corinthians 12:31-13:1-13].
After reading this, she wrote in her journal: "O Jesus... at last I
have found my calling – my calling is to love." ~ Mark Link, S.J.

What are some of the loving things your Knights council has done
for God this month?

*We cannot do great things,
only small things with great love.*
~ Mother Teresa of Calcutta

February 27

UNITY is a jar of pickled cauliflower

The LORD says, "Why spend money on what does not satisfy?
~ Isaiah 55:1-2

In her book, *A Marriage Made in Heaven*, Erma Bombeck describes how she fantasized her 25th wedding anniversary. "I pictured a large white tent with hundreds of guests milling around. The orchestra was playing our song, as my husband and I swayed gracefully on the dance floor.
Actually it turned out quite differently. My kids threw a couple of hamburgers on the grill, gulped them down, and split – leaving me and my husband to clean up. After my husband put away the last things, he came over and said affectionately, "Close your eyes. I have a surprise for you." When I opened them, he was holding a jar of cauliflower, packed in pickle juice. He said softly, "I hid it from the kids, because I knew you liked cauliflower packed in pickle juice."
Erma concluded, "Maybe love is that simple." ~ Mark Link, S.J.

Have you taken the time to show your lady that you love her?

Few happinesses equal the joy of finding a heart that understands.
~ Victor Robinsoll (slightly adapted)

FRATERNITY is continuing the Master's work

[Jesus said to his disciples], "Proclaim the gospel to every crea-
ture." ~ Mark 16:15

Composer Giacomo Puccini was stricken by cancer while working
on his last opera, *Turandot*. He said to his students, "If I don't
finish it, finish it for me." Shortly afterward, he died.
His students carried out his wish. In 1926, Puccini's favorite
student, Arturo Toscanini, directed the premiere in Milan. When
the opera reached the point where Puccini was forced to put down
his pen, Toscanini stopped the music, turned to the audience, and
cried out, "Thus far the Master wrote, but he died." A reverent
silence filled the opera house.
Then Toscanini picked up the baton again, smiled through his tears,
and cried out, "But the disciples finished his work."
At the conclusion of the opera, the audience broke into a tumultuous
applause. ~ Mark Link, S.J.

How prepared and willing are we Knights to help finish our
Master's work? Are we proving it with our council activities?

[The Ascension] does not represent Jesus' removal from earth, but
his constant presence everywhere on earth.
~ William Temple

February 29

PATRIOTISM is renewed courage

So keep up your courage, men… ~ Acts 27:25

A decline in courage may be the most striking feature an outside
observer notices in the West today.

The Western world has lost its civic courage, both as a whole and
separately, in each country, in each government, in each political
party, and, of course, in the United Nations. Such a decline in
courage is particularly noticeable among the ruling and intellectual
elites, causing an impression of a loss of courage by the entire
society.

There remains many courageous individuals, but they have no
determining influence on public life. Political functionaries exhibit
this depression, passivity, and perplexity in their actions and in their
statements, and even more so in their self-serving rationales, as to
how morally justified it is to base state policies on weakness and
cowardice.

Must one point out that from ancient times a decline in courage has
been considered the first symptom of the end?

~ Aleksandr Sozhenitsyn, excerpted from *A World Apart*

As Knights, are we courageous in our responsibilities to society?

*Fear God and keep his commandments, for this is the whole duty of
man.* ~ Ecclesiastes 12:13

March 1

CHARITY can be a great moment wrapped in a small one

I do not call you servants any longer… Instead, I call you friends.
~ John 15:15

I used to drive a cab for a living. It was a cowboy's life, a life for someone who wanted no boss. What I didn't realize was that it could also be a ministry. One night, I responded to a call. When no one responded to my horn, I rang the doorbell. A small woman in her 80s came to the door. She took my arm and we walked slowly to the cab. She kept thanking me for my kindness, and asked, "Can you drive through downtown?"
"It's not the shortest way," I answered quickly.
"Oh, I'm in no hurry," she said. "I'm on my way to a hospice."
I looked in the rearview mirror. Her eyes were glistening.
"The doctor says I don't have very long."
I quietly reached over and shut off the meter. "What route would you like me to take?" I asked.
We drove through the neighborhood where she and her husband had lived when they were newlyweds. Sometimes she'd ask me to slow at a corner and she would stare into the darkness.
We drove in silence to the address she had given me. As I waved goodbye to her, I heard the door slam shut behind me. It was the sound of a life coming to a close. ~ Author unknown

We are conditioned to think that our lives revolve around great moments. But have you ever been caught in a crucial moment beautifully wrapped in what others may consider a small one?

Then their eyes were opened and they recognized Him…
~ Luke 24:31

UNITY is receiving the body and blood of Christ

Every time you eat this bread and drink from this cup, you proclaim the LORD's death until he comes. ~ 1 Corinthians 11:26

Saint Mark ends his account of the Last Supper, saying, "Then they sang a hymn and went out to the Mount of Olives (Mark 14:26)." The disciples felt a deep joy as they walked along under the stars. But it was bittersweet, for Jesus had said many sorrow-tinged things. He said, "This is my body, which is given for you... This is my blood, which is poured out for you (Luke 22:19-20)." Even though Jesus warned his disciples that he was to die violently (Matthew 16:21), they never quite got the point. ~ Mark Link, S.J.

As we reflect on these daily readings, are we getting His point? Are we hearing God's call of the Knights, as the right arm of the Church?

Every time ministers call their people around the table, they call them to experience not only the LORD's presence but his absence as well; they call them to... sadness as well as to joy.
~ Henri J. M. Nouwen

March 3 *Saint Katharine Drexel*

FRATERNITY is a stewardship of treasure

The harvest is large, but there are few workers. ~ Matthew 9:37

Kate Drexel came from a wealthy family in Philadelphia. Riding
through the city one day in the 1880s, Kate saw the tragic plight of
African-American children living in hideous slum conditions.
When she probed their plight, she became convinced that prejudice,
broken promises, and unjust laws were creating a cycle of ignorance
and powerlessness for these children. Kate decided to do
something.
She founded the Sisters of the Blessed Sacrament to work among
African-American and Native American children.
By the time Mother Katharine Drexel died, she had spent nearly $20
million of her own personal fortune on this work. The order she
founded over a hundred years ago continues her work.
Her canonization was granted by Pope John Paul II.
~ Mark Link, S.J.

If you had $20 million to spend as you wished, what is one thing
you would use it for immediately?

*A man's true wealth hereafter, is the good he does in this world to
his fellow man. When he dies, people will say 'What property has
he left behind him?' but the angels will ask, 'What good deeds has
he sent before him?'* ~ Mohammed

March 4

CHARITY is being rescued by the LORD

I love you just as the Father loves me. ~ John 15:9

Someone asked an old chief "Why're you always talking about
Jesus?"
The chief didn't say anything. Instead, he collected some dry grass
and twigs and put them into a circle.
Next he caught a caterpillar, feeding on a nearby clump of weeds.
He placed it inside the circle. Then, he took a match and set fire to
the dry grass and the twigs. As the fire blazed up, the caterpillar
began to search for an escape.
At this point the old chief extended his finger to the caterpillar.
Instantly, it climbed on to it.
He said, "That's what Jesus did for me. I was like the caterpillar,
without hope. Then Jesus rescued me. How can I *not* talk about my
Savior's love and mercy?" ~ Mark Link, S.J.

How grateful are you for what Jesus did for us? How do you show
it concretely?

It wasn't the nails that held Jesus on the cross but his love for us.
~ Author unknown

March 5

UNITY is wishing emeralds were peanuts

These three remain: faith, hope, and love; and the greatest of these is love. ~ 1 Corinthians 13:13

Helen Hayes was not yet a famous actress, when she met her future husband, Charlie MacArthur. She wrote: "I was at a party feeling very shy because there were a lot of celebrities around. I was sitting in a corner alone and a very handsome young man came up to me and offered me some salted peanuts and said, "I wish they were emeralds." And that was the end of my heart. I never got it back."

In the final years of her famous life, Helen was sitting alone again. This time an older Charlie came up to her, gave her a handful of emeralds, and said, "I wish these were peanuts." ~ Mark Link, S.J.

Have you experienced love, as Helen did? Have you expressed it, as Charlie did?

He came into my life as the warm wind of spring awakened the flowers, as the April showers awaken the earth. My love for him was unchanging... strong as death. ~ A. Chennault

March 6

FRATERNITY is putting your life on the line for your brother

The greatest love a person can have for his friends is to give his life for them. ~ John 15:13

Reverend Benny Newton was watching the news when rioting erupted in Los Angeles following the acquittal of the policemen involved in the Rodney King beating.

He rushed to the rioting scene, arriving just after an angry mob had pulled Fidel Lopez from his truck, stripped him, spray-painted him, and began beating him. Throwing himself across Lopez's body, he yelled, "If you kill him, you'll have to kill me too."

When the mob backed-off, Newton drove Lopez to a hospital, where the trucker received 58 stitches in his forehead.

"He put his life in mine," Lopez said, "He saved me."

~ Mark Link, S.J.

Imagine you are Fidel Lopez. What are your thoughts before and after Newton intervened?

You may forget the brother with whom you laughed, but you will never forget the brother with whom you cried.
~ adapted from an Arab Proverb

March 7

PATRIOTISM is touching the nation's heart by song

Sing hymns and psalms to the LORD with praise in your hearts.
~ Ephesians 5:19

Irving Berlin, was the most popular American songwriter of the century. He died in 1989 at the age of 101.
The Berlin family came to New York as part of the tide of Jewish immigrants from Czarist Russia in 1893. A keen observer of the western culture, young Irving began his music career as a singing waiter, parodying hit songs. He went on to write 1,500 tunes and 19 Broadway shows. His "God Bless America" became the nation's second national anthem. His "White Christmas" became history's top-selling song.
A fellow songwriter, Harold Arlen, said of Berlin's songs, "They sound as if they were born that way – God Almighty – not written!"
~ Mark Link, S.J.

What is your favorite patriotic song?

God respects me when I work, but he loves me when I sing.
~ Rabindranath Tagore

CHARITY is Charlie Brown

Everyone who makes himself great will be humbled, and everyone who humbles himself will be made great. ~ Luke 14:11

The cartoon character Charlie Brown is based on a real person. He worked with juvenile delinquents, often housing them temporarily in his own home. After the real Charlie Brown died in 1983, a friend said of him, "He saw his own life as the doing of daily works of charity in imitation of Christ and the saints."

Charles Schulz – the Charlie Brown creator – was a friend of the real Charlie. He sometimes offered him a share of the cartoon profits, but Charlie always refused. He had no big interest in money. Nor did Charlie go about telling people that he was the real Charlie Brown. ~ Mark Link, S.J.

Can you ever recall bragging about yourself or seeking recognition from others? To what extent do you still do it? Why?

Until we lose ourselves, there is no hope of finding ourselves.
~ Henry Miller

March 9

UNITY is the parable of the two sons

*[Jesus told a parable about a father. He said to his son], "'Go and
work in the vineyard today.' 'I don't want to' he answered, but
later he changed his mind and went."* ~ Matthew 21:28-29

The film, *Tom Brown's School Days*, concerns a popular boy who
lived with about a dozen other boys in the dormitory of a British
boarding school.
One night, a new boy innocently knelt beside his bed to say his
prayers. Several older boys poked fun at him.
That night, Tom lay awake thinking about how his mother taught
him to pray nightly – something he no longer did.
The next night, several boys were planning to poke more fun at the
new boy. When bedtime came, however, something unexpected
happened to change their plans. When the new boy knelt down to
say his prayers, so did Tom. ~ Mark Link, S.J.

What is one thing in your life that you should change? What is one
thing in our council that we should change?

When you're through changing, you're through.
~ Bruce Barton

March 10

FRATERNITY goes beyond my own family and friends

Fishermen throw their nets out in the lake and catch all kinds of fish. When the net is full, they pull it to shore and sit down to divide the fish. The good ones go into the buckets, the worthless ones are thrown away. It will be like this at the end of the age.
~ Matthew 13:47-49

Albert Schweitzer was a concert pianist who gave up his career in music to become a doctor and missionary to Africa.
He once said, "It's not enough to say, "I'm a good father. I'm a good husband."… You must do something… for those who have need of help, something for which you get no pay but the privilege of doing it. For remember, you don't live in a world all your own. Your brothers and sisters are here too." ~ Mark Link, S.J.

Do you count your fraternal brothers in your circle of friends?

Yours are the only hands with which God can do his work… Yours are the only eyes through which God's compassion can shine upon a troubled world. ~ Saint Teresa of Avila

March 11

CHARITY is what is needed most at the moment

Love the LORD your God… This is the greatest and the most important commandment. The second most important commandment is like it: "Love your neighbor as you love yourself. ~ Matthew 22:37-39

An old poem by an unknown poet asks this question: "What is Love?" The poet responds by listing six answers. They go something like this.

Love is –
silence – when words would hurt,
patience – when another's hurt,
deafness – when another's mad,
gentleness – when another's sad,
promptness – when need is seen,
courage – when life is mean.

Of the poet's answers of love, which do I score highest on? Lowest? What is one concrete thing I might do to make my love more like Jesus' love?

What does love look like? It has feet to go to the poor and needy. It has eyes to see misery and want. It has ears to hear sighs and sorrows. ~ Saint Augustine

March 12

UNITY is a forest of trees being pruned by the Master

O LORD, you are our Father. We are the clay, you are the potter; we are all the work of your hands. ~ Isaiah 64:7

Like a tree, we must be pruned of a lot of dead branches before we will be ready to bear good fruit. We can think of changed people as trees which have been stripped of their old branches, pruned, cut and bare. But through the dark, seemingly dead branches flow silently and secretly. With the new sap comes new life. With the sun of spring, there are new leaves, buds, blossoms, and fruit, many times better because of the pruning. We are in the hands of the Master Gardener, who makes no mistakes in His pruning.
~ Fr. Pat Umberger

Pray that we may cut away the dead branches of our lives. Pray that we may not mind the pruning, since it helps us to bear good fruit later.

Choose one area of your prayer life which might benefit from attention, such as repentance, faith, zeal, relationship, boldness, humility, contentedness, concern for God's honor. How will you strengthen this area?

Snowflakes are one of nature's most fragile things, but just look what they can do when they stick together. ~ V.M. Kelly

March 13

FRATERNITY is defending the needy, especially the young

If anyone should cause one of these little ones to lose faith in me, [woe to that person]. ~ Mark 9:42

A skinny boy with a shoeshine kit stood at the edge of a sidewalk café. A woman felt a surge of admiration for him for trying to be a man and earn a living.
Just then a man charged out of the café, grabbed the boy, and threw him like a bag of garbage out into the street.
The woman's heart went out to the boy. Why did the man treat the boy so brutally?
He hadn't picked anybody's pocket. He hadn't stolen anyone's purse. He hadn't tried to sell drugs.
As the boy limped off, ashamed and humiliated; the diners went back to eating. The woman wondered: "How will this cruel experience affect his attitude toward work and people?"
~ Mark Link, S.J.

How would you have reacted if you had witnessed this incident? Now, in retrospect, how *should* a Catholic gentleman react?

Give us clear vision that we may know where to stand and for what to stand, because unless we stand for something, we put up with everything. ~ adapted from Peter Marshall

PATRIOTISM is sacrificing all

The greatest love you can have for his friends is to give your life for them. ~ John 15:13

PFC Milton Lee Olive III sacrificed his own life to save four fellow soldiers during the Vietnam War. An enemy grenade landed in the midst of five soldiers. Without thinking twice, Olive smothered it with his own body.

In awarding him the Medal of Honor posthumously, President Lyndon Johnson said:

"In that incredible brief moment… in which he decided to die, he put others first and himself last. I have always believed that to be the hardest but the highest decision that any man is called upon to make." ~ Mark Link, S.J.

What is one of the hardest decisions you were ever called upon to make? What helped you make it?

If you limit your choices only to what seems possible or reasonable, you disconnect yourself from what you truly want, and all that is left is compromise. ~ Robert Fritz

March 15

CHARITY is learning from a childhood memory

Love is patient and kind... Love never gives up.
~ 1 Corinthians 13:4,7

Alan Loy McGinnis tells this story about the author Dr. Norman
Lobsenz. Young Norman's wife was in the midst of a serious
illness, and the ordeal was taking its toll on Norman. One night he
was on the verge of collapse when, suddenly, he recalled an incident
from his childhood.

One night when his mother had taken ill, Norman got up around
midnight to get a drink of water. As he passed his parents'
bedroom, he saw his father sitting in a chair on his mother's side of
the bed. She seemed fast asleep. Norman rushed into the room and
cried, "Daddy, is Mom worse?"

"No, Norman," his father said softly, "I'm just sitting here watching
over her, in case she wakes and needs something."

That long-forgotten incident from his childhood gave Norman all
the strength he needed to carry on. ~ Mark Link, S.J.

What episode from your childhood is a source of strength for you?

The pains of love be sweeter far
Than other pleasures are.
~ John Dryden

March 16

UNITY is sharing Psalm 139

The LORD is… in this place, and I didn't know it. ~ Genesis 28:16

During World War II, Eddie Rickenbacker and a crew of seven crashed into the Pacific. All supplies were lost, except for four small oranges.
After eight days, it rained and they were able to collect a supply of water to drink. On another occasion, a seagull landed on Rickenbacker's head. He caught it for food, which they all shared.
After 21 days, rescue came.
One of the things that kept them going was a prayer session each day. A prayer they prayed often was Psalm 139.

Where could I go to escape from you?
Where could I get away from your presence?…
If I flew away beyond the east
or lived in the farthest place in the west,
you would be there to lead me,
you would be there to help me (Psalm 139:7, 9-10).
~ Mark Link, S.J.

Can you recall a time when your Brother Knights were gathered in prayer and you sensed the Father's presence in a special way?

Closer is He than breathing, nearer than hands and feet.
~ Alfred Lord Tennyson

March 17 *St. Patrick*

FRATERNITY is remembering that Christ is with us

Who shall separate us from the love of Christ? Shall trouble or hardship or persecution or famine or nakedness or danger or sword? ~ Romans 8:35

Christ, be with me, Christ before me, Christ behind me,
Christ in me, Christ beneath me, Christ above me,
Christ on my right, Christ on my left,
Christ where I lie, Christ where I sit, Christ where I arise,
Christ in the heart of every one who thinks of me,
Christ in the mouth of every one who speaks of me,
Christ in every eye that sees me,
Christ in every ear that hears me,
Salvation is of the LORD,
Salvation is of the LORD,
Salvation is of the Christ,
May your salvation, O LORD, be ever with us.
~ Saint Patrick, A Prayer

Patrick was a humble, pious, gentle man, whose total devotion and trust in God should be a shining example to every Knight. He feared nothing, not even death. How can we emulate Saint Patrick's complete trust in God?

The love of God and his fear grew in me more and more, as did the faith, and my soul was roused, so that, in a single day, I have said as many as a hundred prayers and in the night nearly the same.
~ Saint Patrick, during his captivity as a teenage slave in Ireland

CHARITY is bringing a bit of heaven to earth

Why should God reward you if you love only the people who love you? Even the pagans do that... Be perfect just as your Father in heaven is. ~ Matthew 5:48

Gandhi was the guiding star and architect of India's independence. For over 20 years he opposed British rule with programs of nonviolent disobedience. Toward the end of his life, he got many death threats. This caused a friend to quip:
"The saints in heaven have been awaiting Gandhi's arrival for sometime now, but he's making them wait. He's working on his dream of bringing a bit of heaven's perfection to earth before he leaves for heaven."
On January 30th, 1948, Gandhi was shot by an extremist, who didn't share his dream of getting India's factions to live together in mutual love and harmony. ~ Mark Link, S.J.

What bit of heaven's perfection can we as Knights dream of leaving before we depart for heaven?

It is not a calamity to die with dreams unfulfilled, but it is a calamity not to dream. ~ Benjamin E. Mays

March 19 *St. Joseph*

UNITY is following a real man's man

I bow my knees before the Father, from whom every family in heaven and on earth is named. ~ Ephesians 3:14, 15

One of my favorite saints is Saint Joseph, because he was a man's man – a man accustomed to labor, sweat and the burden of supporting a family. Scripture says, "Unless the LORD builds the house, those who build it labor in vain (Psalm 127:1)." It's always struck me that God the Father put His only Son into the care of a carpenter, a builder. And Joseph, in his faith and obedience, allowed God to use his own human talents to build the Living Tabernacle. Joseph protected and taught, formed and provided for, the Redeemer of the world.

Joseph was a living witness of the meaning of manliness; the nobility of human labor; and the dignity of married love. Surely, Jesus must have admired and loved him with all his heart. So if we hope to restore the identity of fathers in our families and in our culture, if we hope to rebuild the integrity of family life in our communities... we should look first to Joseph. We have no better model. ~ Most Reverend Charles J. Chaput, O.F.M. Cap., Archbishop of Denver, Colorado

How can we Knights model our lives after Saint Joseph?

Husbands and fathers... Spend time with your kids. Keep Sunday holy. Pray together. Choose to be faithful. Be the leaders you were meant to be. ~ Most Reverend Charles J. Chaput, O.F.M. Cap., Archbishop of Denver, Colorado

FRATERNITY is built on deeds that withstand the years

Let your hope keep you joyful. ~ Romans 12:12

In 1985, Japan Airlines Flight 123 crashed into a mountain killing 517, the worst single plane crash in air history. Minutes before the jumbo jet hit a mountain, passengers were told it was going to crash. Rescuers found in the wreckage a pocket calendar belonging to an executive of a Japanese shipping company. In his final seconds of life on earth, he had dashed several notes across seven pages of the calendar sharing his thoughts with his family.

I'm very sad.
I'm sure I won't make it.
To think that our dinner last night was the last time.
Be good to each other and work hard.
Kids, help your mother.
~ Mark Link, S.J.

If you were in the same situation, what would you scribble to your family that might surprise them? Would you consider expressing those sentiments now?

A home is built of loving deeds that stand a thousand years.
~ Victor Hugo

March 21

PATRIOTISM is a young man who serves his country

*The LORD bless you and keep you; the LORD make his face to
shine upon you, and be gracious to you; the LORD lift up his
countenance upon you, and give you peace.* ~ Numbers 6:24

All of my students were dear to me, but Mark was one in a million.
He had that happy-to-be-alive attitude that made even his occasional
mischievousness delightful. He talked incessantly. I had to
constantly remind him that speaking out of turn was not acceptable.
What impressed me so much, though, was his sincere response
every time I had to correct him for misbehaving – "Thank you for
correcting me, Sister!" One day, I asked each of my students to list
their classmates on two sheets of paper. Then I told them to think of
the nicest thing they could say about each person and write it down.
I summarized everyone's comments and then gave each student his
or her list. Before long, the entire class was smiling. Years later,
Mark was killed in Vietnam. When I attended the funeral, I had
never seen a serviceman in a military coffin before. Mark looked so
handsome, so mature. When his parents retrieved his personal
effects, they found two worn pieces of notebook paper that had
obviously been taped, folded and refolded many times. I knew it
was the list of nice things his classmates had said about him. That's
when I finally sat down and cried. I cried for Mark and for all of his
friends who would never see him again. ~ Sister Helen P. Mrosla

How is our assembly planning to salute our patriots on Memorial
Day and Independence Day?

Whoever loves God must also love his brother. ~ 1 John 4:21

81

March 22

CHARITY is giving us this day our daily bread

"I am the bread of life," Jesus told them. "Those who come to me will never be hungry. ~ John 6:35

In his book, *Swimming in the Sun*, Albert Haase tells how one afternoon, he was walking through the grounds of the infamous Dachau concentration camp.
Coming to the spot where Barracks 26 once stood, he paused and prayed. That barracks was the prison dormitory where many Catholics were imprisoned by the Nazis in World War II. Each day they were given one meal, consisting of a chunk of bread and a cup of watered-down soup.
Each day one of the prisoners sacrificed their meager bread ration to make possible the celebration of Mass. This 'daily bread' ration was then secretly consecrated by a priest and passed around as communion for prisoners. ~ Mark Link, S.J.

How willing are we as Knights to sacrifice what we have so that others may receive their physical or spiritual "daily bread"?

The effect of our sharing in the body and blood of Christ is to change us into what we receive. ~ Pope St. Leo the Great

UNITY is celebrating the Eucharist – at all costs

Where two or three come together in my name, I am there with them. ~ Matthew 18:20

A religious persecution in 1980 left a region of Guatemala without priests. But the people continued to meet in their churches. Once a month they sent delegates to a part of Guatemala where priests still functioned.
Traveling up to eighteen hours on foot, the delegates put a basket of bread on the altar and celebrated the Eucharist in the name of their parish.
After the Mass, they took the bread home. Now it was the Body of Christ. When the government threatened to close all churches, the people said, "If the authorities forbid us to meet in the churches, we shall gather under the trees of the woods or in the caves of the mountains."
~ Fernando Bermudez, *Death and Resurrection in Guatemala*

Are there more subtle forms of religious persecution going on in your community? If so, what can Knights do to combat them?

If you do not eat the flesh of the Son of Man and drink his blood, you will not have life in yourselves. ~ John 6:53

FRATERNITY is striving for the greater glory of God

Does a person gain anything if he wins the whole world but loses his life? ~ Mark 8:36

A basketball team had just celebrated a prayer service before playing in the state tournament.

During the service, the chaplain said to the team, "The important thing ten years from now won't be whether or not you won the state championship. Rather, it will be what you became in the process of trying to win it."

After the prayer service, the coach said to the players: "Sit down a minute. Our chaplain said something that is bothering me. I wonder what we've become trying to put together a winning season. Have we become more loyal to one another? More brotherly? Better Catholics?

I hope to God that we have. Because if we haven't, we've failed God, we've failed one another, we've failed ourselves."
~ Mark Link, S.J.

This past year, have we become more loyal to one another? More brotherly? True Catholic gentlemen?

You can't turn back the clock. But you can wind it up again.
~ B. Prudden

CHARITY is a steadfast choice for Life

Then the angel said to her, "Do not be afraid, Mary, for you have found favor with God. Behold, you will conceive in your womb and bear a son, and you shall name him Jesus." ~ Luke 1:30-31

The Solemnity of the Annunciation marks the moment when God Himself began redeeming the unborn child – and all of us who once were unborn children – by becoming one Himself. Never can the unborn be considered too small to possess rights, for God Himself was that small.

The Annunciation teaches us the fruitfulness of self-giving. When Mary said "Yes" to "Life", she knew the road ahead would be difficult, yet she embraced the vocation of motherhood. This is precisely the opposite behavior that avoids responsibility, and culminates in abortion. What happened at the Annunciation overcomes the fear and despair that lead to violence. Mary's life gives courage to all mothers who are afraid of the suffering that might lay ahead and assures them that they are not alone.

How is our council, following Mary's example, engaging in active charity and providing alternatives to abortion?

We must be concerned about the nonviolent affirmation of the sacredness of all human life if we are to have peace on earth and good will toward men... Man is a child of God, made in His image, and therefore must be respected as such... When we truly believe in the sacredness of human life, we won't trample over people with the iron feet of oppression, and we won't kill anybody.
~ Dr. Martin Luther King, Christmas Eve, 1967

UNITY is looking at life through loving eyes

Those who trust in the LORD for help will find their strength renewed. They will rise on wings like eagles. ~ Isaiah 40:31

Nelda Bonner was dying of cancer. In her final months, sleep became difficult. So she would write in a journal. Her five children found it after her death. It contained over 40 handwritten pages of memories. Her are some excerpts:
"In a strange way, I have been happier this last year than I have ever been. I have a peace and calmness that I have never had before. I have discovered what my real relationship with God is... Your daddy and I are closer than we have ever been. He has been my rock. I have learned to appreciate more than ever small things: a few hours of feeling good... the lovely faces of my grandchildren. I glory in the beauty around me – I truly look at the world through the eyes of love." ~ Mark Link, S.J.

Need we wait until we are on our deathbed before we appreciate the truly important things in our lives?

Adversity brings us back to earth, kindly pulling us by the ear to remind us of what is truly important.
~ Author unknown

FRATERNITY is taking your turn in formation

Whoever wants to be first must place himself last of all and be the servant of all. ~ Mark 9:35

Twice a year geese migrate in a V formation, as a flock. Philip Yancey explains:
"That's the secret of their strength... cooperating as a flock, geese can increase their flight distance by 71-percent... The lead goose cuts a swath through the air resistance, which creates a helping uplift for the two birds behind him. in turn, their beating makes it easier on the birds behind them... Each bird takes his turn as the leader. The tired birds fan out to the edges of the V for a breather, and the rested ones surge forward to the point of the V to drive the flock onward." ~ *Campus Life*

Are you ready to assume the point in the V formation of our council? Is our council ready to assume the lead in the V formation of our parish? The Catholic Church?

O God, help us to be masters of ourselves that we may be servants of others. ~ Sir Alec Paterson

March 28

PATRIOTISM is hanging in and doing your best

As long as it is day, we must do the work of him who sent me; night is coming when no one can work. ~ John 9:4

President Harry S. Truman once said: "The greatest epitaph in the country is right here in Arizona. It's in Tombstone, Arizona, and the epitaph says, "Here lies Jack Williams. He done his damndest." I think that is the greatest epitaph a man could have. Whenever a man does the best he can, then that is all he can do; and that is what your President has been trying to do for the last three years for this country." ~ Mark Link, S.J.

What motivates Knights to do the best they can for God and country?

Let us be up and doing,
With a heart for any fate;
Still achieving, still pursuing,
Learn to labor and to wait.
~ Henry Wadsworth Longfellow

March 29 *Anniversary of the Knights of Columbus (1882)*

Soldiers of Christ

Endure hardship with us like a good soldier of Jesus Christ.
~ 2 Timothy 2:3

Soldiers are identified by their uniforms. Spies and undercover
agents disguise themselves, hoping to slip in without being noticed.
The LORD doesn't need undercover Christians. He needs those
who wear His uniform and proudly identify themselves with Him.
Do you act as a "secret believer" – one who unveils your
Christianity only when it is non-threatening? In hostile situations,
do you cover up your true identity? This kind of clandestine
discipleship makes it easy to deny the LORD in difficult times.
When the apostle Peter tried to secretly follow the LORD at a
distance, on three occasions he denied that he knew Jesus.
To come out of your foxhole, you must first decide to be identified
with Jesus Christ as your LORD and Savior. No more secrecy, no
more undercover discipleship. Straightforwardly proclaiming your
allegiance to the LORD is practical evidence of your faith.
~ Carman, adapted from *Raising the Standard*

Do your friends and coworkers know that you are Catholic? Do
they know you are a Knight? Are you a clandestine Knight in
hostile situations?

When people hear us speak God's word,
they marvel at its beauty and power;
when they see what little impact it has on our daily lives,
they laugh and poke fun at what we say. ~ a 2nd century Christian

March 30

UNITY is one body, one spirit in Christ

All of us… are one body, for we all share the same loaf.
~ 1 Corinthians 10:17

Astronauts Aldrin and Armstrong had just landed on the moon.
While Armstrong prepared for his moonwalk, Aldrin unpacked
bread and wine. Aldrin wrote: "I poured the wine into the
chalice… In the one-sixth gravity of the moon the wine curled
slowly and gracefully up the side of the cup. It was interesting to
think that the very first liquid ever poured on the moon and the very
first food eaten there were communion elements. I sensed
especially strong my unity with our church back home, and the
Church everywhere." ~ *Guideposts* - Treasury of Hope

What is one thing the Knights might do to build a stronger sense of
unity in our parish? In our local community?

*In Jesus Christ, true God and true man… rests our hope for real
humanity. Not by ourselves, but insofar as we are members of the
Body of Christ.* ~ Karl Barth

March 31

FRATERNITY is sharing your gift with others

Happy are those whose greatest desire is to do what God requires;
God will satisfy them fully! ~ Matthew 5:6

The great American concert violinist, Fritz Kreisler, said: "I was
born with music in my system. It was a gift from God. I didn't
acquire it. So I do not even deserve thanks for the music. Music is
too sacred to be sold, and the outrageous prices charged by musical
celebrities today are truly a crime against society. I never look upon
the money as my own. It is public money. It is only a fund
entrusted to me for proper disbursement... In all these years of my
so-called success in music, my wife and I have not built a house for
ourselves. Between it and us stand all the homeless in the world."
~ Mark Link, S.J.

How fully do you agree with Kreisler? Do you share God's gifts to
you with your brethren?

Serve one another with whatever gift each of you has received.
~ 1 Peter 4:10

April 1 *April Fool's Day*

CHARITY is a fool for Christ

For the message of the cross is foolishness to those who are perishing, but to us who are being saved it is the power of God.
~ 1 Corinthians 1:18

I once saw a man in Los Angeles wearing a sign that said, "I'm a fool for Christ. Whose fool are you?"
I thought at the time, "That's the most stupid thing I've ever seen."
But one night many years later it would be revealed to me that God – who is more than just an image on a piece of wood – loved me.
And though I had shunned Him all my life, I realized my desperate need of Him. It was then that I understood the truth of that odd sign I had seen years before: the cross is foolishness to those who are perishing.
That night I knelt at the foot of the cross and believed in Jesus. I have been a fool for Christ ever since. ~ John Wimber, adapted

Has such a revelation ever come to you? How does our council promote a spirituality that brings us closer to Christ?

So then do not be foolish, but understand what the will of the LORD is. ~ Ephesians 5:16-18

April 2

UNITY is seeing the LORD in many faces and many places

I urge you, then, to make me completely happy by... being one in soul and mind. ~ Philippians 2:2

On the seventh and last night of the bike trip for AIDS, Mark Bosco wrote in his journal:
"The words of novelist Alice Walker came to me as I finished the last few miles – 'I think it annoys God if you walk by the color of purple in a field somewhere and don't notice it.'
This whole trip became for me an exercise in noticing things – the beauty of creation as I pedaled past mountains, farms, and beaches... the diversity of God's people forming a community of friendship and support in the face of a terrible disease... My faith in God and his people has been renewed... The ride gave me the gift of noticing my LORD alive in so many places, in so many faces." ~ Mark Link, S.J.

Have you ever seen the LORD alive in your Brother Knights' faces?

Place yourself at one another's service.
~ Galatians 5:13

April 3

FRATERNITY is fellow warriors

I went past the field of the sluggard, past the vineyard of the man who lacks judgment; thorns had come up everywhere, the ground was covered with weeds, and the stone wall was in ruins. I applied my heart to what I observed and learned a lesson from what I saw: A little sleep, a little slumber, a little folding of the hands to rest – and poverty will come on you like a bandit and scarcity like an armed man. ~ Proverbs 24:30-34

Saint Paul challenges all of us as men to finish the race and to be on our guard. He knows that even if we've built a positive legacy to this point, there are wolves waiting at the door, ready to tear it from our grip and steal it away. He knows that we can lose our testimony as a role model in a single unguarded moment.

Don't let anyone rob a lifetime of influence on your wife and your children. Don't let moral poverty sneak up on you like a slinking wolf and rip away your witness for Jesus Christ. Guard your heart! Guard it in the limitless power of God's indwelling Spirit.

But don't stand guard alone. You need fellow warriors to pray for you, walk with you, and remind you of what you already know. And there are brothers out there who need the same thing from you! An arm around the shoulder. A brotherly nudge in the right direction. God warns us, and we warn each other. God strengthens us, and we strengthen each other. ~ Gary Rosberg

Are you and our council brothers well-positioned to stand guard together?

Character may be manifested in great moments, but it is made in small ones. ~ Phillip Brooks

April 4

PATRIOTISM is waging war against evil

Christ Jesus… gave himself to redeem all mankind.
~ 1 Timothy 2:5-6

This month, back in 1865, the slain body of President Lincoln lay in state in Cleveland, Ohio. It was on its way from Washington, DC to Springfield, Illinois, where it would be buried.
In the long line of people filing past the body was a poor black woman and her little son. When they reached the president's body, the woman lifted up her son and said in a hushed voice, "Honey, take a long, long look. That man died for you."

What that mother said about Lincoln, every mother could say to her child about Jesus. Both Jesus and Lincoln tell us that waging war against evil involves great personal suffering – even the loss of one's own life. ~ Mark Link, S.J.

Against what modern evil should the Knights be willing to wage war and suffer much – even losing our lives, if necessary?

It's important that people know what you stand for. It's equally important that they know what you won't *stand for.*
~ Author unknown

April 5

CHARITY, UNITY AND FRATERNITY is the Passion of the Christ

For thou, O LORD, art good and forgiving, abounding in steadfast love to all who call on thee. ~ Psalm 86:5

THE PASSION OF THE CHRIST a movie directed by Mel Gibson, has depicted the last 12 hours of Jesus Christ's life, in no way that the film industry has ever dramatized before. It underscores the emotion, pain and passion of the crucifixion of Jesus Christ. Anyone who has seen the movie came out of the theatre understanding better just how incredible his love for us is. Everything about the Son of God comes down to this: he forgives us because he loves us. As we all know love is the cornerstone of the virtue of Charity. If you have seen the movie, especially with others in a movie theatre, the sense of unity and fraternity that it offers is profound.

The next time you receive the Body and Blood of Christ, remember that it is his actual Body and Blood, and that despite how dramatic the movie might have been, it still pales in comparison to receiving and experiencing the Eucharist itself. ~ a Sir Knight

How do you feel and what do you think when your are receiving the Body and Blood of Christ? Do your reverence the Eucharist whenever you are in its presence – the presence of Christ?

So we, who are many,
are one body in Christ,
and individually members one of another.
~ Romans 12:5

April 6

UNITY is a house of prayer

Them I will bring to my holy mountain and make joyful in my house of prayer; their holocausts and sacrifices will be acceptable on my altar, for my house shall be called a house of prayer for all peoples.
~ Isaiah 56:7

Dorothy Day died in New York City in 1980. The *New York Times* called her the most influential person in the history of American Catholicism. There's now a movement to canonize her for her personal life of poverty and for her work among the poor.
In her book, *From Union Square to Rome*, Day wrote that before her conversion to Catholicism she used to go to early morning Mass at St. Joseph's Church on Sixth Avenue. What attracted her were the people kneeling in prayer. She says, "I longed for their faith. So I used to go in and kneel in the back pew." She was drawn to St. Joseph's because it was clear it was a "house of prayer." ~ Mark Link, S.J.

Would a visitor to our parish church witness the same devotion and faith as Day witnessed at St. Joseph's? Does our council help make our parish a place of welcome for all? What would a newcomer say about our parish?

In prayer we should unite ourselves to the community.
~ The Talmud

April 7 *St. John the Baptist de la Salle (1651-1719)*

FRATERNITY is leading little brothers to Christ

Let the little children come to me, and do not hinder them, for the kingdom of God belongs to such as these. ~ Luke 18:16 NIV

John was a French priest who became famous as a teacher of underprivileged boys. When he became aware of the needs of poor children, he felt himself called to respond. John would later give away his share of the family fortune. He began training a group of young men as teachers, thus beginning the order known today as the Christian Brothers. John successfully introduced several new educational methods and established colleges for training teachers. His success in training delinquent and underprivileged boys provoked bitter opposition from secular schoolmasters, who resented his emphasis on Christian values. Ignoring his critics, John urged his teachers to treat their students with love, compassion, and concern for their spiritual well-being. One of the lessons we learn from John is that our calling from God may at first seem unpleasant, but if we persevere, we will learn to love the life God intends for us. John initially didn't want to work with children, but he obeyed the LORD's will, and ended up being very happy and fulfilled in his educational ministry. Another lesson, as John learned, was that educating young people is an important way of serving Christ – especially by preparing them for eternity through an emphasis on faith and morality. ~ J.M. Guerin

Knights are the big brothers of Squires. What has our council planned for this year to support and mentor our Squires Circle?

The Savior has only good things to say about children.
~ Author unknown

April 8

PRAY until something happens

…Whoever believes in Him shall not perish, but have eternal life. ~ John 3:16

A man was sleeping when the Savior appeared. The LORD told him there was work to be done, and showed him a massive rock which he was to push with all his might. For many years the man toiled. The Adversary sensed his despair and placed thoughts into his weary mind: "You are never going to move it."
"Why kill myself over this?" the man thought. He decided to make it a matter of prayer and take his troubled thoughts to the LORD. "I have labored long and hard in Your service. Yet, I have not budged that rock by half a millimeter. Why am I failing?"
The LORD responded compassionately, "When I asked you to serve me, your task was to push against the rock with all your strength. Never once did I mention that I expected you to move it. And now you come to me, thinking that you have failed. But now you are strong and muscled. Through opposition your abilities now surpass that which you used to have. Your calling was to be obedient and to exercise your faith in Me, and you have done so. I, my friend, will now move the rock."
By all means, exercise the faith that moves mountains, but know that it is God who moves them. ~ Author unknown

Do you entertain thoughts from the Adversary when you grow weary?

When everything seems to go wrong, just PUSH! When the job gets you down, just PUSH!
P.U.S.H. – Pray Until Something Happens ~ Author unknown

April 9

UNITY is brothers helping one another

*If there is a poor man among your brothers... do not be hardhearted
or tightfisted toward him.* ~ Deuteronomy 15:7

The parable of the rich man and the poor man (Luke 16:19-31) inspired the stirring homily of Pope John Paul II at Yankee Stadium
in 1979. He said, "We cannot stand idly by, enjoying our own
riches and freedom if, in any place, the Lazarus of the 20th century
stands at our doors... The rich man and Lazarus are both human
beings, both of them equally created in the image and likeness of
God, both of them equally redeemed by Christ."
~ Mark Link, S.J.

What caused the rich man to be condemned? How have your
values changed since you became a Knight? How do you think
God might want them to change some more?

*The poor of the United States and of the world are your brothers
and sisters in Christ. You must never be content to leave them just
the crumbs of the feast. You must give of your substance, and not
just of your abundance.*
~ Pope John Paul II

April 10

FRATERNITY is Brother Knights praying as one

When you pray and ask for something, believe that you have received it, and you will be given whatever you ask for.
~ Mark 11:24

Jim Johnson was sent to save a failing hotel. The situation was so bad that Jim decided upon desperate measures.
Each night he drove to a hill overlooking the hotel. He parked, sat in the car, and prayed for twenty minutes. He prayed for the hotel guests, behind the lighted windows. He prayed for the employees and their families. He prayed for himself.
Gradually, changes started to take place in the hotel. A new spirit radiated from its employees. New warmth greeted each new guest. Hope permeated the operation. Within a year, the hotel was back on its feet.
Norman Vincent Peale, who tells the story, ends with this thought:
If the prayer of one person could revitalize a hotel, think what the prayer of an entire nation could do for the world.
~ Mark Link, S.J.

When was the last time our council gathered for a prayer vigil or recited the rosary?

Prayers travel more strongly when said in unison.
~ Gaius Petronius

April 11 *St. Stanislaus (1030-1079)*

PATRIOTISM is fighting political and social injustice

The LORD gives strength to his people. ~ Psalm 29:11 NIV

The Polish bishop and martyr, St. Stanislaus, spent seven years studying canon law and theology. He earned a doctorate, but he refused it out of humility. When his parents died, Stanislaus gave away his inheritance, and was ordained a priest.
Stanislaus' great eloquence and piety generated a spirit of renewal and conversion in the local community. When he became bishop in 1072, Stanislaus soon found himself embroiled in political affairs. He was outspoken in his attacks upon political and social injustices of the immoral King Boleslaus II, who warred with his neighbors and oppressed the peasantry. In 1079, the bishop excommunicated Boleslaus. The enraged king ordered his soldiers to murder Stanislaus; when they refused, he killed the bishop with his own hands while Mass was being celebrated. Because of Stanislaus' popularity, King Boleslaus was forced to flee to Hungary, where he's said to have spent the rest of his life doing penance in a Benedictine monastery. St. Stanislaus is the patron of Poland.
~ J.M. Guerin

St. Stanislaus teaches us that we must use our influence to oppose injustice and become involved in politics if necessary. From a Catholic perspective, is a complete separation of Church and state always possible?

Patriotism consists not in waving the flag, but in striving that our country shall be righteous as well as strong.
~ James Bryce

April 12

CHARITY is clothing yourself with humility

*... In your relations with one another, clothe yourselves with
humility, because God is stern with the arrogant but to the humble
he shows kindness... Cast all your cares on Him because He cares
for you.* ~ 1 Peter 5:5-7

Years ago, Don Shula, legendary coach of the Miami Dolphins, was
vacationing in a small town in Maine.
One rainy afternoon, Shula, his wife, and five children went to the
town's only theater. When they walked in, only six other people
were there. To a person, however, they stood up and applauded the
Shula family.
As the Shulas sat down, a man came running up and shook the famous coach's hand.
"How did you recognize me?" Shula asked him.
"Mister, I don't know who you are," he replied. "All I know is that
the manager announced before you came in with your family that
unless five more people showed up, there wouldn't be a movie today." ~ Mark Link, S.J.

Humility creates in us a capacity for the closest possible intimacy
with God. How do you handle humbling experiences when they
come unexpectedly into our lives?

*Once the game is over, the king and the pawn go back into the same
box.* ~ Italian Proverb

April 13

UNITY is God protecting His people

*Do not be afraid – I am with you! I am your God – let nothing
terrify you! I will make you strong and help you; I will protect you
and save you.* ~ Isaiah 41:10

Dr. Sheila Cassidy left England and practiced medicine among the
poor in Chile. Then one day she was arrested by the Chilean secret
police for treating a revolutionary leader.
She was taken into custody, tied down, and tortured for four days
by having electrodes attached to her body. When she was
eventually released, she explained her courage this way:
"I think it was the fact that prayer had become an integral part of
my life before I became a prisoner that made it possible for me to
face the unknown with a calm that surprised even me."
~ Mark Link, S.J.

Of all the peoples conquered by Babylon (see Isaiah 41), only the
Jews retained their religious, ethnic, and political identity. How
might this be a witness to the Knights of Columbus? How might
the Knights relate to Israel's call to be His servant?

Who has God, lacks nothing. God alone is enough.
~ Saint Teresa of Avila

April 14

FRATERNITY is boyhood memories

*I am writing to you, little children, because your sins have been
forgiven you for His name's sake.* ~ 1 John 2:12

A priest is walking down the street one day when he notices a
small boy trying to press a doorbell on a house across the street.
The doorbell is just outside the reach of the young man.
After watching the boy's efforts, the priest steps smartly across the
street. He walks up behind the little fellow and, placing his hand
kindly on the child's shoulder, leans over and gives the doorbell a
solid ring.
Crouching down to the child's level, the priest smiles benevolently
and asks, "And now what, my little man?"
To which the boy replies, "Now we run!" ~ Author unknown

Recall a favorite boyhood memory. Were you mischievous?
Today, are you more likely to err on the side of doing what you
shouldn't or not doing what you should?

The wildest colts make the best horses.
~ Plutarch

April 15

CHARITY is working unseen

... The greatest among you should be like the youngest, and the one who rules like the one who serves. ~ Luke 22:26

Exalt Christ.
Use a sharp knife with thyself. Say little, serve all, pass on.
This is true greatness, to serve unnoticed and work unseen.
Oh, the joy of having nothing and being nothing,
seeing nothing but a Living Christ in Glory,
and being careful for nothing but His interests down here.
~ J.N. Darby

Service is one of the hallmarks of knighthood and the greatest is he who serves others (Matthew 23:11). How generously do you serve others?

Service is the stairway by which we mount to the throne of God.
~ Author unknown

April 16

UNITY is finding God

When you pray, go to your room, close the door, and pray to your Father, who is unseen. And your Father, who sees what you do in private, will reward you. ~ Matthew 6:6

Rabbi David Wolpe authored the book, *Teaching Your Child about God*. He tells a story about a boy who began wandering into the nearby woods. This concerned the child's father, so one day he said, "I have noticed that each afternoon you wander off into the woods. What do you do in such a dangerous place?"

The child said, "I go there to find God."

"That is a good thing; I'm glad that you are searching for God," said the father. "But, my child, don't you know that God is the same everywhere?" "Yes," the boy answered, "but I'm not." ~ Mark Link, S.J.

What is the point of Rabbi Wolpe's story? Is there a place where you readily find God?

Oh, help me, LORD, to take the time to set all else aside, That in the secret place of prayer I may with Thee abide. ~ Author unknown

April 17

FRATERNITY is total devotion to the LORD

Therefore, I urge you, brothers, in view of God's mercy, to offer your bodies as living sacrifices, holy and pleasing to God – this is your spiritual act of worship. ~ Romans 12:1

When the Spanish explorer Hernando Cortez landed in Mexico in 1519, he was intent on conquest. To ensure the devotion of his men, he set fire to his fleet of eleven ships. With no means of retreat, Cortez's army had only one direction to move, into the Mexican interior. Cortez understood the price of commitment and he paid for it.

The apostle Paul also understood the price of dedication. After assuring us of our victory in Christ, he calls on us to burn our ships, bridges, or anything else that ties us to our destructive former life. Furthermore, he challenges us to commit ourselves completely to God (see above scripture).

Is Paul asking a lot? Yes! But he's not asking too much. He begins his exhortation with the word 'therefore' because he wants to point us back to everything he's written in the previous eleven chapters. In those chapters, he explained that God offers us forgiveness, acceptance, freedom from the dragon, a wonderful future, and the power needed for a victorious life. In light of all that, God wants our total devotion. ~ Bill Perkins

It's important to realize that God extends His mercy without strings to all who believe (Ephesians 2:8,9). But does our refusal to devote ourselves to God short-circuit His power in our lives?

To seek God, is the greatest adventure. To find Him, the greatest human achievement. ~ R. Simon

April 18

PATRIOTISM is working for peace

Happy are those who work for peace; God will call them his children! ~ Matthew 5:9

Although Truman hastened the war's end with his controversial decision to drop the atom bomb, he ordered a "peace statement" to be made on the nation's presidential seal.
It was used to show an eagle with arrows (war) in one talon and the olive branch (peace) in the other. Early versions had the eagle face the arrows. Truman ordered all future versions to show the eagle facing the olive branch, to symbolize that our nation was turned toward peace, not war. ~ Mark Link, S.J.

What are some of the things pointing our nation in the wrong direction? Sir Knights, how can we move the nation in the right direction?

O God... help us to keep in mind the real causes of war: dishonesty, greed, selfishness, and lack of love. Drive them out of this ship, so that we may be a pattern of the new world for which we are fighting.
~ Lord Hugh Beresford, Royal Navy, 1941

April 19

CHARITY is the everlasting love of the LORD

Therefore do not worry about tomorrow, for tomorrow will take care of itself. ~ Matthew 6:34

When you are tired and discouraged from fruitless efforts...
God knows how hard you have tried.
When you've cried so long and your heart is in anguish...
God has counted your tears.
If you feel that your life is on hold and time has passed you by...
God is waiting with you.
When you don't know where to turn...
God has a solution.
When nothing makes sense and you are confused or frustrated...
God has the answer.
When you have much to be thankful for...
God has blessed you.
When something joyful happens and you are filled with awe...
God has smiled upon you.
When you have a purpose to fulfill and a dream to follow...
God has opened your eyes and called you by name.
Remember that wherever you are or whatever you are facing...
GOD KNOWS.
~ Fr. Pat Umberger

Why pray when you can worry? What causes you the most worry? What are the signs that indicate you are worrying too much? What is God saying to us through the above verse?

Without courage, all other virtues lose their meaning.
~ Winston Churchill

April 20 *Columbine High School, Littleton, Colorado (1999)*

In memory of all those we lost at Columbine

And whenever you stand praying, if you have anything against anyone, forgive him… ~ Mark 11:25

If God is causing all things in your life to work together for good, then you can thank Him for whatever you're encountering. God is in charge. God is in control. And when your life seems but a wasted heap, remember that He works wonders with raw materials. It pleases the LORD when we subjugate our will to His: "LORD, I submit this to You. I don't know how to deal with it, so I just thank You for it and I believe Your Word." ~ Charles Stanley

The answers we search for won't come from the White House or the courthouse – we must start in *our* house. Do you know where your children are?

Columbine, friend of mine,
Peace will come to you in time.
~ The Cohen Brothers

April 21

FRATERNITY is realizing that giving is a privilege

Whoever receives anyone I send receives me, also; and whoever receives me receives him who sent me. ~ John 13:20

Ensworth Reisner remembers a minister who had very little money and was just scraping by. One day, a destitute family came to him. The minister was moved to pity and gave them all the money he had on hand. Then, as they left, he said, "Thank you for the privilege of letting me help you."
Reisner says, "Those remarkable words taught me an important lesson. When people give you the opportunity to help them, they give you the opportunity to be like God. And for that we should give them thanks." ~ Mark Link, S.J.

What keeps us, as Knights, from having the same attitude that Ensworth Reisner has?

God has given us two hands – one to receive with and the other to give with. We are not made cisterns for hoarding; we are channels made for sharing. ~ Billy Graham

April 22 *Death of Brother Barnabas, Squires Founder (1929)*

CHARITY is training faithful young men for Knighthood

For you know the gracious act of our Lord Jesus Christ, that for your sake he became poor although he was rich, so that by his poverty you might become rich. ~ 2 Corinthians 8:9

In 1923, Christian Brother Barnabas McDonald, a noted expert in the field of social welfare work with young people, created an official junior organization for the Knights of Columbus, the Columbian Squires. He formed the Squires as a faithful group of young Catholic men between the ages of 12 and 18. Approximately 26,000 Squires belong to more than 1,000 Circles internationally. The Squires are active throughout the United States, Canada, the Philippines, Mexico, Puerto Rico, and Guam. In 1995, Circles donated more than $300,000 in charitable contributions and volunteered over 460,000 hours of community service to such causes.
Squires engage in leadership activities in four major areas: Spiritual, Service, Circle and Membership. Knowing that they have other activities (school, sports, jobs and dates), they do what they can, when they can and have fun doing it! ~ A Sir Knight

From Jesus' example in the above passage, what prompts you to be more generous with your time for young Squires? What inhibits you?
With prom season approaching, would our council consider sponsoring a Squires alcohol awareness campaign for our community, traditionally known as "Dying for a Drink"?

You are the bows from which our children as living arrows are sent forth. ~ Kahlil Gibran

April 23

UNITY is the poor and the rich dancing together

[They place on] people's backs loads that are heavy... yet they aren't willing even to lift a finger to help them carry those loads.
~ Matthew 23:4

Cesar Chavez has been called a "modern-day Moses" for migrant workers. He brought unity to their ranks in Florida and helped them achieve their first labor contract. It brought justice to the poorest of the poor. He died on this date in 1993 and was carried to his rest by over 35,000 marchers amid dancing and mariachi music. Sons, grandsons, and celebrities rotated as pallbearers, carrying the plain white pine coffin that was built by his brother. One of the gifts presented at Mass was a short-handled hoe, the backbreaking tool that was banned, thanks largely to Chavez's efforts.
~ Mark Link, S.J.

To be a man is to suffer for others.
God help us to be men! ~ Cesar Chavez

How do you account for the incredible display of unity generated at the Chavez funeral?

Blessed is the influence of one, true, loving human soul on another.
~ George Elliot

FRATERNITY is shining forth in a crisis situation

Teach me, LORD, what you want me to do. ~ Psalm 86:11

Singer Pearl Bailey died in 1990. Her heart was as big as her body. Her spirit truly shined when an Amtrak train with 400 passengers on board jumped the track in Mansfield, Ohio, slamming into an embankment.

Amid the wreckage and confusion, a familiar voice rang out calmly, "This is Pearl, honey! Don't worry! Everything's going to be all right!"

Dressed only in a night robe and sneakers, she took a leadership role, becoming a big sister to the injured passengers, calming and helping them. "She was something out there!" said one of the rescue workers. ~ Mark Link, S.J.

What kind of brother are you in ordinary situations? Perhaps more importantly, what kind of brother are you in crisis situations?

No personal consideration should stand in the way of performing a public duty. ~ Author unknown

April 25

PATRIOTISM is citizens lifting together

Behold, how good and how pleasant it is for brothers to dwell to-gether in unity! ~ Psalm 133:1-2

Ages ago a flock of a thousand quails lived together in a forest in India. They would have been happy, but they were in great dread of their enemy, the quail hunter. He would trick them by mocking their call and then capturing them with a great net.

The wise quail said, "Brothers! When the fowler throws his net over us, let each one put his head through a mesh in the net and then all will lift it up together and fly away with it!"

The next day, the fowler threw his net, and the birds escaped as they had planned. This continued for many days, and the fowler's wife grew angry. The fowler explained, "The trouble is that all the birds are working together and helping one another."

A few days later, one of the quails accidentally trod on the head of one of his brothers. Then they began to argue about who was lifting most of the weight of the nets. The fowler saw his chance and cast his net over the quails once more. They were still boasting and quarreling, forgetting to work the net together. So the hunter lifted the net himself and took his catch home.
~ *Jataka* tales, adapted

In our common affairs, one of the basic truths of citizenship is that we pull and lift together or we perish. Do you find Christian community in our council? What hinders it?

Any kingdom divided against itself will be ruined, and a house divided against itself will fall. ~ Luke 11:17 NIV

CHARITY is strengthened by His power

I pray that out of his glorious riches he may strengthen you with power through his Spirit in your inner being... ~ Ephesians 3:16

Behold, LORD, an empty vessel that needs to be filled. My LORD, fill it. I am weak in the faith; strengthen thou me. I am cold in love; warm me and make me fervent that my love may go out to my neighbour. I do not have a strong and firm faith; at times I doubt and am unable to trust thee altogether. O LORD, help me. Strengthen my faith and trust in thee. In thee I have sealed the treasures of all I have. I am poor; thou art rich and didst come to be merciful to the poor. I am a sinner; thou art upright. With me there is an abundance of sin; in thee is the fullness of righteousness. Therefore, I will remain with thee of whom I can receive but to whom I may not give. Amen. ~ Martin Luther

Have you been through a difficult time, only to find that your endurance has strengthened your faith?

If He bids us carry a burden, He carries it also.
~ Charles Spurgeon

April 27

UNITY is a fortified unit

... make my joy complete by being like-minded, having the same love, being one in spirit and purpose. ~ Philippians 2:2

Redwood trees are the giants of the forest. They tower above the earth at heights of over three hundred feet. Unlike most trees, which send their roots to a depth equaling their height, redwoods send their roots outward, intermingling their roots with one another. Together they form a fortified unit, a secure stronghold that allows these giants to withstand high winds.

That is how strength is achieved among men as well, by working together as a unified whole. Men working together bring strength, whether dealing in the workplace, leading families at home, or serving in churches. Unfortunately, individualism among men prevails in the church. In fact, the individual approach has produced a generation of isolated men at church. The individualism imitates the independence and surface relationships among men in American society... We weren't created to live in isolation. But we often act as if we were!... Men, we need each other! ~ Pete Richardson, excerpted

As our ranks continue to grow, UNITY is a constant struggle within every council. When was the last time our council enjoyed widespread participation in a council activity or event?

We must learn to live together as brothers or perish together as fools. ~ Dr. Martin Luther King, Jr.

April 28

FRATERNITY is standing shoulder to shoulder

Do not be afraid; do not be discouraged. Go out to face them
tomorrow, and the LORD will be with you.
~ 2 Chronicles 20:17 NIV

I've stepped over the line. I am out of the comfort zone.
The decision has been made. I am a follower of Jesus Christ.
I won't look back, let up, slow down or back away.
I am finished with low living, small planning, smooth knees, tame
visions, chintzy giving and dwarfed goals.
I no longer need pre-eminence, prosperity, positions or popularity.
I don't have to be right, first, recognized, praised or rewarded.
I now learn by faith, love by patience, lift by prayer and labor by
power. My face is set, my gait is fast.
My goal is heaven, my road is rough, my Guide reliable.
I cannot be bought, compromised, detoured, lured away, turned
back, diluted or delayed.
I will not flinch in the face of adversity, negotiate at the table of the
enemy or meander in the maze of mediocrity.
I must go on until He comes to get His own, He will have no
problem recognizing me, because I have dedicated my life to being
a believer committed to doing whatever it takes.
~ Author unknown

As Knights, we not only strive to serve others, but to spiritually
grow closer to God. What has our council done this year in terms
of spiritual growth?

All life is the management of risk, not its elimination.
~ Walter Wriston

April 29

CHARITY is a gift from God if we are willing to receive it

Ask and you will receive, so that your joy may be complete.
~ John 16:24

We need not let ourselves think that we cannot do something useful or that we never will be able to accomplish a useful task. The fact is that we can do anything in the field of human relationships, if we are willing to call on God's supply of strength. The supply may not be immediately available, because we may not be entirely ready to receive it, but it will surely come when we are properly prepared for it. As we grow spiritually, a feeling of being plentifully supplied by God's strength will possess us and we will be able to accomplish many useful things. ~ Fr. Pat Umberger

Pray that we may claim God's supply of strength by our faith in Him. Pray that it shall be given to us when we are ready to receive it.

What sorts of spiritual programs can our council implement to increase our supply of God's strength and enable us to accomplish more good works?

I know of no great men except those who have rendered great service to the human race. ~ Voltaire

April 30

UNITY is simple faithfulness to Him

Be faithful to me... and I will give you life as your prize of victory.
~ Revelation 2:10

A neighborhood grocery store is owned by a couple of simple
means. Although they don't talk a lot about God, they live in His
presence.
Their love for each other makes their store a holy place. Customers
leave the store feeling more human... closer to God.
After a long, twelve-hour day, the couple puts things in order for
the next day, turns off the lights, and bolts the door. Then they go
home, have a glass of wine, watch TV, and say their simple prayers
to a friendly God or light a candle to the Madonna. Sometimes
they play cards or reminisce. Then they go to bed.
~ James Kavanaugh, adapted

Are there any people in your life who exhibit this kind of simple
faith? Have they influenced your perspective on life?

God has not called me to be successful; he has called me to be
faithful. ~ Mother Teresa of Calcutta

May 1 *St. Joseph the Worker*

Labor of Love for Him

For where your treasure is, there also will your heart be.
~ Matthew 6:20-21

"May Day" was celebrated throughout the Communist world as a way of supposedly honoring the role and importance of laborers in Marxist countries. The Communist conception of work as an end in itself was, of course, very different from the Christian understanding. In 1955, to highlight this difference, Pope Pius XII instituted the feast of St. Joseph the Worker. Joseph, the husband of Mary and the foster-father of Jesus, spent a lifetime laboring as a carpenter. His primary motivation for working wasn't a quest for riches or status, but a desire to serve God and to care for his family in a loving way. Joseph never worked any miracles; he never made any important speeches; he wasn't a public figure, but was known only as a humble carpenter (Matthew 13:55). Joseph labored in obscurity, but was nonetheless given an important part in God's plan.
Work is not intended to be an end in itself or a path to earthly riches; rather, it's meant to glorify God and to help us prepare for eternity. Honest and humble labor is a source of true human dignity. ~ J.M. Guerin

Do you labor only for material gain or does your work glorify God?

Socialism… cannot be brought into harmony with the dogmas of the Catholic Church… ~ Pope Pius XI (Achille Ratti), from the encyclical, *Quadragesimo Anno* (1931)

May 2

PATRIOTISM is praying for our nation

If my people, upon whom my name has been pronounced, humble themselves and pray, and seek my presence and turn from their evil ways, I will hear them from heaven and pardon theirs sins and revive their land. ~ 2 Chronicles 7:14

Every important event in Jesus' life found Him in prayer.

Jesus prayed at His baptism (Luke 3:21).
He prayed at the start of His ministry (Mark 1:35).
He prayed before picking the twelve (Luke 6:12).
He prayed before asking His disciples the question,
"Who do you say I am?" (Luke 9:18).
He prayed before going to Jerusalem (Luke 9:29).
He prayed in the garden (Luke 22:41).
He prayed on the cross (Luke 23:34).
He prayed before teaching His disciples how to pray (Luke 11:1).

What role does prayer play in the important events in our lives?

Be joyful in hope, patient in affliction, faithful in prayer.
~ Romans 12:12

Prayer is like the turning on of an electric switch.
It does not create the current;
it simply provides the channel through which the electric current may flow. ~ Max Handel

CHARITY is sharing the Good News with others

Rather, blessed are those who hear the word of God and keep it.
~ Luke 11:28

James is sometimes referred to as St. James "the Lesser," to distinguish him from St. James "the Greater," who was also an apostle and the brother of St. John, James' brother. St. Jude was also an apostle, and their mother Mary was a close relative of the Blessed Virgin; for that reason, James was sometimes called the brother (cousin) of the LORD. But James' holiness came not from being related to Jesus in a biological way, but in a spiritual one – and this is a relationship Our LORD offers to every one of His followers.

When Jesus called Philip as an apostle, his first impulse was to share the news with his friend, Nathanael, describing Jesus as "the One of Whom Moses spoke" (John 1:43-49). At the Last Supper, it was Philip who asked Jesus to show them the Father (John 14:8-9); he, like the other disciples, was slow to realize the union between God the Father and Christ. But Philip's example reminds us that, as Good News, the Gospel is meant to be shared with others; every Christian is called to evangelize in one way or another. ~ J.M. Guerin

Do we hear the Good News at every council meeting and how are we sharing it with others?

Be bold and mighty forces will come to your aid.
~ Basil King

UNITY is building a temple

So then you are no longer strangers and sojourners, but you are fellow citizens with the holy ones and members of the household of God, built upon the foundation of the apostles and prophets, with Christ Jesus himself as the capstone. Through him the whole structure is held together and grows into a temple sacred in the LORD; in him you also are being built together into a dwelling place of God in the Spirit. ~ Ephesians 2:19-22

Charles Schulz, author of the *Peanuts* cartoons, once said, "How can you go to something that you are already a part of? If you are a Christian, you *are* the Church."

Someone else said, "That's precisely my problem with the Church. How can I believe that Christ founded it, when I see so many second-rate Christians mutilate its teachings so badly?"

To that, someone replied, "That's like saying, 'How can I believe in the musical talent of Beethoven, when I hear so many second-rate musicians mutilate his Ninth Symphony so badly?' Beethoven's music isn't on trial; the second-rate musicians are."

~ Mark Link, S.J.

When people see us minister to God, they marvel at His beauty and power; but when they see what little impact He has in our lives, they laugh at what we believe. Do you consciously maintain your bearing as a Catholic gentleman at all times? What kind of witness to the Knights are you presenting to others?

The only way the world knows anything about Christ is by watching His followers.
~ Steve Lawhead

May 5

FRATERNITY is seeking our share of happiness together

*Be merciful, just as your Father is merciful. Do not judge, and you
will not be judged; do not condemn, and you will not be condemned.
Forgive, and you will be forgiven; give, and it will be given to you.
A good measure, pressed down, shaken together, running over, will
be put into your lap; for the measure you give will be the measure
you get back.* ~ Luke 6:36-38

Happiness cannot be sought directly; it is a by-product of love and
service. Service is a law of our being. With love in our heart,
there is always some service to other people. A life of power and
joy and satisfaction is built on love and service. Persons who hate
or are selfish are going against the law of their own being. They
are cutting themselves off from God and other people. Little acts
of love and encouragement, of service and help, erase the rough
places of life and help to make the path smooth. If we do these
things, we will surely have our share of happiness.
~ Fr. Pat Umberger

Pray that we may give our share of love and service. Pray that we
may not grow weary in our attempts to be righteous.

Based on the above verse, what part of your life could you improve
upon?

He who helps in the saving of others, saves himself as well.
~ Hartmann Von Aue

May 6

CHARITY is helping my fellow man

Having nothing, and yet possessing everything.
~ 2 Corinthians 6:10 NIV

A king once fell gravely ill. He grew worse with each passing day.
His servants were ready to give up hope when the king's old
nursemaid spoke up.
"If you can find a happy man," she said, "take the shirt from his
back, and put it on the king – then he will recover."
His messengers rode far and wide throughout the kingdom, and yet
nowhere could they find a happy man. No one seemed content;
everyone had some kind of complaint. If a man was rich, he didn't
have enough. If he was not rich, it was someone else's fault.
Finally one night the king's son was passing a small cottage when
he heard someone say: "Thank you, LORD. I've finished my
daily labor, and helped my fellow man. I've eaten my fill, and now
I can lie down and sleep in peace." The prince rejoiced in having
found a happy man at last. He gave orders to take the fellow's shirt
to the king, and of course pay the owner as much money as he
wished.
But when the king's messengers went into the cottage, they found
the happy man was so poor he had no shirt at all.
~ Author unknown

Learning how to work and learning how to be satisfied often seem
to go hand in hand. What needs to change in your life in order to
be a happy man with a shirt on your back?

The wise man carries his possessions within him.
~ Bias of Priene

May 7

UNITY is people of the light

Believe in the light... while you have it, so that you will be the people of the light. ~ John 12:36

Anne Herbert was sitting in a restaurant in Sausalito, California, when she wrote down a phrase she'd been mulling over for days. Now the phrase is seen everywhere on bumper stickers, business cards, and at the bottom of letters. One woman saw it spray-painted on a warehouse 100 miles from her home. When she got home, she tried to recall it to write it down, but it wasn't quite right. So she drove all the way back to copy it.
The phrase that appeals to so many reads:

"Practice random kindness and senseless acts of beauty."

Herbert believes that "random kindness" can trigger a tidal wave of good in the world, just as "random violence" triggers evil. Maybe that's why the phrase is seen everywhere. It touches something deep in the heart; it appeals to the very best in us.
~ Fr. Pat Umberger

What "random kindness" or "senseless act of beauty" can you commit today?

Like all revolutions, guerrilla goodness begins slowly, with a single act. Let it be yours. ~ Anonymous

May 8

FRATERNITY is feeling the presence of the Holy Spirit

*The people honored Joshua all his life, just as they had honored
Moses.* ~ Joshua 4:14

Alec Guinness played the British colonel in *The Bridge on the
River Kwai*. His autobiography, *Blessings in Disguise*, describes a
moving episode that began to thaw his anti-Catholicism and
prepare the way for his becoming a Catholic.
He was in a film being shot in France. One night, dressed as a
priest, he was walking to the film site. A small boy ran up,
grabbed his hand, swung it playfully, and prattled on nonstop.
Alec wrote: "He obviously took me for a priest and so to be
trusted. Suddenly with a 'Bon soir, mon pere'... he disappeared... I
was left with an odd calm sense of elation.
Continuing my walk, I reflected that a Church which could inspire
such confidence in a child, making its priests... so easily
approachable could not be as scheming and creepy as so often made
out." ~ Mark Link, S.J.

What kind of reverence do you have for persons and things linked to
God? How are Knights passing on this reverence to younger
generations?

*Shine through me and be so in me that every soul I come in contact
with may feel your presence in my spirit.*
~ John Henry Newman

May 9

PATRIOTISM is a nation united by noble leadership

Wherever you go, I will go; wherever you live, I will live.
~ Ruth 1:16

Imagine the following. A dynamic leader emerges in our world. The leader's charisma cuts across all national and social boundaries. Everyone trusts this person and recognizes that the "hand of God" rests upon this person. He gives a speech with compassion and understanding, spelling out programs for curbing corruption, reducing drug traffic and crime, revitalizing ghetto areas, reforming the prison system, and erasing poverty. Even the most realistic politicians are impressed by the leader's grasp of the problems and insights for dealing with them. The leader ends his address by asking for volunteers at every level and in every area of his proposed programs. ~ Mark Link, S.J.

Who has been a "Ruth" to you (see above verse and Ruth 1) – someone who has gone out of their way to be there for you in times of need? What impact has that person had on you? When has our assembly, collectively and individually, been faithful and supportive in a Brother Knight's time of need?

You see things as they are and ask "Why?"
But I dream things that never were and ask "Why not?"
~ George Bernard Shaw

CHARITY is an outstretched hand

I stretch out my hands to You; My soul longs for You, as a parched land. ~ Psalm 143:6

A nurse escorted a tired, anxious young man to the bedside of an elderly man. "Your son is here," she whispered to the old man. He was heavily sedated because of the pain of his heart attack. He dimly saw the young man standing outside his oxygen tent.
He extended his hand and the young man wrapped his fingers tightly around it, squeezing a message of encouragement. All through the night the young man held the old man's hand, offering gentle words of hope.
As dawn approached, the old man died. The young man placed the lifeless hand he had been holding on the bed, and then he went to notify the nurse.
"Who was that man?" He asked.
The startled nurse replied, "I thought he was your father."
"No," he answered. "I never saw him before in my life."
"Then why didn't you say something?" asked the nurse.
He replied, "I also knew he needed his son, and his son just wasn't here. When I realized he was too sick to tell whether or not I was his son, I knew how much he needed me..." ~ Author unknown

When charity is given out the door, God puts it back through the window. Recall an instance where you performed a charitable act and you received great joy from it.

Only great souls know the grandeur there is in charity.
~ Jacques BéNigne Bossuet

May 11

UNITY is stewardship of time, talent and treasure

A generous man will prosper; he who refreshes others will himself be refreshed. ~ Proverbs 11:25

The most contented and successful businessmen of my acquaintance are those who say sincerely: "God owns my business." Each of them acknowledges a responsibility to be as good an employee as possible for God. What they have learned is an attitude of trust – the belief that God knows what's best for us, His children. Putting our entire lives into His hands (yes, even our bankbooks and our mortgage payments!) will not result in some kind of catastrophe. Have you thanked God for your home? When you go to the grocery store, are you consciously grateful that you can pay for your family's needs? Have you asked God to bless your automobile with safety of operation? Have you offered to use it as He directs? Do you feel that tithing is giving God something of yours – or do you see it as returning to Him a fraction of what is already His? ~ Brock Thoene, *Protecting Your Income and Your Family's Future*

What are the possessions God has given you? What things are you most frightened of losing – your job, your savings, your standard of living? What financial plans are of greatest concern to you – your children's education, owning your own business, retiring comfortably?
Take all of these and consciously dedicate them all to His service. Trust completely in His ownership and planning.

It is not how much one makes but to what purpose one spends. ~ John Ruskin

FRATERNITY is joining forces with the Church

Instead, seek his kingdom, and these other things will be given you besides. ~ Luke 12:31

The first century martyrs, Saints Nereus and Achilleus, were Roman soldiers and members of the elite Praetorian Guard, entrusted with the responsibility of defending the Roman Emperor and persecuting Christians. Upon their dramatic conversion to Christianity, they were arrested, taken to the island of Terracina, and martyred. Aside from this, nothing else is known about them. Their unexpected conversions are a vivid reminder of the power of the Gospel and of divine grace. No matter how bleak a situation may appear, God is able to bring about amazing changes in fortune, validating Jesus' promise that the gates of hell shall not prevail against the Church (Matthew 16:18).
Pope St. Gregory the Great (d. 604) said on the feast of Nereus and Achilleus, "These saints despised the world and trampled it under their feet when peace, riches and health gave it charms." Like them, we are called to seek God's Kingdom first, and not the wealth and success this world offers (Luke 12:31-34).
~ J.M. Guerin

How would your life be different if you sought God's Kingdom first, instead of wealth and success?

The highest reward for a man's toil is not what they get for it, but what they become by it.
~ John Ruskin

May 13 *Fatima (1917)*

LOVE is possessing a sacred flower

Give thanks to the LORD… His love is eternal. ~ Psalm 118:1

On this date in 1981, in Fatima, Portugal, Pope John Paul II said to
the million people attending:
"On this very day last year… in Rome, the attempt on my life was
made in mysterious coincidence with the anniversary of the first
apparition at Fatima on May 13th, 1917. I seemed to recognize in
the coincidence of the date a special call to come to this place. And
so today I am here."
After Mass, the Holy Father asked Mary, the mother of Jesus, to
intercede for the world as she did for the married couple at Cana.
He ended by asking the Spirit for this grace:
"Let there be revealed once more in the history of the world the
infinite power of merciful love." ~ Mark Link, S.J.

How is the infinite power of God's love being revealed through the
works of the Knights right now?

Divine love is a sacred flower,
which in early bud is happiness,
and in its full bloom is heaven.
~ E.L. Hervey

May 14

UNITY is focusing our lives on truly worthy matters

What profit would there be for one to gain the whole world and forfeit his life? ~ Matthew 16:26

In 1917 Theodore Roosevelt expressed well the priority in each of our lives to attend church in community. He suggested that in this world a churchless community, a community where men have abandoned and scoffed at or ignored their religious needs, is a community on the rapid downgrade. He argued that while marriages could be dissolved through divorce, if done so on a wide scale, would mean the complete moral disintegration of our society.

He admonished all to attend Sunday church as a family. He acknowledged the argument of many who do not go, that they can worship anywhere, that it didn't need to be done in Church. But he went on to say "I also know as a matter of cold fact the average man does *not* thus worship or thus dedicate himself."

We should listen closely to our pastor's sermons. You may not always hear a good sermon, but it will be a sermon by a good man who wants the best for our eternal lives.

How does the above verse influence the way you make priorities in your faith life? Is attending church each week a priority?

I count him a great man who inhabits a higher sphere of thought, into which other men rise with labor and difficulty.
~ Ralph Waldo Emerson

May 15 *St. Isidore the Farmer (1070-1130)*

FRATERNITY is setting an example for your fellow workers

He has showed you, O man, what is good. And what does the
LORD require of you? To act justly and to love mercy and to walk
humbly with your God. ~ Micah 6:8

St. Isidore is the patron saint of farmers and rural communities.
Isidore was born in Madrid; as a young boy, he went to work for a
wealthy landowner. He would labor there for the rest of his life.
He was a model worker and a very devout Christian. Every day he
rose early in the morning to attend Mass – sometimes, according to
fellow workers, showing up late for work because he spent too
much time in prayer. Isidore would pray while plowing in the
fields, and it's even said that angels would sometimes help him
with his work.
Many of us desire to build a successful career, changing jobs when
better opportunities arise and perhaps even becoming our own
bosses. God's grace can be experienced in such a lifestyle, but this
measure of success is not required for holiness. St. Isidore had no
need to become independent, for he realized that he was ultimately
working for Christ. He also showed us that work and prayer can be
combined. This might mean arranging our schedule so as to
attend daily Mass; it also means praying while working. St. Isidore
worshipped God in both these manners, thereby sanctifying his
work and influencing those around him. ~ J.M. Guerin

Is there any aspect of this great saint's life that we Knights can
emulate?

Humility is the only true wisdom by which we prepare our minds for
all the possible changes of life. ~ George Arliss

136

May 16

PATRIOTISM is paving the way for generations yet to come

LORD, I put my hope in you; I have trusted in you since I was young. ~ Psalm 71:5

When the Civil War broke out, Oliver Wendell Holmes volunteered for the Union and was wounded three times in three different battles.
After the war, he graduated from Harvard Law School, became a Supreme Court justice in 1902, and served until his death in 1935.
He said in a speech late in his life:
"As I grow older, I grow calm... I do not lose my hopes... I think it probable that civilization will somehow last as long as I care to look ahead... I think it not improbable that man, like the grub that prepares a chamber for the winged thing it has never seen... may have cosmic destinies he does not understand."
~ Mark Link, S.J.

What experience with God in the past gives you confidence now that He will be with you in the future? At the rate our assembly is currently moving, what do you foresee as our assembly's destiny?

Behind the cloud the starlight lurks,
Through showers the sunbeams fall;
For God, who loveth all His works,
Has left His hope for all.
~ John Greenleaf Whittier

May 17

CHARITY is a child's angel

She is clothed with strength and dignity, and she laughs at the days to come. She opens her mouth in wisdom, and on her tongue is kindly counsel. She watches the conduct of her household. Her children rise up and praise her. Give her a reward for her labors, and let her works praise her. ~ Proverbs 31

Once upon a time there was a child ready to be born. One day the child asked God:
How am I going to live on earth being so small and helpless?
Among the angels, I chose one for you. She will care for you.
But, here in Heaven, I don't do anything else but sing and smile.
Your angel will sing for you and will also smile for you every day. And you will feel your angel's love and be happy.
And what am I going to do when I want to talk to You?
Your angel will place your hands together and teach you to pray.
I've heard that on earth there are bad men. Who will protect me?
Your angel will defend you even if it means risking its life.
But I will always be sad because I will not see You anymore.
Your angel will teach you the way to come back to Me.
At that moment there was much peace in Heaven, but prayers from earth could already be heard. The child asked softly:
Oh God, please tell me my angel's name.
Your angel's name is of no importance, you will call her: "Mommy"

Are we Knights attending to our Ladies and our Ladies Auxiliary?

Everything comes to us from others. To be is to belong to someone.
~ Jean Paul Sartre

May 18

UNITY is a council working for the LORD

But they that wait upon the LORD shall renew their strength;
they shall mount up with wings as eagles;
they shall run and not be weary;
and they shall walk and not faint. ~ Isaiah 35:4

Glenn Van Ekeren gives seminars on maximizing human potential.
He is fond of telling the story about a basketball coach who had the
rare art of inspiring teams with the courage to fight back when
things looked impossible. During the halftime of one difficult
game, he stood before the team and yelled, "Did Michael Jordan
ever quit?"
The team yelled back, "No!"
The coach yelled, "Did Cal Ripken, Jr. ever quit?"
The team yelled, "No!"
"What about the Wright brothers? Did they quit?"
"No!" yelled the team.
Then the coach shouted, "And what about Elmer McAllister. Did
he ever quit?"
There was an awkward pause.
Then the team captain said, "Coach, we never heard of him."
"Of course you didn't!" shouted the coach. "He quit!"
~ Mark Link, S.J.

What objective might our council be on the verge of giving up on?
Would a different approach prevent us from quitting?

Great things happen when men and mountains meet.
~ William Blake

FRATERNITY is tapping into the power of prayer

God purposely chose what the world considers nonsense in order to shame the wise, and he chose... what the world looks down on... to destroy what the world thinks is important.
~ 1 Corinthians 1:27–28

Young Joseph of Cupertino labored under a learning disability and was considered dull and clumsy. When he tried to enter religious life, he was turned down by one monastery after another.
Finally, in spite of his disability, a Franciscan group agreed to accept him.
Joseph acquired enough knowledge to be ordained a priest. Eventually, many miracles were attributed to him and many credible people, including Pope Urban VIII, saw him "levitate" while praying. His constant admonition to people was "Pray, pray, pray!"
~ Mark Link, S.J.

What is the greatest challenge I face when it comes to prayer?

If you are a stranger to prayer, you are a stranger to power.
~ Author unknown

May 20 *St. Bernardine of Siena (1380-1444)*

CHARITY is making His name the theme of your life

God greatly exalted him and bestowed on him the name that is above every name. ~ Philippians 2:9

St. Bernardine of Siena was known for his popularity with ordinary people. He once cared for an elderly woman who constantly pronounced the name "Jesus" with great devotion. Bernardine was profoundly affected, and decided to make the name of Jesus the theme of his own life. When Siena was struck by a plague, Bernardine nursed the sick until he himself became ill. After recovering, he became a Franciscan monk, and was ordained a priest in 1404. Bernardine spent a dozen years in solitude and prayer, and was then sent forth as a preacher. Bernardine was especially known for his devotion to the Holy Name of Jesus (see above verse), and he devised a symbol – *IHS* (the first three letters of the name Jesus in Greek) – to represent it. The symbol began to replace the superstitious symbols of the day. When a manufacturer of playing cards complained that the saint's preaching against gambling was depriving him of his livelihood, Bernardine told him to start making medallions with the *IHS* symbol. The man took this advice – making more money than ever and finding a holier way to make a living. ~ J.M. Guerin

St. Bernardine of Siena shows how deep our devotion to Jesus can be. How might we foster this profound devotion in our council?

Take the name of Jesus with you, child of sorrow and of woe;
Joy and comfort will be given to you; take it then, where'er you go.
~ L. Baxter

UNITY is the power of the Holy Spirit

My teaching and message were not delivered with skillful words...
but with convincing proof of the power of God's Spirit.
~ 1 Corinthians 2:4

TV celebrity Malcolm Muggeridge interviewed Mother Teresa of
Calcutta. The verdict of the videotaped interview was that it was
hardly usable.
Mother Teresa's delivery was halting and her accent was thick.
One BBC official, however, felt that the interview had a mysterious
power and decided to air it on a Sunday night. Response to the
program was amazing – both in terms of mail and contributions.
What came through was not "skillful words" but "the power of
God's Spirit" speaking through Mother Teresa – the same power
that Paul talks about in today's Bible reading. ~ Mark Link, S.J.

Can you recall a time when the Spirit seemed to strengthen and
guide our council in some situation?

As the earth can produce nothing without the energizing power of
the sun, so we can do nothing without the energizing power of the
Spirit. ~ Author unknown

May 22

FRATERNITY is sharing our lives and love with God

I pray that your love will keep on growing more and more, together with true knowledge and perfect judgment, so that you will be able to choose what is best. ~ Philippians 1:9–10

The Spiritual Exercises of Saint Ignatius contains this guideline for life:
"I believe we were created to share our life and love with God and other people forever. I believe that God created all other things to help us carry out this lofty purpose. I believe, therefore, that we should use the other things God created, insofar as they help us carry out the purpose for which we were created and to abstain from them insofar as they hinder us from doing this. Therefore, we shouldn't prefer, out of hand, certain things to others, for example, health to sickness, wealth to poverty, honor to dishonor, or a long life to a short one. Our sole norm for preferring a thing should be how well it helps us attain the end for which we were created."
~ Mark Link, S.J.

How do the above verses make you feel about the uncertainties in your life? How do you discern what is "true knowledge and perfect judgment (see above verse)"?

The strength of a person consists in finding out the way God is going, and going that way. ~ Henry Ward Beecher

May 23

PATRIOTISM is trusting a worthy leader

Stand firm and steady… Nothing you do in the LORD's service is ever useless. ~ 1 Corinthians 15:58

At the end of the Revolutionary War, the new United States owed back pay to the soldiers, men who had fought long and hard for the nation's freedom. Mutiny was close at hand. There was only one man who could influence them.

On March 15th, 1783, George Washington met with the armed forces. They had revered him during the lean, hard years of fighting; now, they glared at him with restless eyes. Washington spoke of his own dedicated service. He begged them not to "open the flood gates of civil discord, and deluge our rising empire in blood." He appealed to their honor and glory thus far. Then he paused. His audience did not seem moved. Washington produced a letter from the government that he started to read slowly. He stumbled and stuttered. Then Washington pulled from his pocket something his men had never seen him use before – spectacles. "Gentlemen, you must pardon me," he said quietly. "I have grown gray in your service, and now find myself growing blind."

This humble act touched his soldiers where words had failed. After the general left, the men voted to give Congress more time.
~ William Bennett, adapted

What was the underlying reason the men were persuaded to be patient a while longer?

My first wish would be that my military family should consider themselves as a band of brothers, willing and ready to die for each other. ~ General George Washington

May 24

CHARITY is attending to the rocks

I commanded you at that time all the things that you should do.
~ Deuteronomy 1:18

A teacher was speaking to a group of business students about time management. Using a wide-mouthed Mason jar, he filled it with a dozen fist-sized rocks. Then he asked, "Is this jar full?"
Everyone in the class said, "Yes."
"Really?" He then poured some gravel into the jar as he shook it, causing the gravel to work its way between the big rocks. Then he smiled and asked, "Is the jar full?"
By this time the class was on to him. "No," one of them answered.
"Good!" he replied. Then he used a bucket of sand to fill the gaps left between the rocks and the gravel. Once more he asked, "Is this jar full?"
"No!" the class shouted.
Once again he said, "Good!" Then he poured water into the jar until it was filled to the brim. Then he asked, "What is the point of this illustration?"
One eager beaver raised his hand and said, "No matter how full your schedule is, you can always fit some more things into it!"
"No." the speaker replied, "If you don't put the big rocks in first, you'll never get them in at all." ~ Author unknown

What are the big rocks in your life? Time with your loved ones, your faith, your finances, a cause? What are the big rocks in our council agenda?

Try not to become a man of success, but rather try to become a man of value. ~ Albert Einstein

May 25

UNITY is handling difficult situations with finesse

*As you enter a house, wish it peace. If the house is worthy, let your
peace come upon it; if not, let your peace return to you. Whoever
will not receive you or listen to your words – go outside that house
or town and shake the dust from your feet.*
~ Matthew 10:12-14

Schoolchildren were cutting across the lawn of an elderly couple,
wearing an ugly path in it. At first this only annoyed the couple.
But soon annoyance turned into anger. The couple knew something
had to be done. The situation was wrecking their peace of mind.
The couple's solution was beautiful. They put crushed gravel on the
path, lined it with flowers, and set a bench next to it. Then one
afternoon, as when school let out, they sat on the bench and greeted
the children.
The children responded wonderfully. They thanked the couple for
the path and sat and chatted with them. ~ Mark Link, S.J.

Maybe we can't preach the gospel by word, but we can preach it
by example as the elderly couple did. How do we handle situations
that threaten to destroy our peace of mind?

LORD, help us deal with ugly situations in a beautiful way.
~ Author unknown

FRATERNITY is running the race

*Therefore, since we are surrounded by so great a cloud of wit-
nesses, let us also lay aside every weight, and sin which clings so
closely, and let us run with perseverance the race that is set
before us.* ~ Hebrews 12:1

Catholic faith continually reminds us that we are not chess players
in a dark room lit by a single light bulb, absolutely alone with God,
but rather that we are being cheered on and helped by a huge
heavenly stadium full of saints, virgins, martyrs and ordinary
blokes who "fought the good fight" and "finished the race" under
circumstances just like ours. Frustrated with your job? So were a
million saints who soldiered through to heavenly glory. In pain,
lonely, frightened, confused? They've been there too and they are
shouting to you from the stands, "You can make it! We did! And
we know you can too! God will save you as he saved us!" So run
the race with perseverance and drop all the discouraging junk the
world hands you. God will be with you every step of the way! He
is your coach, you trainer, your cheerleader and your biggest fan!
~ Dr. Scott Hahn and Jeff Cavins

How should Knights "run the race"? What does hardship
demonstrate about a Knight's relationship to God? What comfort
do you get from knowing that a "cloud of witnesses" is watching
you run the Christian race?

*Servant of God, well done! well hast thou fought
The better fight, who single hast maintain'd
Against revolted multitudes the cause of truth.*
~ John Milton, *Paradise Lost*

May 27

CHARITY is allowing loved ones to go through life's struggles

But seek first his kingdom and his righteousness; and all these things shall be added to you. ~ Matthew 6:33

One day a small opening appeared on a cocoon. As the butterfly struggled to bust through the tiny hole, a man sat waiting to see the butterfly appear. As a show of compassion, he took a pair of scissors and snipped off the remaining bit of the cocoon. The butterfly then emerged easily – but it had a swollen body and small, shriveled wings.

The man continued to watch the butterfly expecting, at any moment, the wings would enlarge and expand. Neither happened. The butterfly spent the rest of its life crawling around with a swollen body and shriveled wings. What the man did not understand is that the restrictive cocoon and the struggle required of the butterfly are nature's way of forcing fluid from its body into its wings. That way, it would be ready for flight once it achieved freedom from the cocoon. Sometimes struggles are exactly what we need in our lives. If we went through our days without any obstacles, it would cripple us – we would not be as strong as what we could have been. And, we could never fly. ~ Author unknown

Do we sometimes bail our children out of a difficult situation, depriving them of a life lesson?

Every good and excellent thing in the world stands moment by moment on the razor-edge of danger and must be fought for – whether it's a principle, or a home, or a country.
~ Thornton Wilder

May 28

UNITY is communion with God

I am convinced that neither death, nor life, nor angels, nor rulers, nor things present, nor things to come, nor powers, nor height, nor depth, nor anything else in all creation, will be able to separate us from the love of God in Christ Jesus our LORD.
~ Romans 8:38-39

We can withdraw into the calm of communion with God. We can rest in that calm and peace. When the soul finds its home of rest in God, it is then that real life begins. Only when we are calm and serene can we do good work. Emotional upsets make us useless. The eternal life is calmness and when we enter into that, then we live as an eternal being. Calmness is based on complete trust in God. Nothing in this world can separate us from the love of God.
~ Fr. Pat Umberger

Pray that we may wear the world like a loose garment. Pray that we may keep serene at the center of our being.

How could the forces in the above verses disrupt our trust in God's love?

All things proclaim the existence of God.
~ Napoleon Bonaparte

May 29

FRATERNITY is approbation from the Holy Father

... You are all brothers. ~ Matthew 23:8

Speaking extemporaneously at the Vatican in 1973, Pope Paul VI said: "Tell your sons, your grandsons; tell the people that the pope loves the Knights of Columbus." Earlier he remarked: "Indeed you have been brothers to the poor, to the sick, to the young, to the aged and to the underprivileged. In the name of all those whom you have helped by your brotherly compassion, we thank you from our heart... Even more admirable have been your insistence upon the supremacy of God and your fidelity to the vicar of Christ. In truth you can call yourselves "brothers" because you call God your Father and have declared yourselves ready to do His will and serve His cause. In 1978, the Holy Father called the Knights "an immense force for good... We rely on you, on each of you, on the Order itself – to bring holiness to the world, to live the Gospel values in your families, to transmit them to your children with the infectious conviction of joyful faith. Christ needs you to bring fraternal concern to your neighborhoods, to exemplify justice in your communities, to spread peace and truth in the world."
~ *These Men They Call Knights*

How dedicated are you, personally, to the noble ideals of Knighthood? How does our council manifest its respect and love for the Successor of Peter, the Pastor of the Universal Church?

Why, that's a nation. The nation of Columbus! You should have representation at the United Nations! ~ Pope John Paul II, when told the Knights and their families numbered over five million strong in 1979.

May 30

PATRIOTISM is trusting in Him even in the face of evil

They said to one another, "Here comes that dreamer... Let's kill him... Then we will see what becomes of his dreams.
~ Genesis 37:19-20

One night, Dr. Martin Luther King, Jr., was just about to doze off when the phone rang.
A voice on the other end said, "Listen, nigger, we've taken all we want from you. Before next week, you'll be sorry you ever came to Montgomery."
Dr. King hung up. Suddenly, all of his fears came crashing down on him. He got up and heated a pot of coffee.
Then he sat down at the kitchen table, bowed his head, and prayed: "People are looking to me for leadership, and if I stand before them without strength and courage, they too will falter. I am at the end of my powers. I have nothing left. I've come to the point where I can't face it alone."
At that moment, Dr. King felt God's presence as he had never felt it before. ~ Mark Link, S.J.

When do you feel closest to God: in time of need, joy, love or prayer?

I am the LORD your God;... Do not be afraid; I will help you.
~ Isaiah 41:13

May 31

CHARITY is understanding the brevity of life

Moreover, when God gives any man wealth and possessions, and enables him to enjoy them, to accept his lot and be happy in his work – this is a gift of God. He seldom reflects on the days of his life, because God keeps him occupied with gladness of heart.
~ Ecclesiastes 5:19-20

I go for long walks in the woods a lot, and I ask myself if I'm handling [all this success] the way it ought to be handled. I don't know why it happened to me. God has a purpose for it. We are able to contribute an awful lot of money to His work, and maybe that's why. But I firmly believe it will be over one of these days – five years from now, ten years from now. The books will stop selling for whatever reason. All of this is temporary…
One of my best friends in college called me one day and told me that he had terminal cancer. I couldn't believe it. I asked him, "What do you do when you realize that you are about to die?" He said, "It's real simple. You get things right with God, and you spend as much time with those you love as you can. Then you settle up with everybody else." That left an impression with me.
~ John Grisham

As Knights, we are fortunate to have a fraternity of brothers to lean on. How can we teach each other to get things right with God and settle up with everyone *before* the end is near?

A good character is the best tombstone. Those who loved you and were helped by you will remember you when forget-me-nots have withered. Carve your name on hearts, not on marble.
~ C.H. Spurgeon

June 1

UNITY is becoming part of the mix

*The Kingdom of heaven is like this. A woman takes some yeast
and mixes it with a bushel of flour until the whole batch of dough
rises.* ~ Matthew 13:33

A teacher told her class, "When I was a girl, my grandma gave me a
big cucumber inside a bottle with a narrow neck. She said she'd
tell me a 'big secret' when I figured out how she got it into the
bottle. One day I was walking in Grandma's garden, and I saw a
bottle into which she had inserted a vine with a tiny cucumber on
it. Now I knew how she got the cucumber in the bottle; she grew it
there.
Then Grandma told me her 'big secret.' She said a 'good habit'
formed in childhood is like a tiny cucumber inserted in a bottle – or
like a tiny bit of yeast inserted in dough. The habit grows so big and
strong inside you that no one can take it away from you."
~ Mark Link, S.J.

What is one good habit, formed in childhood, which has grown
bigger in you? What are some good habits and/or bad habits our
council is forming?

*First we form habits, then they form us. Conquer your bad habits,
or they'll eventually conquer you.* ~ Dr. Rob Gilbert

153

June 2

FRATERNITY is resisting the temptation to withdraw inward

Even though our physical being is gradually decaying, our spiritual being is renewed day after day. ~ 2 Corinthians 4:16

Psychologist Julius Segal worked with the 52 Americans held captive by Iran for 444 days in the early 1980s.
He listed four reasons why some of them not only survived the ordeal but also grew stronger as a result of it.
First, they resisted the temptation to withdraw into themselves.
Second, they helped other captives. Shifting attention from their own woes and reaching out to help others had a remarkable healing effect on them. Third, they kept control of their lives. One captive invited his guards to sit down each time they entered his room.
"This was my space," he said. "They were my guests." This tiny gesture helped him stay in control and resist becoming a passive victim. Lastly, they learned to tap inner powers through prayer and meditation. ~ Mark Link, S.J.

Which of these four guidelines would be most helpful in crisis situations?
How ready and willing are we to help the wife and children of a Brother Knight when disaster strikes?

Start by doing what's necessary; then do what's possible; and suddenly you are doing the impossible.
~ Saint Francis of Assisi

June 3

CHARITY is sharing God's gift with the world

... Be rich in good works... ~ 1 Timothy 6:18

Although Henri Matisse was nearly 28 years younger than Auguste Renoir, the two great artists were dear friends and frequent companions. When Renoir was confined to his home during the last decade of his life, Matisse visited him daily. Renoir, almost paralyzed by arthritis, continued to paint in spite of his infirmities.

One day as Matisse watched the elder painter working in his studio, fighting torturous pain with each brush stroke, he blurted out:

"Auguste, why do you continue to paint when you are in such agony?"

Renoir answered simply:

"The beauty remains; the pain passes."

And so, almost to his dying day, Renoir put paint to canvas. One of his most famous paintings, *The Bathers*, was completed just two years before his passing, 14 years after this disabling disease struck him. ~ Mark Link, S.J.

Is our council aware of the God-given talents of its brethren? Do we use them toward the greater honor and glory of God?

Man's mind stretched to a new idea never goes back to its original dimensions. ~ Oliver Wendell Holmes

June 4

UNITY is a cornerstone

Did you never read in the Scriptures, 'The stone which the builders rejected, this became the chief corner stone; this came about from the LORD, and it is marvelous in our eyes'? ~ Matthew 21:42

A second-century story concerns a king who tried to get an influential subject to denounce Jesus.

The king said, "If you don't reject your Jesus, I will be forced to banish you."

The subject replied, "My dear king, you can't banish me from Jesus. He remains with his followers forever."

The king showed irritation and said, "If you don't denounce this Jesus, I'll seize everything you treasure."

The subject said, "The only thing I truly treasure is stored in heaven. There's no way you can seize it."

The king erupted and shouted, "You leave me no choice but to kill you." The subject said, "My dear king, I am already dead. I died with Jesus in baptism and share His own Divine life. You cannot kill me. You cannot kill Him." ~ Mark Link, S.J.

At different times in your life, how have you received Jesus?
Is Jesus like a cornerstone (the foundation in your building), or is He like a millstone (a weight that drags you down) in your life?

Faith is the act of trust by which one being, a sinner, commits himself to another being, a Savior.
~ Horace Bushnell

FRATERNITY is avoiding 'cannots'

Kind words bring life, but cruel words crush your spirit.
~ Proverbs 15:4

You cannot bring about prosperity
by discouraging thrift.
You cannot help small men
by tearing down big men...
You cannot lift the wage earner
by pulling down the wage payer.
You cannot help the poor man
by destroying the rich.
You cannot keep out of trouble
by spending more than your income.
You cannot further the brotherhood of man
by inciting class hatred.
You cannot establish security
on borrowed money.
You cannot build character and courage
by taking away men's initiative and independence.
You cannot help men permanently
by doing for them what they could and should do for themselves.
~ William J. H. Boetcker

Which of the above "cannots" is a problem in today's world?
Which are you most guilty of?

Two things are bad for the heart –
running up stairs and running down people
~ Bernard Baruch

June 6

PATRIOTISM is a backbone

*Jesus saw a very poor widow dropping in [the Temple treasury]
two little copper coins. He said, "I tell you that this poor widow
put in more than all the others... She... gave all she had to live on."*
~ Luke 21:2-4

Journalist Leo Aikman said there are four kinds of "bones" in every
organization.
First, there are the Wishbones.
They see the problem, talk about it, and hope that someone will do
something about it.
Second, there are the Jawbones.
They see the problem, talk about it, talk about it some more, but do
little else.
Third, there are the Knucklebones.
They see the problem, talk about it, and criticize what's being done
about it.
Finally, there are the Backbones.
They see the problem, study it prayerfully, roll up their sleeves, and
do what needs to be done. ~ Author unknown

One of the persistent challenges facing the leadership of the
Knights is a lack of widespread involvement on the part of council
members. Are you a backbone of your council or assembly? If
not, what kind of "bone" are you?

Laziness is nothing more than the habit of resting before *you get
tired.* ~ Mortimer Caplan

June 7

CHARITY is knowing God will see

Whatever you do, do your work heartily, as for the LORD rather than for men. ~ Colossians 3:23

Long ago in ancient Greece an aged sculptor was laboring over a block of stone. He carved with utmost care, probing the rock with his chisel, chipping away a fragment at a time, gauging the marks with sinewy hands before making the next cut. When it was finished, the piece would be hoisted high into the air and set on top of a towering shaft, and so would become the capital, or uppermost part, of a column. And the column would help support the roof of a lofty temple.

"Why spend so much time and effort on that section?" asked a government official who passed by. "It will sit fifty feet high. No human eye will be able to see the details."

The old artist put down his hammer and chisel, gazed steadily at his questioner, and replied: "But God will see it!"

~ as told by William Bennett

Does this story remind us who the really important audience is as we go about our daily work?

A work of art that is good in itself glorifies God because it reflects God. ~ Flannery O'Connor

June 8

UNITY is praying to Him

*Peace is what I leave with you; it is my own peace that I give you...
Do not be worried and... afraid.* ~ John 14:27

Piri Thomas waited until his young prison cell mate was asleep.
Then he knelt and prayed aloud to God. When he finished, a voice
added, "Amen!" It was his young cell mate.
"I believe in Dios, also," said the kid. "Maybe you don't believe it,
but I used to go to church, and I had the hand of God on me. I felt
always like you and I feel now... quiet, peaceful."
Then Thomas asked the kid, "What's it called, chico, this what we
feel?" "It's Grace by the Power of the Holy Spirit," the kid said.

Thomas wrote: "I didn't ask any more. There in the semi-darkness,
I found a new sense of awareness... I fell asleep thinking that I
heard the kid crying softly. 'Cry, kid,' I thought, 'I hear even
Christ crying.'"
~ Piri Thomas, excerpted from *Down These Mean Streets*

When was the last time our council prayed together with the fervor
of Piri Thomas and the kid?

*Acquire inward peace, and a multitude around you will find their
salvation.* ~ Saint Seraphim

June 9

FRATERNITY is relishing the brotherhood of the men

[Some soldiers heard David say he'd love a drink of water from a certain well. They sneaked through the enemy's lines,] drew some water from the well, and brought it back to David. But he... poured it out as an offering to the LORD and said, "I could never drink this! It would be like drinking the blood of these men who risked their lives!" ~ 1 Chronicles 11:18–19

An old story concerns a king's knight. He came upon a spring of delicious water. After filling his leather canteen with it, he began the daylong journey home to present it to the king. The king drank it with great relish and thanked him profusely.

After the subject left, the king's advisor asked for permission to take a drink of water. When he did, he nearly spit it out, because it was tepid and terribly stale.

He turned to the king and asked, "Why did you pretend to relish the water?"

The king replied, "It wasn't the water that I was relishing; it was my knight's love." ~ Author unknown

What is the most memorable fraternal deed your Brother Knights have done for you? Have you returned an act of kindness to a Brother Knight in some way?

God doesn't want our deeds; God wants the love that prompts them. ~ Saint Teresa of Avila

June 10

CHARITY is ending well

Better is the end of a thing than its beginning; and the patient in spirit is better than the proud in spirit. ~ Ecclesiastes 7:8

Socrates said that the love of wisdom was the practice of death. A Greek story about a rich king who boasted of his wealth and then found himself beggared concludes, "Call no man happy till he is dead."

If this seems to be a very gloomy view of life, that indicates how far we have drifted from the realities that surround us. In the words of Bob Halligan, Jr. of the band *Ceili Rain*, all of us have a date to "lay down in the back of that long, black Cadillac". Getting ready for that date is ultimately what we are all in the business of doing. Our end matters far more than our beginning. We start from a wide variety of circumstances that we have no control over. To be proud of our beginnings is to take silly credit for our gifts from God, like being proud of our hair color. To receive grace is to humbly thank God for his gift in Christ Jesus. It is to end well, no matter how we start. ~ Dr. Scott Hahn and Jeff Cavins

What are you expecting your life's work will give you in the end?

Man wants to live, but it is useless to hope that this desire will dictate all his actions. ~ Albert Camus

June 11

UNITY is playing hide-and-seek in tall grass

Jesus prayed: Father! May they be in us, just as you are in me and I in you. May they be one, so that the world will believe that you sent me. ~ John 17:21

Bill Russell is a basketball legend. He grew up in Monroe, Louisiana. There his father worked long hard days. But his father was a strong man, and would return home each night still full of energy. Bill wrote:
"He'd call to my brother, mother and me. We would follow him to the fields where the grass grew tall as wheat, and the four of us would play hide-and-seek... When it was time to go home, my father would reach down and pick me up under one arm and mybrother under the other. Then he would lean down so my mother could crawl up on his back. Then he would run all the way home, carrying his whole family, as if we weighed nothing."
~ *Second Wind*

How is this image of Russell's father an image of God our Father and the human family?

Father! To God himself we cannot give a holier name.
~ William Wordsworth

June 12

FRATERNITY is fellowship with our brothers and faith in the LORD

I waited patiently for the LORD's help; then he listened to me and heard my cry... He taught me to sing a new song. ~ Psalm 40:2, 4

"As I write this, I'm at 35,000 feet... The airplane was an hour and a half late. People are grumpy... downright mad. Flight attendants are apologizing... The sports film on golf just broke down and so did the nervous systems of half the men on board. It's a zoo... For a change, I refused to be hassled by today's delay. I asked God to keep me calm, cheerful, relaxed and refreshed. Know what? He did. He really did! No pills. No booze... Just relaxing in the power of Jesus."
~ Charles Swindoll, *Growing Strong in the Seasons of Life*

When have you I refused to be hassled and simply given it to Christ? Have you ever been frustrated by something related to our council? What was the outcome?

We must wait for God long and meekly –
in wind and wet, in the lightning and the thunder, in the cold and in the dark. Wait, and he will come. He never comes to those who do not wait. ~ Frederick W. Faber

June 13 *St. Anthony of Padua*

Holding God up to the world

Christ Jesus, who, though he was in the form of God, did not regard equality with God as something to be exploited, but emptied himself, taking the form of a slave, being born in human form, he humbled himself and became obedient to the point of death – even death on a cross. ~ Philippians 2:6-8

In San Antonio, Texas, there is a large and lovely statue of St. Anthony of Padua, the patron saint of the city. The statue was a gift of Portugal (Anthony's birthplace) to San Antonio. It stands in a public park along the San Antonio River in the heart of the city. The Christ child in Anthony's arms stands on the Bible and his arms are extended in the shape of the cross as if embracing the whole world – as if Anthony is saying: "I hold up to all, as Savior of the world, this humble God of self-emptying love!"
The image of Anthony holding the divine infant is a symbol and model for each of us. The image inspires us to go through life clinging to the wonderful mystery of the humble, self-emptying Christ, who accompanies us as a servant of our humanity and of the world's healing. ~ J.M. Guerin

How can we, as Knights, go through life carrying an imaginary God-child in our arms – and holding Him up to the world?

The divine self-giving revealed in Jesus' Incarnation is comparable to God's supreme act of love embodied in Jesus' self-giving on the cross. ~ Father Raymond Brown

June 14 *Flag Day*

CHARITY is a pledge of allegiance

Blessed is the nation whose God is the LORD... ~ Psalm 33:12

Patriotism is a positive attitude for believers. The Pledge of Allegiance reads:
I pledge allegiance to the flag of the United States of America and to the Republic for which it stands, one nation under God, indivisible, with liberty and justice for all.
Patriotism to our nation is a secondary allegiance under the general umbrella of covenant loyalty to God. We are submitted to God's authority, and are therefore submitted to every authority that He allows on earth (Romans 13:1-7). In the allegiance to the country in which we dwell, we have a covenantal obligation to seek its welfare. *Seek the peace of the city... and pray to the LORD for it; for in its peace you will have peace* (Jeremiah 29:5-7). When we pledge allegiance to the flag of the United States, we are not doing it in a blind loyalty which says, "My country – right or wrong." We recognize the flag as a symbol of the nation in which we are living temporarily. As we show commitment and submission to every human organization, we also demonstrate our integrity by showing patriotism to our country. ~ Keith Intrater, excerpted

Our country has laws that are in direct conflict with Church teaching. How do you reconcile your allegiance to God and country? What is our assembly doing to affect change in these laws?

The people are the masters of both Congress and the courts, not to overthrow the Constitution, but to overthrow the men who pervert it. ~ Abraham Lincoln

June 15

UNITY is the human family

*[One day Jesus came to John for baptism. John said,] "I ought to
be baptized by you..." Jesus said, "Let it be so for now."*
~ Matthew 3:14–15

John had told people to be baptized as a sign of their commitment
to turn from sin and back to God. This raises a question:
Why was the sinless Jesus baptized?
By becoming one of us, Jesus became a member of our sinful
human family.
He would not separate himself from us – even in our sinfulness.
Thus, he teaches us an important lesson. We cannot separate
ourselves from our sinful human family either, especially from its
"family" sins:
disregard for the poor,
disrespect for life in all forms,
discrimination against human differences. ~ Author unknown

If Jesus was crucified for our "family" sins, what should we as
Knights do about these sins?

*No man is worth his salt who is not ready at all times to risk his
body, to risk his well-being, to risk his life, in a great cause.*
~ Theodore Roosevelt

FRATERNITY is being a source of strength

The father of a righteous man has great joy; he who has a wise son delights in him. ~ Proverbs 23:24

All foster fathers need only look to Saint Joseph for strength. We know Joseph was a man of faith, obedient to whatever God asked of him without knowing the outcome. When the angel came to Joseph in a dream and told him the truth about the child Mary was carrying, Joseph immediately and without question or concern for gossip, took Mary as his wife.

When the angel came again to tell him that his family was in danger, he immediately left everything he owned, all his family and friends, and fled to a strange country with his young wife and baby. He waited in Egypt without question until the angel told him it was safe to go back.

When looking for the epitome of fatherhood, one need look no further than Saint Joseph himself. ~ Author unknown

How can our council apply Saint Joseph's example to our Columbian Squires Circle?

It doesn't matter who my father was; it matters who I remember he was. ~ A. Sexton

June 17

CHARITY is rededication to a new beginning

When Jesus was twelve years old... [he spoke with teachers in the Temple] All who heard him were amazed. ~ Luke 2:42-47

At four, Ayinde Jean-Baptiste memorized Martin Luther King's "I Have A Dream" speech. At twelve, he mesmerized a vast throng of men gathered in Washington, DC, for the Million Man March with a two-minute oration on fatherhood. Ayinde wrote it with the help of his father and mother. An excerpt reads:
"When you stop making excuses, when you start standing with our mothers, when you stick it out with our families... then we can build a new nation... My fathers... you must rededicate yourselves to a new beginning." ~ Mark Link, S.J.

How can our council encourage strong father figures, and renewed emphasis on family life? How can we encourage the involvement of the Knight's Lady and children in our commitment to the life of Catholic knighthood?

Dad has left home. He won't come back until it dawns on him that the most profound satisfactions in his life arise from being a father first, and only after that a top golfer or a big shot.
~ Philip Wylie

June 18

UNITY is understanding God's love and forgiveness

How can I give up? ~ Hosea 11:8

The prophet Hosea speaks of God's love and forgiveness in a touching way.

Speaking in God's name, he says:

When *Israel* was a child, I loved *him* and called *him* out of Egypt...
But the more I called to *him*, the more *he* turned away from me...
Yet I was the one who taught Israel to walk...
How can I abandon [*Israel*]?...
My heart will not let me do it!
My love for *you* is too strong.
I will not punish *you* in my anger...
For I am God and not man.
I, the Holy One, am with *you*.
I will not come to *you* in anger (Hosea 11:1-3, 8-9).
~ Mark Link, S.J.

How does this passage impact you when you re-read it in a whisper, imagining that God is saying '*The Knights*' or *your name* in place of the words referring to *Israel* (in *italics*)?

*[LORD,] your goodness and love will be with me all my life;
and your house will be my home as long as I live.*
~ Psalm 23:6

June 19 *African American Emancipation Day (1865)**

Preserve the UNITY

*Make every effort to preserve the unity which has the Spirit as its
origin and peace as its binding force. There is but one body and
one Spirit, just as there is but one hope given all of you by your
call.* ~ Ephesians 4:3-4

John Howard Griffin dyed his skin black, shaved his head, and
posed as a black man in the South in the pre-civil-rights days.
One day, he asked for a Catholic church. He was given directions
to the nearest "*colored* Catholic church."
"There's no such thing as a colored Catholic church," Griffin
replied.
His informant said, "You don't really believe that, do you?…
You're going to find that a lot of white Catholics look on you as a
nigger first and a Catholic second, no matter what the Archbishop
says." ~ John H. Griffin, excerpted from *Racist Sins of Christians*

Ideally, Knights look upon *all* Christians as being equal members
of the Body of Christ. But how do we react when blind-sided by
some form of racism and bigotry?

*Father!… may they be one, so that the world will believe that you
sent me.* ~ John 17:21

* Juneteenth, or June 19th, 1865, commemorates the day a Yankee
troop informed Texas slaves of their freedom, two years *after* the
Emancipation Proclamation.

PATRIOTISM is remembering our forefathers founded our nation based on principles from God

Be watchful, stand firm in your faith, be courageous, be strong.
~ 1 Corinthians 16:13

One simple fact often overlooked is that Christian, and especially Catholic, faith is not supposed to be a cakewalk. The gospel is replete with exhortations to "be courageous, be strong." This is not the sort of exhortation one receives at vacation resorts or mattress testing sites. It is the sort of thing one hears in athletic training, or before a trial, or in preparation for some rigorous voyage. And that is because the Christian walk is a place of training, trial and travel. We are going somewhere and we need to be prepared to get there. That somewhere is Heaven and it will require everything of us just as it required everything of God. Not that we earn it, of course, but rather that we must be ready to receive fully what God has given.
~ Dr. Scott Hahn

Today, ask God to help you be courageous and strong in your faith, that you may fully receive into yourself the love of the Blessed Trinity. In your turn, stand firm against public policy that is contrary to Catholic teachings.

Name one instance this year where our council or assembly was compelled to take a stand against public policy.

The only thing necessary for the triumph of evil is for good men to do nothing. ~ Attributed to Edmund Burke, statesman

CHARITY is God being there with you

The Spirit of the LORD God is upon me, because the LORD has anointed me to bring good tidings to the afflicted; he has sent me to bind up the brokenhearted, to proclaim liberty to the captives, and the opening of the prison to those who are bound.
~ Isaiah 61:1

If you are afflicted, brokenhearted, or captive, this is the sign, not of your rejection by God, but of his special tender love for you. In Christ Crucified, God is right there next to you. He will never abandon you, just as he did not abandon Jesus even at the hour of abandonment itself. Even at the very bottom, God is there. And he knows the way out. He walked out himself on Easter morning.
~ Dr. Scott Hahn and Jeff Cavins

Choose one area of your spiritual life which might benefit from attention – repentance, faith, zeal, relationship, boldness, humility, contentedness, concern for God's honor. How will you strengthen this chosen area?

We ought always to thank God for you, brothers, and rightly so, because your faith is growing more and more, and the love every one of you has for each other is increasing.
~ 2 Thessalonians 1:3

June 22

UNITY is celebrating the Body and Blood of Christ

And now I am no more in the world, but they are in the world, and I am coming to thee. Holy Father, keep them in thy name, which thou hast given me, that they may be one, even as we are one.
~ John 17:11

Among other things, Mass is the sacrament of the unity of the Body of Christ. When someone tells us "I'll be there in spirit!", we know they really mean, "I won't be there." Jesus knew that too, which is why he did not leave us as orphans but remains with us, not only in Spirit, but in the sacramental presence of the Holy Eucharist. In the same way, he now calls us to be members of one another, not just "in spirit" but for real. That means we are not only "together" in our hearts, but really together in the same room, offering the same prayers, making the same physical gestures, hearing the same Scriptures, offering the same bread and wine and receiving the same Body and Blood of Christ. As we do this, we are, by the promise of Christ, joined not only to each other but with God Himself. And our unity, according to the above Scripture, is to be the same as the unity that exists between Father and the Son in the Godhead. Today, thank God for the miraculous unity of the Body of Christ and for his even more miraculous gift of unity with God the Father, Son and Holy Spirit!
~ Dr. Scott Hahn and Jeff Cavins

What kind of unity exists between God and Jesus that we should emulate within our council (see John 17)? When was the last time our council celebrated Mass together?

In union there is strength. ~ Aesop

June 23

FRATERNITY is listening to the heart

I beg you to be kind and listen to our brief account. ~ Acts 24:4

Erma was waiting for her flight. It felt good just sitting and
reading a book, with no one to bother her.
Just then a woman sat down and said, "Bet it's cold in Chicago."
Erma said coldly, "Probably."
The woman kept talking, and Erma kept responding coldly.
Then the woman dropped the bombshell. She was taking her
husband back to Chicago. He had died after 53 years of marriage.
Erma's heart sank. She closed her book, held the woman's hand,
and listened.
When the call to board came, they walked arm in arm to the plane.
Then they went to their assigned seats, which were a few rows
apart.
As Erma buckled up, she heard the woman say to the person next
to her,
"Bet it's cold in Chicago."
Erma found herself praying: "Dear God, help the person next to her
listen kindly." ~ Mark Link, S.J.

Recall one person who crossed your path in need of kindness?
Did you extend it?

I'm going your way, so let us go hand in hand...
Let us help one another while we may.
~ William Morris

June 24

CHARITY is preparing the way of the LORD

And you, child, will be called prophet of the Most High, for you will go before the LORD to prepare his ways. ~ Luke 1:76

Joel Weldon, an expert on human potential, likes to tell about the Chinese bamboo tree. This unusual plant takes five years to emerge from the soil. All during these five years, however, it has to be watered and fertilized. Once the plant emerges, it skyrockets to a height of 90 feet in six short weeks. The plant's rapid growth is made possible by the elaborate root system that developed during its five years of germination.

John the Baptist, like Jesus, spent 30 years preparing for his ministry. It was the most important time of his life. For during this time he was putting down the elaborate spiritual root system that made possible his fruitful ministry in later life.

~ Author unknown

What kind of spiritual roots are we as Knights growing? Does our council put an emphasis on the spiritual growth of each Knight?

If I had eight hours to chop down a tree, I'd spend six sharpening my ax. ~ Abraham Lincoln

June 25

UNITY is honoring the living bread of life

What Moses gave you was not the bread from heaven; it is my Father who gives you the real bread... I am the living bread that came down from heaven. If anyone eats this bread, he will live forever. ~ John 6:32, 51

Each year, Catholics celebrate the feast of the Body of Christ. Sometimes it includes an outdoor procession. Here is how an African bishop described his experience during a rainstorm in Nigeria in 1986:
"The people danced and sang in the rain. It was the first time I recall the Blessed Sacrament being carried... to the sound of ... cheering and clapping. Everyone was drenched. No one thought of seeking shelter or running away. Judges, lawyers, doctors, mothers, children stood their ground as if nothing was happening except the Eucharist. I have not seen anything like it here or anywhere else." ~ *America* magazine

Do we sometimes forget that the consecrated bread is truly the Body of Christ?

Jesus cannot be our Savior unless he is first our LORD.
~ Hugh C. Burr

June 26

FRATERNITY is digging up those rocks

[Jesus said of his disciples' failure to stay awake and pray,] "The spirit is willing, but the flesh is weak." ~ Mark 14:38

There's an old story about a farmer who was perennially plagued by a large rock located in the center of his field. Apart from the inconvenience of plowing around it each year, he sometimes forgot it and damaged equipment on it.
He swore that he would take time off some day and dig it out once and for all. But he kept putting it off year after year. One day he decided to act. To his surprise, the rock was almost totally on the surface and quite easily removed.
He thought to himself, "Why did it take me so long to get around to digging it up? How much grief I could have saved myself had I removed it right away!" ~ William Bennett

What rocks has our council procrastinated in removing this year?

Work as though everything depends on you;
pray as though everything depends on God.
~ attributed to St. Ignatius of Loyola

178

Living the Life of God

The plans of the diligent lead to profit as surely as haste leads to poverty. ~ Proverbs 21:5

St. Cyril, later recognized as a great teacher of the Church, began his career as Archbishop of Alexandria with impulsive, often violent, actions. He pillaged and closed the churches of the Novatian heretics, participated in the deposing of St. John Chrysostom and confiscated Jewish property in retaliation for their attacks on Christians. His style would later hurt him as he championed the cause of orthodoxy against the heresy of Nestorius, who declared that Mary could not be the mother of the one Person who is truly God and truly human. Eventually, Cyril learned to practice moderation and overcome Nestorius and his teachings. He was later declared a doctor of the Church.

The lives of the saints are valuable not only for the virtue they reveal but also for the less than admirable qualities they overcome. Holiness is a gift from God to be used in our daily lives. We try to respond to God's gift, but sometimes with a lot of zigzagging. If Cyril had been more patient and diplomatic, the Nestorian Church might not have risen and maintained power so long. ~ J.M. Guerin

How can we as Knights live our lives as saints – growing out of immaturity, narrowness and selfishness – living the life of God?

The Eucharist consummates our kinship with the Word, our communion with the Father, our sharing in the divine nature.
~ St. Cyril, adapted

June 28

CHARITY is a thunderbolt

For thou, O LORD, art good and forgiving, abounding in steadfast love to all who call on thee. ~ Psalm 86:5

When it all comes down to it, this is the most astonishing fact about God: that he forgives and loves us. If that seems like a commonplace, then we haven't really encountered God. As Peter Kreeft said long ago, that the "god" of feel-good religion should love us is a commonplace. What else should such a simpering, nice, harmless little fellow do. His only creed is "Niceness is Nice" so of course he "loves" us. It's his duty. But that the real God loves us... that the power who hurled Andromeda and made the tiger and shatters the cedars with lightning... who was steeped in Eternity when the dinosaurs came and went like a flash in the pan. That this God loves us, forgives us, and bothers his tender head about us to the degree that he is willing to be crucified for us: that is a thunderbolt. Rejoice in the glory and mercy of that Thunderbolt. ~ Dr. Scott Hahn and Jeff Cavins

Does God answer all of your prayers?

Don't think so much about who is for or against you, rather give all your care, that God be with you in everything you do.
~ Thomas á Kempis

June 29 *Sts. Peter & Paul*

UNITY through humbleness and obedience

[The LORD] said to me, "My grace is sufficient for you, for power is made perfect in weakness." I will rather boast most gladly of my weaknesses, in order that the power of Christ may dwell with me.
~ 2 Corinthians 12:9

Saints Peter and Paul were the two greatest apostles, and the two most important leaders of the early Church. Peter was a fisherman, and followed Jesus throughout His public ministry. Paul persecuted the early Church before his conversion. Peter was largely uneducated; Paul's careful education helped him become one of the greatest religious thinkers of all history.

Peter was directly appointed by Christ in the presence of the other apostles (Matthew 16:18-19); Paul received his authority from Christ during a personal conversion and spiritual experience (Acts 22:6-10, 14-16). Both men considered themselves to be profoundly unworthy (Luke 5:8; 1 Corinthians 15:9), yet each was capable of fulfilling his mission – only through Christ's grace (Luke 22:31-32; 2 Corinthians 12:7-10). ~ J.M. Guerin

The LORD can do great things through us, as long as we remain humble and obedient – as St. Paul said, "In weakness there is strength". In what ways can you overcome your own human weaknesses in order to receive God's grace?

Wink at small faults, for you have great ones yourself.
~ Scottish Proverb

181

June 30

FRATERNITY is choosing followers

[Jesus chose Simon and Andrew], James and John, Philip and
Bartholomew, Matthew and Thomas, James son of Alphaeus, and
Simon (...the Patriot), Judas son of James, and Judas Iscariot.
~ Luke 6:14–16

To: Jesus of Nazareth
From: Jerusalem Business Consultants, Inc.

We have reviewed the resumés of your candidates for managerial
posts. We recommend you continue your search. Peter is too
emotional and prone to faulty snap judgments (Luke 22:33).
James and John lack a team spirit and are prone to be hotheads
(Matthew 20:20–21, Luke 9:54). Thomas will miss meetings and
is a skeptic. Simon is a left-wing political zealot who would fight
constantly with Matthew, an establishment tax collector, currently
under investigation by our bureau.
The only candidate you should retain is the highly motivated and
competitive, Judas Iscariot. ~ Inspired by similar accounts

What do you think Jesus was looking for most in those He chose to
be His twelve apostles?
How do you decide whether or not to invite a potential candidate to
become a Knight? Do you do so just to increase membership? Is
the lowest common denominator your only criteria for knighthood?

I do not judge as people judge. They look at the outward
appearance, but I look at the heart. ~ 1 Samuel 16:7

July 1

CHARITY is drawing near to God

Draw near to God, and he will draw near to you. ~ James 4:8

The grace of God can cure disharmony and disorder in human
relationships. We can put our affairs, with their confusion and their
difficulty directly into God's hands. God can begin to effect a cure
of all the disharmony and disorder. We can believe that God will
cause us no more pain in the doing of it than a physician, who
plans and knows that he can effect a cure, would cause his patient.
We can have faith that God will do all that is necessary as
painlessly as possible. But we must be willing to submit to God's
treatment, even if we cannot now see the meaning or purpose of it.
~ Fr. Pat Umberger

We pray that we may willingly submit to whatever spiritual
discipline is necessary. We pray that we may accept whatever it
takes to live a better life.

How can drawing closer to God strengthen our council and
assembly?

*The achievements of an organization are the results of the
combined effort of each individual.*
~ Vince Lombardi

July 2

UNITY is gathering the flock through kindness

He will not argue or shout… He will not break off a bent reed, nor put out a flickering lamp. ~ Matthew 12:19–20

Someone described Cardinal Bernardin as "the kindest, gentlest man I ever knew." Thousands of people in Chicago agreed. The front-page story of his burial described how people stood in the cold, waiting, in some cases, for half a day and three deep.
"An eerie, respectful silence followed the cortege as it snaked through the city… People held signs, lit candles, rang bells and held pictures. At Wabash Avenue and Randolph Street, a roller blader in skin-tight purple and yellow jumpsuit stood with head bowed, hands in prayer… A boy in a blue winter jacket held up a sign he had colored on a sheet of orange paper.
"Bye, Joe," it said. "You have everlasting life."
~ *Chicago Tribune*

Cardinal Bernardin practiced what Fredrick W. Faber preached years ago:
"Kindness has converted more sinners than zeal, eloquence and learning." What council activities are planned which reach out to men in our parish, and encourage them to join our ranks?

The strength of a team can be seen in the strength of its leaders.
~ Vince Lombardi

July 3 *St. Thomas*

FRATERNITY is doubting and then believing

*Receive the holy Spirit. Whose sins you forgive are forgiven them,
and whose sins you retain are retained.* ~ John 20:22-23

Like the other apostles (except for Judas Iscariot), Thomas was
from Galilee, and – in spite of his weakness – was committed to
being a follower of Christ.
Thomas is best known for his initial unwillingness to believe in
Jesus' Resurrection; instead of accepting the testimony of others,
he demanded to see the Risen LORD for himself (John 21:24-29).
His statement of doubt ("unless I see and touch, I will not
believe"), however, was later replaced by an expression of faith
("my LORD and my God!"). Also, Thomas had on an earlier
occasion expressed a willingness to die for Christ (John 11:16).
According to legend, St. Thomas did indeed die for Christ, being
martyred in southern India after spending some years there as a
missionary. ~ J.M. Guerin

Spiritual growth is not always a steady progression; it often has ups
and downs. We, like St. Thomas, tend to be doubtful, but do we
have to see the Risen LORD in order to genuinely believe in Him?

*Help row the other's boat across, and lo!
thine own has reached the shore.*
~ Hindu Proverb

July 4 *American Independence Day*

PATRIOTISM is one nation under God

Proclaim liberty throughout all the land unto all the inhabitants thereof. ~ Leviticus 25:10 – inscribed on the Liberty Bell

Take this day to reflect on our nation's religious roots –
The Declaration of Independence is the official and unequivocal affirmation by the American people of their belief and faith in God. It affirms God's existence as a "self-evident" truth that requires no further discussion or debate. The nation created by the great Declaration is God's country. The rights it defines are God-given. The actions of its signers are God-inspired. The Declaration contains five references to God - God as supreme Lawmaker, God as Creator of all men, God as the Source of all rights, God as the world's supreme Judge, and God as our Protector on whom we can rely. It declares that each of us is created equal. This means equally endowed with unalienable rights. It does not mean that all are born with equal capabilities. Nor does it mean that all of us can be made equal, as Communist dogma alleges. As the modern discovery of DNA now confirms, each of God's creatures is unequal and different in every other way from every other person. The Declaration of Independence proclaims that life and liberty are the unalienable gifts of God - natural rights - which no person or government can rightfully take away. It affirms that the purpose of government is to secure our God-given unalienable individual rights, and that government derives its powers from the consent of the governed. Our Declaration reduced government from master to servant, for the first time in history. ~ *Crosswalk*

If we ever forget that we are One Nation Under God, then we will be a Nation gone under. ~ President Ronald Reagan

July 5

FREEDOM isn't free; FREEDOM is 56 brave men

Blessed is the nation whose God is LORD, the people chosen as his very own. ~ Psalm 33:12

Have you ever wondered what happened to some of the 56 men who signed the Declaration of Independence?

Five signers were captured by the British as traitors, and tortured before they died. Twelve had their homes ransacked and burned. Two lost their sons serving in the Revolutionary Army; another had two sons captured. Nine of the 56 fought and died from wounds or hardships of the Revolutionary War.

They signed and pledged their lives, their fortunes, and their sacred honor. What kind of men were they?

Twenty-four were lawyers and jurists. Eleven were merchants. Nine were farmers and large plantation owners. But they signed the Declaration of Independence knowing full well that the penalty would be death if they were captured. ~ Author unknown

Like the men who signed the declaration, our assembly is composed of men of ordinary means. Is that all we share in common with our forefathers or are we prepared to uphold their patriotic convictions even at the expense of all that we hold dear?

For the support of this declaration, with firm reliance on the protection of the divine providence, we mutually pledge to each other, our lives, our fortunes and our sacred honor.
~ Signers of the Declaration of Independence, 1776

July 6 *St. Maria Goretti (1890-1902)*

UNITY is being touched by God's grace

This is how my heavenly Father will treat each of you unless you forgive your brother from your heart. ~ Matthew 18:35

Maria Goretti was known for her cheerful and holy disposition. While home alone one day, Maria was assaulted by Alessandro Serenelli, an eighteen-year-old neighbor. She resisted his sexual advances. Enraged, the young man repeatedly stabbed her with a dagger.
Maria was taken to a hospital, where she forgave her attacker and expressed concern for her family; she later died.
Serenelli was sentenced to prison for thirty years. For the next eight years he was unrepentant, but then he had a dream in which Maria was gathering flowers and presenting them to him.
Moved by this experience, Alessandro's life changed; his first action upon being released from prison was to visit Maria's mother and beg forgiveness. On Christmas Day, 1937, Alessandro received communion side by side with Mrs. Goretti, and he was present in St. Peter's Square when Maria was canonized in 1950.
~ J.M. Guerin

Even the most hardened sinner can be touched by God's grace, as witnessed by Serenelli's repentance in prison. Does his conversion serve as an argument for abolishing the death penalty? Where does Christ, Himself executed as a capital criminal, command us to stand on the issue of capital punishment?

The weak can never forgive. Forgiveness is the attribute of the strong. ~ Mahatma Gandhi

FRATERNITY is serving God with determination

Turn back and serve God with ten times more determination.
~ Baruch 4:28

Jane Goodall is an expert on wildlife and conservation. She has lectured at Yale University and written for the *New York Times*. In a moment of candor, she confessed:
"When I left home and faced the realities of the world, I put my thoughts of God in cold storage for a while, because I couldn't reconcile what I believed, deep inside, with what was going on around me.
But that early period when God was as real as the wind... left me an inner peace, which as I grew older, swelled – until, perforce, I had to open my mind to God again." ~ Mark Link, S.J.

Do you trust that God has a wonderful plan for your life or do you feel somewhat dubious? How does He communicate his plans for you – are they always clear, sometimes clear or never clear? What role does Scripture, counsel, hunches, prayer and circumstances play?

With peace in the soul,
we can face the very worst experience.
Without peace in the soul,
we can't even face the simple task of writing a letter.
~ adapted from an anonymous British psychiatrist

July 8

CHARITY is a simple lesson that hits home with our children

Train a child in the way he should go, and when he is old, he will not turn from it. ~ Proverbs 22:6

According to a recent radio report, a middle school in Oregon was faced with a unique problem.
A number of girls were beginning to use lipstick and would put it on in the bathroom. That was fine, but then they were pressing their lips to the mirrors leaving dozens of little lip prints.
Finally the principal decided that something had to be done. She called all the girls to the bathroom and met them there with the custodian.
She explained that all these lip prints were causing a major problem for the custodian who had to clean the mirrors every day. To demonstrate how difficult it was to maintain the mirrors, she asked the custodian to clean one of the mirrors.
He took out a long-handled brush, dipped it into the toilet and scrubbed the mirror.
Since then there have been no lip prints on the school's mirrors.
~ Author unknown

What kind of child to your Heavenly Father have you proven to be? Whose faith do you have now: Your own? Your parents? None at all?

Do not handicap your children by making their lives easy.
~ Lazarus Long

July 9

UNITY is knowing the Good Shepherd

I am the good shepherd. As the Father knows me and I know the
Father, in the same way I know my sheep and they know me.
~ John 10:14–15

In ancient England, dinner guests used to entertain other guests
after meals. At one dinner an actor was present and did a fabulous
rendition of Psalm 23, "The LORD is my Shepherd." Everyone
stood and applauded.
Then a guest noticed the aunt of the host dozing in the back of the
room. The old woman was deaf and had missed almost all of the
entertainment.
The guest shouted, "Auntie, come up and do something."
Everyone applauded.
She recited the same psalm. When she finished, there wasn't a dry
eye in the room. Later, the guest asked the actor, "Your rendition
was fabulous. So why were we so moved by the aunt?"
He replied, "Simple – I know the psalm, but old auntie knows the
Shepherd." ~ Mark Link, S.J.

How does it make you feel to think of God caring for us as the
Good Shepherd?

The King of love my Shepherd is,
Whose goodness faileth never;
I nothing lack if I am His
And He is mine forever.
~ Sir Henry William Baker

July 10

FRATERNITY is generating power through prayer

Jesus made the disciples get into the boat and go on ahead to the other side of the lake, while he sent the people away. After sending the people away, he went to a hill by himself to pray.
~ Matthew 14:22–23

Nobel Prize winner Dr. Alexis Carrell wrote a book called *Man the Unknown*. In it, he makes this striking statement:
"Prayer is the most powerful form of energy we can generate...
The influence of prayer on the human mind and body is as demonstrable as secreting glands... Only in prayer do we achieve that complete and harmonious assembly of body, mind, and spirit which gives the frail human reed its unshakable strength."
~ Mark Link, S.J.

What is one effect that regular prayer has had on your life? When was the last time our Brother Knights gathered in prayer for a worthy cause?

When we pray we link ourselves to the inexhaustible motive power which spins the universe. We ask that a part of this power be apportioned to our needs. ~ Alexis Carrel

July 11 *St. Benedict (circa 480-547)*

PATRIOTISM is community involvement through God's call

You see that a person is justified by what he does and not by faith alone. ~ James 2:24

The founder of the Benedictine Order, St. Benedict came from a distinguished Italian family (his sister was St. Scholastica). He studied in Rome, but disturbed by the city's sinful and chaotic nature, he chose to live as a hermit at the age of twenty. Soon afterwards some monks asked Benedict to be their leader; though this initial experiment failed (as the monks were upset by Benedict's high standards, and even tried to poison him), the saint was enthusiastic over the idea of monasticism: monks living together in a community, combining contemplation, work, and shared prayer. The Benedictine Rule emphasizes *ora et labora* ("prayer and work"). The saint performed many miracles, and when he died, he was buried in the same grave as his sister. He could never have imagined the monasteries established under his influence played a vital role in preserving Western culture during the Dark Ages, and the Rule of Benedict has guided many monks and religious up to this day. ~ J.M. Guerin

Benedict teaches us that great things can be done for God through a life properly balanced between prayer, study, and labor, with elements of community involvement. Is our assembly's mission plan balanced across the board? Or do we have an imbalance – perhaps too much emphasis on good works and not enough on spiritual building initiatives?

As the flower is before the fruit, so is faith before good works
~ Richard Whately

July 12

CHARITY is a servant of God

Whoever serves me must follow me, and where I am, there also will my servant be. The Father will honor anyone who serves me. ~ John 12:26

The film, *Chariots of Fire*, is about Eric Liddell, a Scott, and Britain's top 100-meter runner and a cinch to win the gold in the 1924 Paris Olympics. Deeply religious, Liddell never ran on Sunday.
When the Olympic schedule was released, he was shocked. The 100-meter event was scheduled for Sunday. In spite of incredible pressure put upon him by the British press, Eric refused to compete. He switched to the 400-meter race, a race he had never run in his life.
Just before the race, an American runner, Jackson Scholz, handed Liddell a note. It contained this sentence from John 12:26: "My Father will honor anyone who serves me."
Seconds later, Eric won the 400-meter event. Still clutched in his hand was the note Jackson Scholz had given him.
~ Mark Link, S.J.

How loyal are we in serving Jesus?

Those who trust in the LORD... will run and not grow weary.
~ Isaiah 40:31

July 13

UNITY is following God's guidance

Do not love the world or the things in the world. The love of the Father is not in those who love the world; for all that is in the world – the desire of the flesh, the desire of the eyes, the pride in riches – comes not from the Father but from the world. And the world and its desire are passing away, but those who do the will of God live forever. ~ 1 John 2:15-17

Functioning on a material plane alone can take us away from God. We can also try to function on a spiritual plane. Functioning on a spiritual plane as well as on a material plane can make life what it should be. All material activities are valueless in themselves alone. But all activities, seemingly trivial or of seemingly great moment, are all alike if directed by God's guidance. We can try to obey God as we would expect faithful, willing servants to carry out directions. ~ Fr. Pat Umberger

Pray that the flow of God's spirit may come to us through many channels. Pray that we may function on a spiritual plane as well as on a material plane.

Are all human desires contrary to God's will? Why?
In what areas does love for the world compete with love for God: In our use of money? Time? Priorities? Relationships? Ambitions?

In His will is our peace.
~ Dante Alighieri

July 14 *Blessed Kateri Tekakwitha (1656-1680)*

FRATERNITY is every culture receiving the Good News

He who has ears, let him hear. ~ Matthew 11:15

Known as the "Lily of the Mohawks," the Native American, Kateri Tekakwitha, was born near modern-day New York State. When Kateri was four, she was stricken with smallpox which left her with a pock-marked face and partial blindness. Kateri became skilled at decorating leather moccasins and clothing, but her relatives treated her like a slave. When Jesuit missionaries visited her village, she was too shy to ask for religious instruction. One of the priests, noticing her piety, spoke to her about Jesus. Kateri was delighted, and she was later baptized. Because she thereafter refused to work on Sundays, her relatives accused her of laziness and disrespect, and treated her severely. This, and the harsh penances she practiced, seriously affected her health, but she responded to every difficulty with love and patience as she grew in grace and virtue. Helped by other sympathetic Indians, she escaped to a Catholic settlement near Montreal; she later made a vow of perpetual virginity – something unheard of for an Indian maiden. Though only twenty-four, Kateri became very weak, and died during Holy Week 1680. Immediately afterwards, her pock-marked face took on a new beauty, her spiritual beauty, and she was buried on Holy Thursday. ~ J.M. Guerin

Sometimes people might be eager to hear the Gospel, but too shy to ask about it. When have you shared the Good News with someone whom you suspected might respond?

It is the grand endeavor of the gospel to communicate God to men.
~ Horace Bushnell

July 15

CHARITY is a signal from God

Call upon me in the day of trouble; I will rescue you, and you shall honor me. ~ Psalm 50:15

The only survivor of a shipwreck was washed up on a small, uninhabited island. He prayed feverishly for God to rescue him, and every day he scanned the horizon for help, but none seemed forthcoming.

Exhausted, he eventually managed to build a little hut out of driftwood to protect him from the elements, and to store his few possessions.

But then one day, after scavenging for food, he arrived home to find his little hut in flames, the smoke rolling up to the sky. The worst had happened; everything was lost. He was stunned with grief and anger.

"God, how could you do this to me!" he cried.

Early the next day, however, he was awakened by the sound of a ship that was approaching the island. It had come to rescue him.

"How did you know I was here?" asked the weary man of his rescuers.

They replied, "We saw your smoke signal." ~ Author unknown

Recall a time when you were discouraged when things were going bad, only to find out that God was at work in your life.

Happiness is easy. It is letting go of unhappiness that is hard. We are willing to give up everything but our misery.
~ Hugh Prather

July 16

UNITY is living in harmony with God

Do you not know that you are God's temple and that God's Spirit dwells in you? ~ 1 Corinthians 3:16

God's spirit is all around us all day long. We have no thoughts, no plans, no impulses, no emotions that God does not know about. We can hide nothing from God. We need not make our conduct conform only to that of the world and need not depend on the approval or disapproval of others. God sees in secret, but rewards openly. If we are in harmony with God, doing our best to live the way we believe God wants us to live, we can be at peace.
~ Fr. Pat Umberger

Pray that we may always feel God's presence. Pray that we may realize this presence constantly all through the day.

Paul tells the Corinthians as a church they are God's temple. How is our council a dwelling place for God's Spirit?

I never yet have known the Spirit of God to work where the LORD's people were divided. ~ D.L. Moody

FRATERNITY is God leading us where He wants us to go

Moses, however, said to the LORD, "If you please, LORD, I have never been eloquent, neither in the past, nor recently, nor now that you have spoken to your servant; but I am slow of speech and tongue." ~ Exodus 4:10

Daniel Harrington is a biblical scholar. When asked where he finds God, he said:
"I stutter… As a young boy I read in a newspaper that Moses stuttered. I looked it up in the Bible, and sure enough in Exodus 4:10, Moses says to God: '… I am slow of speech and slow of tongue.'"
But Harrington found much more than this. He found the story of God's self-revelation to Moses and of God's commissioning of Moses to speak that self-revelation to the world.
Harrington ended, "I found God in the Bible, and I have continued to do so ever since."
Then he added this caution:
"The encounter with God through the Bible cannot be programmed or forced... God takes the initiative in this relationship and leads us where he wants us to go." ~ James Martin

What concerns do you still harbor about doing God's will or following his lead? What do you hear God saying about your excuses? When was the last time we consulted the Bible at a council meeting? How many times have you read the Bible, cover-to-cover?

Pull the string, and it will follow wherever you wish. Push it, and it will go nowhere at all. ~ Dwight D. Eisenhower

July 18

PATRIOTISM is not a call to arms, but a call to peace

Nation will not take up sword against nation, nor will they train for war anymore… ~ Isaiah 2:4

Whenever I think of my past, I cannot help but think of the mystery of my survival. Why was I still alive, when men all around me had died like flies in four years of conflict?

I came to feel ashamed of my former godless idea that man's own ability were his only trustworthy guides. In my early life, religion had little place in my thinking. In the Navy, the former "War Catechism" became the sum total of my ideology…

In an editorial column, I came across this calling: "Oh people of Japan, if there is any one of you who has not yet read the Bible, please read the first thirty pages with an open mind. Surely there is something there that will touch your heart."

For me, this was a voice from Heaven. I came to the Gospel of Luke where I faced the scene of the crucifixion of Christ. "Father, forgive them for they know not what they do." Jesus prayed for the very soldiers who were about to thrust His side with a spear… I am not ashamed to say that my eyes filled with tears. Immediately I accepted Jesus as my personal Savior… The fervent prayer that I send to all mankind is that there will not be another Pearl Harbor.
~ Mitsuo Fuchida, lead pilot in the raid on Pearl Harbor, *From Pearl Harbor to Golgotha*

Have you ever had a life-changing revelation?

The world will be safe and secure in its peace only when nations adopt the principles of Christ and play fair with them.
~ William Person Merrill

CHARITY is kissing boo-boos

For we are God's workmanship, created in Christ Jesus to do good
works, which God prepared in advance for us to do.
~ Ephesians 2:10

When was the last time you kissed a child's boo-boo? Have you
ever listened to a friend as they complained about their job? When
your wife has had a rough day, do you rub her back, buy her
favorite ice cream, suggest a movie out together? Do you have a
reputation for being someone who can be counted on when things
go wrong? If you answered yes, congratulations! You've been
practicing a spiritual work of mercy. The work of mercy we
practice by kissing cuts or bringing home peach swirl is
"comforting the afflicted." Sometimes we think we have to
volunteer our summers in Ethiopia to help the afflicted. But when
we think of mercy that way, we are setting ourselves up to feel
guilty because we're not Mother Teresa.
When you think about it, though, neither was Jesus. When he
comforted the afflicted, he didn't take-off for India; he went down
the street in his hometown and started comforting. He cured the
deaf guy on the corner; he soothed his friend's relatives when they
mourned; he leaned back and listened to the woman at the well.
In other words, he kissed boo-boos, and offered a friendly ear.
~ Boston College Newsletter

How is our council practicing spiritual works of mercy in our local
community?

Catholicism is the spirit of Jesus Christ at work in the world.
~ Author unknown

July 20

UNITY is one mankind under God

You can look at the earth and the sky and predict the weather;
why, then, don't you know the meaning of this present time?
~ Luke 12:56

On this date in 1969, the world watched on TV as astronauts Neil
Armstrong and Ed Aldrin landed on the moon. Six hours later, both
men were walking on its powder-like surface.
Later, Aldrin said of the scientific feat of landing someone on the
moon:
"It was more than a team of people and government and industry
working together... It is my hope that people will keep this whole
event in their minds and see beyond the minor details and technical
achievements to the deeper meaning behind it all: a challenge, a
quest, the human need to recognize that we are all one mankind
under God." ~ *LIFE*

What deeper meaning might the scientific feat of landing a man on
the moon hold for our nation? For our world?

Because of what you have done the heavens have become a part of
man's world. And as you talk to us from the Sea of Tranquility, it
inspires us to redouble our efforts to bring peace and tranquility to
Earth. For one priceless moment, in the whole history of man, all
the people on this Earth are truly one. One in their pride in what
you have done. One in our prayers that you will return safely to
Earth. ~ Richard Nixon to Neil Armstrong after the successful
Moon landing

July 21

FRATERNITY is Matthew 25

Come and possess the kingdom which has been prepared for you...
I was a stranger and you received me...
I was sick and you took care of me...
Whenever you did this for one of the least important of these
followers of mine, you did it for me. ~ Matthew 25:34-40

Two young men were canoeing on a river in the Canadian wilds.
One day they both became ill. Fortunately, they spotted a trapper's
cabin. They beached their canoe and walked up to the cabin. It
was unlocked. In one corner was a cot. On it lay an open Bible
with a note. It read:
Your cabin saved my life. I was seriously ill and needed shelter.
Your cabin provided it. I have no money with which to repay you.
I can only promise you God's blessing. Read the passage from
Matthew 25.
Later, one of the young men said, "I'd read that passage many
times, but I never really understood it until that day."
~ Mark Link, S.J.

When have you been hungry, thirsty, a stranger, in need of clothes,
sick or imprisoned, and someone reached out to you? In these six
areas, where do you find yourself serving most naturally? In which
areas do you have the most trouble reaching out?
In what ways does our council minister to the areas Jesus specified
in Matthew 25?

God has given us the choice whether or not we follow Him;
but in reality, we are always at His mercy.
~ Author unknown

July 22 *St. Mary Magdalene*

CHARITY is showing our love for Him

... Go to my brothers and tell them, 'I am going to my Father and your Father, to my God and your God.' ~ John 20:17

The name Magdalene means "from Magdala," a village on the shores of the Sea of Galilee. Mary Magdalene is the woman out of whom Jesus drove seven demons (Mark 16:9, Luke 8:2).
This Mary was present at the crucifixion of Jesus (Mark 15:40).
She was also present at his burial (Mark 15:47).
Some think she's the sinful woman who anointed Jesus' feet at Simon's house (Luke 7:36-50). But this is only speculation.
Likewise, some think she was the sister of Martha and Lazarus (John 11:1, 12:3). But again, this is only speculation.
This much is certain. She is someone who loved Jesus deeply. In the final analysis this is all that matters. ~ J.M. Guerin

How does our council exhibit our deep love for Jesus?

Mature love says, 'I need you because I love you.'
Immature love says, 'I love you because I need you.'
~ Erich Fromm

23 July

UNITY is doing our part in God's work

But I do not count my life of any value to myself, if only I may finish my course and the ministry that I received from the Lord Jesus, to testify to the good news of God's grace. ~ Acts 20:24

We can have a singleness of purpose to do our part in God's work. We need not let material distractions interfere with our job of improving personal relationships. It is easy to become distracted by material affairs, so that we lose our singleness of purpose. We do not have time to be concerned about the many concerns of the world. We can concentrate and specialize in what we can do best. ~ Fr. Pat Umberger

Pray that we may not become distracted by material affairs. Pray that we may concentrate on doing what we can do best.

How would you complete the following sentence?
The one thing I must accomplish at any cost is _____

In the march to do God's will, are the Knights in the front of the pack, stragglers, or onlookers?

All work that is worth anything is done in faith.
~ Albert Schweitzer

July 24

FRATERNITY is doing as the fishermen do

The people... listened to the message with great eagerness, and every day they studied the Scriptures. ~ Acts 17:11

In his *Journal of a Soul*, John XXIII describes an experience he had during a retreat in Turkey. He wrote:

"Every evening from the window... I see an assemblage of boats on the Bosporus; they come round from the Golden Horn in tens and hundreds... a most impressive spectacle of color and lights. These lights glow all night and one can hear the cheerful voices of the fishermen...
The other night towards one o'clock, it was pouring with rain, but the fishermen were still there... What a vision of work, zeal, and labor... We must do as the fishermen of the Bosporus do."
~ Mark Link, S.J.

To what extent do I labor more zealously at succeeding in material undertakings than I do at succeeding in spiritual ones?

I have complete confidence in the gospel; it is God's power to save all who believe. ~ Romans 1:16

PATRIOTISM is ministering to our brothers in arms

Whoever wishes to come after me must deny himself, take up his cross, and follow me. ~ Mark 8:34

During the Vietnam War, Father Capodanno would listen to the confessions of young Marines. The words of absolution, marked by the sign of the cross, were followed by reassurance that together they would see each other through this time of trial. Father Vincent would then present the young man with one of the hundreds of Saint Christopher medals he had made.

Legend says that Christopher, meaning "Christ bearer," was a giant of a man who made his living carrying people across a river. One day, a small child asked him for a lift. When Christopher placed him on his shoulders, he found the child was unbelievably heavy. When they finally reached the other side, Christopher was astounded to discover that the child was Christ carrying the weight of the whole world. For Catholics, the story of Saint Christopher taught a double lesson of compassion for those who suffer and the reality of Christ's presence in the soul. To this day, many Marines cherish the medal given to them by Father Vincent.

~ Fr. Daniel L. Mode, adapted from *The Grunt Padre*

Father Vincent's Saint Christopher medals reminded his men of their dignity and worth as sons of their Heavenly Father. How can our assembly convey the same message to our brethren?

All of my efforts will be devoted to the people I'm serving.
Their lives, both troubles and joys, will be my life.
~ Father Vincent R. Capodanno, Medal of Honor Recipient

July 26 *Sts. Joachim & Anne*

CHARITY is the love and support of spouses and parents

Love the LORD your God; follow him faithfully; keep his commandments; remain loyal to him; and serve him with all your heart and all your soul. ~ Joshua 22:5

The New Testament makes no mention of the Virgin Mary's parents by name, but a second century apocryphal writing, the *Protoevangelium of James*, gives an account of Mary's birth, and is the source of the names Joachim and Anne. Though the accuracy of this tradition can be questioned, Mary's parents must have been God-fearing persons who provided an atmosphere which nourished Our Lady's perfect love and humility. Joachim and Anne are the patron saints of grandparents. Though they never met their grandson Jesus while on earth, they played an important, behind-the-scenes role in preparing for the coming of His Kingdom. Joachim and Anne show us sainthood does not require fame or recognition. Though they remain virtually unknown even today, they helped prepare for Christ's coming simply by fulfilling their duty as spouses and parents. By loving and supporting other people whom God has called to do great things, as Joachim and Anne did for their daughter, we also learn that holiness does not always involve the performance of great deeds. ~ J.M. Guerin

How can we apply the lives of these saints to our own personal lives as husbands and fathers? How does our council support persons whom God has called to do great things?

Pray for all parents that they may provide the loving home and faithful teaching that you provided your daughter.
~ Prayer to the Parents of Our Lady – Saints Joachim & Anne

July 27

UNITY is honoring everyone

It is God's will that by doing right you should silence the ignorance of the foolish. As servants of God, live as free people, yet do not use your freedom as a pretext for evil. Honor everyone. Love the family of believers. ~ 1 Peter 2:15-17

We can remember that in spiritual matters, we are only instruments. It is not ours to decide how or when we are to act. God plans all spiritual matters. It is up to us to make ourselves fit to do God's work. All that hinders our spiritual activity can be eliminated. We can depend on God for all the strength we need to overcome those faults which are blocks. We can keep ourselves fit, so that God can use us as a channels for God's spirit.
~ Fr. Pat Umberger

Pray that our selfishness may not hinder our progress in spiritual matters. Pray that we may be a good instrument for God to work with.

Are you spiritually developing yourself so that you may be a instrument of God?

The religion of Jesus begins with the verb "follow" and ends with the word "go." ~ Author unknown

FRATERNITY is serving others and finding our Father

The one who is righteous by faith shall live. ~ Romans 1:17

A.J. Cronin began his professional career as a physician. Later he turned to writing. In *Adventures in Two Worlds*, he says that as a medical student he felt "superior" to those gullible, uneducated folks who still clung to "outworn myths." He could only "smile" at their faith in the existence of God and the human soul. Then he added:

"But when, as a qualified doctor, I went out into the world, to the mining valleys in South Wales and... assisted at the miracle of birth [and] sat with the dying in the still hours of the night... I lost my superiority, and this, though I was not then aware of it, is the first step toward finding God." ~ Mark Link, S.J.

Why would this be the first step toward finding God?
To what extent might it apply to your life?

I sought my soul – but my soul I could not see.
I sought my God – but my God eluded me.
I sought my brother – and I found all three.
~ Anonymous

CHARITY is being faithful to our calling

I may be able to speak the languages of human beings and even of angels, but if I have no love, my speech is no more than a noisy gong...
Love is patient and kind;
it is not jealous or conceited or proud;
love is not ill-mannered or... irritable;
love does not keep a record of wrongs;
love is not happy with evil, but is happy with the truth.
Love never gives up... Love is eternal. ~ 1 Corinthians 13:1, 4–8

Saint Paul's beautiful passage on love was a favorite of Jefferson, Lincoln, and Franklin D. Roosevelt.
The famous journalist William Allen White requested it be read at the funeral services of his daughter when she was tragically killed at the age of eighteen.
It has been a guide for life and a source of comfort to countless people since it was penned 2,000 years ago. ~ Mark Link, S.J.

Which of Paul's descriptions of love do you find most challenging?

The ancient words of Paul [on love] have always seemed to me to hold the complete answer to all human living.
~ Marjorie Rawlings

July 30

UNITY is keeping our lives in perspective

He has told you, O mortal, what is good; and what does the LORD require of you but to do justice, and to love kindness, and to walk humbly with your God? ~ Micah 6:8

Simplicity is the keynote of a good life. We can choose the simple things always. Life can become complicated if we let it be so. We can be swamped by difficulties if we let them take up too much of our time. Every difficulty can be either solved or ignored and something better substituted for it. We can love the humble things of life. We can reverence the simple things. Our standard need never be the world's standard of wealth and power.
~ Fr. Pat Umberger

Pray that we may love the simple things of life. Pray that we may keep my life uncomplicated and free.

Are we Knights obeying Micah 6:8?

The only important decision we have to make is to live with God; He will make all the rest. ~ Author unknown

July 31 *St. Ignatius of Loyola*

FRATERNITY is Knights following St. Ignatius

*You spoke to me, and... your words filled my heart with joy and
happiness.* ~ Jeremiah 15:16

The leg of Ignatius took nine months to heal and left him with a
lifelong limp. While recuperating, he occupied his time
daydreaming and fantasizing. He called for romances and books of
chivalry, but the only two books to be found in the house were a
life of Christ and a collections of saints' lives. Slowly, Ignatius
conceived an admiration for what he found there. He still dreamed
of glory, but now it was to be God's glory. He still ambitioned
serving a king... but the king was no longer an earthly one.
~ Thomas Clancy, adapted from *Ignatius Loyola: A Soldier-Saint*

How can we as Knights take greater strides toward living the
chivalrous lives of Catholic gentlemen?

God says to us: With thy very wounds I will heal thee.
~ The Talmud

PATRIOTISM is leaving the world in good hands

Only be careful, and watch yourselves closely so that you do not forget the things your eyes have seen or let them slip from your heart as long as you live. Teach them to your children and to their children after them. ~ Deuteronomy 4:9

The most compelling question that every Christian man must ask is this: What am I doing today that will be an influence for Jesus Christ in the next generation? We cannot hold onto the world, we can only hand it to others. It's as if you are a father with your arms wrapped around your young son's shoulders, helping him get the feel of the bat. Swing and miss. Swing and connect. Swing and miss. There is no glory in that moment – only hints of glory as a pattern is established. It may be years before your boy can swing for the fence. Someday, though, he will stand at the plate where the balls are hard and fast. It's a game where they call real strikes, and some men strike out. When your son hits that home run in the game that counts, you may not be around to see it. But there will be a piece of you in that swing. That's your reward for leaving the world in good hands. ~ Howard Hendricks and William Hendricks

What kinds of activities can our assembly engage in to leave the world in good hands? Are we mentoring Columbian Squires to be tomorrow's leaders?

A good character is the best tombstone. Those who loved you and were helped by you will remember you when forget-me-nots have withered. Carve your name on hearts, not on marble.
~ C.H. Spurgeon

August 2

CHARITY is paying the price of a legacy

A good name is more desirable than great riches; to be esteemed is better than silver or gold. ~ Proverbs 22:1

No matter how hard a man works, no matter how much wealth and notoriety a man accumulates, it is always a fair question to ask, *What will I leave behind?*

What we leave behind is called *legacy*. It is more than "Salesman of the Year" plaques. And certainly more than a wooden box planted six feet deep. It's the footprints we leave at a workplace or institution, and the fingerprints we leave in the lives we love.

Deep in the soul of every man is the desire to leave behind a good name. A name that makes people nod in affirmation. For a man to be able to look into the eyes of his wife and children and to be able to see them looking back with respect, admiration, trust, loyalty – that is enough to make most of us hallucinate. That is a living legacy. And that is what every man should long for.

A living legacy is the product of consistent hard choices – integrity, sensitivity, humility, responsibility, fidelity, and charity. There are no shortcuts. No such thing as microwave maturity. It is held out to each of us – ours for the taking – as long as we are willing to pay the price.

~ Fred Hartley, adapted from *Men and Marriage*

Is there a way for a Knight to build his legacy through council activities and events? Would your brothers nod in affirmation if your name came up in conversation?

That person proves his worth who can make us want to listen when he is with us and think when he is gone. ~ Grit

August 3

UNITY is salvation for our children

Children's children are a crown to the aged, and parents are the pride of their children. ~ Proverbs 17:6

You cannot give quality time unless you give a quantity of time. You need to be there. Be alert for those priceless irreplaceable moments when your child needs to belt down a strong gulp of Dad. To be honest, most of the time you spend with your children will be wasted. What they do is suddenly – no one can predict when – open up, and take a long swig of Dad. Then they go back to their preoccupation and put you in a holding mode again.

In a national survey, men complained that 'time' keeps them from being the family shepherd they want to be. It may be true that men are overscheduled and exhausted. But it's not a question of time. A man does what he wants to do. His busy schedule reveals his priorities, not his unavailability. He chooses his top priorities and makes sure they get scheduled.

Is any career worth the life of your child? When put in this way, of course not. The problem is that men don't see their choice in stark black-and-white terms. They make gray choices not knowing they darken gradually. The subtle lie is he doesn't have to choose, he can have it all if he plays his cards right. Double up here, cut corners there, and juggle the rest.

My advice, men, is save your children. The world is full of fathers who will sell out their family for bucks and booty. Well, let them. Let the dead bury the dead. But, not you. A holy calling and ordination summons you to practice the profession of fatherhood.
~ Dave Simmons, adapted from *Dad the Family Counselor*

Fathers, do you hear the call?

August 4 *Columbian Squires Anniversary (1925)*

FRATERNITY is a father's affirmation

Fathers, do not embitter your children, or they will become discouraged. ~ Colossians 3:21

Somewhere between the ages of three to five, little boys are "discovered" by their fathers. At that age, children begin to "function" better. Most men know better what to do with children when they function. Now that a little boy plays more productively, a father can step in and begin to teach him to "do" some things. About this time, a little boy recognizes a kinship with his father and begins to form an identity as a male. Our fathers teach us how to work. Our fathers show us how to do things together. Our fathers teach us to take risks. All of these are great lessons. And if you were one of a fortunate few, perhaps your father was also tender and nurturing. His affirmations helped your self-confidence to grow strong. Our fathers lay the groundwork for the next generation. ~ Dick Brian Klaver, *Men at Peace*

Fathers, do you fit the description above?
Knights, how can we lay the groundwork for the next generation through our Squires? Would our council consider sponsoring a Squires service project such as "Crusade against Poverty" or "Project Build"?
For councils not currently sponsoring a Squires Circle –
What better way to inject youthful leadership into our Order than by setting up a Circle as a feeder organization for Knights?

I cannot think of any need in childhood as strong as the need for a father's protection.
~ Sigmund Freud   217

August 5

CHARITY is the unconditional love of the Father

Because you are sons, God sent the Spirit of his Son into our hearts, the Spirit who calls out, "Abba, Father." ~ Galatians 4:6

Our understanding of God as the Father is affected by our experiences with our own father. So many young people in America today grow up without a father in their life. Can we blame them then for not understanding the heavenly Father?

God says, "If you will listen to me, I will seal you with My Spirit of adoption. You will be a joint heir through Christ. You will no longer be an orphan, but My child." God seals us by His Spirit.

God desires an intimate relationship with us His children. Through this intimacy, God can shape our view of Him and our view of how we think He sees us. We will begin to realize how much God loves us. We can experience the depth of His unconditional love for us. We can go confidently into His presence, addressing Him intimately as "Abba, Father." We can enjoy the knowledge that He will hear us, speak to us, and meet our needs.
~ Doug Stringer

How are we being positive role models for our children? How can we share our image of God the Father with junior leadership in the Squires?

The father who does not teach his son his duties is equally guilty with the son who neglects them. ~ Confucius

August 6

UNITY is a Knight and his Lady as one

His left arm is under my head, and his right arm embraces me.
~ Song of Songs 2:6

To most women affection symbolizes security, protection, comfort,
and approval, vitally important commodities in their eyes.
When a husband shows his wife affection, he sends several
messages to her –

I'll take care of you and protect you. You are important to me, and
I don't want anything to happen to you.

I'm concerned about the problems you face, and I am with you.

I'm so proud of you.

Men need to understand how strongly women need these
affirmations and that there can hardly be enough of them. From a
woman's point of view, affection is the essential cement of her
relationship with a man.
~ Willard Harley, adapted from *His Needs, Her Needs*

Do you send these messages of affection to your Lady?

And now these three remain: faith, hope and love.
But the greatest of these is love.
Husbands, love your wives, just as Christ loved the church and
gave himself up for her.
~ 1 Corinthians 13:13, Ephesians 5:25

August 7

FRATERNITY is fathers on their knees

Come, let us bow down in worship, let us kneel before the LORD our Maker... ~ Psalm 95:6

I want to ask you, Dad: When was the last time your children saw you on your knees, seeking direction from God? That's an unmistakable lesson to a child. To be a spiritual man you must take time to talk to Him and to listen to him through His Word. The regularity of this meeting, not its length, is the important thing. When you're running late, pause long enough to get on your knees and tell the LORD, "I am committing this day to you. Late as I am, I am not leaving this house without getting on my knees before You." God will reward that commitment.
Your attitude of mind covers your home. When your attention is focused on the Truth, you are exercising the mind of Christ. When I think as Christ thinks, I am loving my wife and children more faithfully; I am more sensitive to the needs of those around me. Apart from Christ, you cannot be the man, the husband, and the father you can be. ~ Charles Stanley, *A Man's Touch*

A prayer of commitment and a Bible verse is a good way to launch every new day. Would this commitment lay the groundwork for a longer period of meditation and Bible study later on? Would our council benefit from a Bible study group open to all men of the parish, not just Knights?

Jesus grew in wisdom and stature, and in favor with God and men (Luke 2:52). *Jesus grew mentally, physically, spiritually and socially. What a powerful example of a life fully lived!*
~ J.A. Lacy

220

August 8

PATRIOTISM depends on the character of its citizens

*I have strength to face all conditions by the power that Christ gives
me.* ~ Philippians 4:13

I sought for the greatness
and genius of America
in her vast world commerce,
and it was not there.
Not until I went
into the churches of America
and heard her pulpits,
aflame with righteousness,
did I understand the secret
of her genius and power.
America is great
because she is good,
and if America ever ceases to be good,
America will cease to be great. ~ Alexis de Tocqueville

Tocqueville was a great observer of early American democratic
life. In what areas today would he be critical of the state of the
union?

*A patriot without religion in my estimation is as great a paradox as
an honest man without the fear of God. Is it possible that he whom
no moral obligations bind, can have any real good will towards
men? Can he be a patriot who, by an openly vicious conduct, is
undermining the very bonds of society?.... The Scriptures tell us
"righteousness exalteth a nation."*
~ A. Adams

August 9

CHARITY is our children teaching us faith

I tell you the truth, anyone who will not receive the kingdom of God like a little child will never enter it." And he took the children in his arms, put his hands on them and blessed them.
~ Mark 10:15-16

We were crowded in the cabin,
Not a soul would dare to sleep –
It was midnight on the waters,
And a storm was on the deep.

So we shuddered there in silence –
For the stoutest held his breath,
While the hungry sea was roaring
And the breakers talked with Death.

But this little daughter whispered,
As she took his icy hand,
"Isn't God upon the ocean,
Just the same as on the Land?"

Then we kissed the little maiden,
And we spoke in better cheer,
And we anchored safe in harbor
When the morn was shining clear.

~ James T. Fields , *The Captain's Daughter*

Do you notice when your children teach you how to draw your family to Christ?

We speak of educating our children. Do we know that our children also educate us? ~ Mrs. Sigourney

August 10

UNITY is pleasing your wife

Husbands, in the same way be considerate as you live with your wives, and treat them with respect as the weaker partner and as heirs with you of the gracious gift of life, so that nothing will hinder your prayers. ~ 1 Peter 3:7

Affection is so important for women that they become confused when their husbands don't respond in kind. A wife may call her husband at work, just to talk. She often feels disappointed when he cuts it short. It doesn't mean he doesn't love her; he simply has different priorities because of a different set of basic needs. My needs for protection, approval, and care are not the same as hers, nor are they met in similar ways. I've had to discover these differences and act accordingly. When we walk through a shopping center, it is important to her that we hold hands, something that would never occur to me. But I'm glad to do so, because I know she enjoys that and it says something she wants to hear. If that simple act makes her feel loved and cherished, I would be a fool to refuse to do it. I promised to care for her when I married her, and I meant every word of it. If she explains how I can best give her the care she wants, I'm willing to learn, because I want her happiness. ~ Willard Harley, *His Needs, Her Needs*

Are you willing to learn from your wife? Are you being true to your wedding vows?

Men never remember, but women never forget. ~ Author unknown

It is better to live in a corner of a roof than in a house shared with a contentious woman. ~ Proverbs 21:9

August 11

FRATERNITY is brothers praying for brothers

For where two or three have gathered together in My name, I am there in their midst. ~ Matthew 18:19-21

An inscription near the tomb of Saint Philomena tomb read "Peace be with thee, Philomena." Near her bones was discovered a small glass vial, containing the remains of blood. Because it was a popular custom of the early martyrs to leave symbols and signs such as these, it was determined that St. Philomena was a virgin and a martyr. She was venerated by other saints such as St. John Vianney, St. Madeleine Sophie Barat, St. Peter Eymard, and St. Peter Chanel. After hundreds of other miraculous cures, she was beatified in 1837. The pope dubbed her the Patroness of the Living Rosary and the Patroness of the Children of Mary. She is the only person recognized as a saint solely on the basis of her powerful intercession, although revelations regarding her life have been recorded. ~ J.M. Guerin

How often do we as brothers gather in prayer and ask for the intercession of the Blessed Virgin Mary, the angels, and the saints?

Illustrious Virgin and Martyr, Saint Philomena, Behold me kneeling in spirit before you. Full of confidence in your protection, I beseech you to intercede for me. From heaven, please look upon us. Spouse of Jesus Christ, console me in my troubles, strengthen me in temptations, protect me in the dangers which surround me; obtain all the graces necessary for me, especially [your intentions], and assist me at my death. Amen.
~ Prayer for the intercession of St. Philomena

August 12 *Birth of Father Michael McGivney (1852)*

KNIGHTHOOD is a deep commitment to our principles

Be on your guard, stand firm in the faith, be men of courage, be strong. ~ 1 Corinthians 16:13

In 1881, Father McGivney began to explore the idea of a Catholic, fraternal benefit society. In an era when parish clubs and fraternal societies had wide popular appeal, the young priest felt there should be some way to strengthen religious faith and at the same time provide for the financial needs of families overwhelmed by illness or death of the breadwinner. Father McGivney had suggested "Sons of Columbus" as a name for the Order. This would bind Catholicism and Americanism together through the faith and bold vision of the New World's explorer (*see October 12th entry*). The word "knights" replaced "sons" because Irish-born Civil War veterans wanted to apply a noble ritual in support of the emerging cause of Catholic civil liberty. The Order's principles in 1882 were UNITY and CHARITY. The concepts of FRATERNITY and PATRIOTISM were added later. These Columbus-linked themes "reverberated with pride in the American promise of liberty, equality and opportunity."
~ Father Gabriel B. O'Donnell, OP, adapted

What would Father McGivney say about our council? Are we charitable beyond our parish walls? Are we unified as the right arm of the Church? Are we fraternally bonded in Catholic brotherhood? Are we actively patriotic beyond simple flag-waving?

Give yourself to the LORD; trust in him, and he will help you.
~ Psalm 37:5

August 13

UNITY is a loving father

These commandments that I give you today are to be upon your hearts. Impress them on your children. Talk about them when you sit at home and when you walk along the road, when you lie down and when you get up. ~ Deuteronomy 6:6-7

Parents are responsible not only for the physical needs of their children, but also for spiritual growth (Deuteronomy 6:4-9; 32:45-47). No parents are perfect. There will be problems, but the important thing is to build mutual understanding with our children. Love must be evident when correction is necessary. It is a happy husband-wife relationship and their evident oneness in Christ that leads children toward faith in Him and makes for a happy, wholesome family life.

Paul, writing to Timothy, gives the strongest possible admonition and warning to husbands and fathers, "If any provide not for his own and especially for those of his own house, he hath denied the faith, and is worse than an infidel (1 Timothy 5:8)." This provision need not be confined to material things, but also to time and energy and concern. One father was made aware of this when he was thumbing through his *Day-Timer* one evening. His young son, seeing the small book by which his father's life was ordered and controlled, said, "Daddy, could you put my name in there?"
~ Billy Graham

Are you participating in the spiritual growth of your children?

Please be patient.
God is not yet finished with me.
~ Words on a child's T-shirt

August 14 *Death of Father Michael J. McGivney (1890)*

SAINTHOOD is a life of humility and good works

Let your light shine before men in such a way that they may see your good works, and glorify your Father who is in heaven.
~ Matthew 5:16

A Guild has been established to advance the cause for the beatification and canonization of Father Michael McGivney. The Guild continues to gather evidence on Father McGivney's reputation and character as a servant of God. As a Knight, you are encouraged to join our founder's Guild.

God, our Father, you called your priest, Father Michael J. McGivney, to be an apostle of Christian family life and to lead the young to the generous service of their neighbor.
We humbly ask that you glorify your servant, Father McGivney, on earth according to the design of your holy will.
Through his intercession, grant the favor I now present (*here make your request*). Through Christ our Lord. Amen.
~ Canonization Guild for Father Michael J. McGivney

Our Father, Hail Mary, Glory be . . .

The road to canonization is long and arduous. What is our council and assembly actively doing to promote the cause for Father McGivney?

The source of our brotherhood is found in the heart of a zealous young priest, and from that heart followed a movement that neither time nor adversity has destroyed. ~ Father Gabriel B. O'Donnell

August 15

Assumption of the Blessed Virgin Mary

And coming to her [Mary], he [the angel Gabriel] said, "Hail, favored one [kecharitomene]." ~ Luke 1:28

Mary was exempted from bodily corruption because, by an entirely singular privilege, she completely overcame sin by her Immaculate Conception. Jesus ascended to Heaven by His own power as Creator and LORD. Mary was taken to Heaven by the power of God, raised aloft by grace, not by nature. Pope Pius said, "Christ has overcome sin and death by His own death… However, in accord with His general rule, God does not wish to grant the full effect of victory over death to the just until the end of time shall have come... Yet God wished that the Blessed Virgin Mary be exempt from this general law. For she, by a completely singular privilege, conquered sin in her Immaculate Conception, and thus was not liable to that law of remaining in the corruption of the grave, nor did she have to wait for the end of time for the redemption of her body (AAS 42. 754)." ~ J.M. Guerin

Mary responded to God with her "fiat" – totally giving herself over to His will, when she said, "I am the handmaid of the LORD; let it be done unto me according to Your will." How do you respond without reservation to the will of God?

Finally the Immaculate Virgin, preserved free from all stain of original sin, when the course of her earthly life was finished, was taken up body and soul into heavenly glory, and exalted by the LORD as Queen over all things, so that she might be the more fully conformed to her Son, the LORD of lords and conqueror of sin and death. ~ Pius XII, Munificentissimus Deus

August 16

CHARITY is a nickel

*How can a young person live a pure life? He can do it by obeying
your word. With all my heart I try to obey you, God. Do not let me
break your commands. I have taken your words to heart so I
would not sin against you.* ~ Psalm 119:9-11

David Brenner grew up poor in Philadelphia. He didn't expect a
graduation gift when he finished high school. Yet, he received one
he never forgot.
"Some of my friends got some neat gifts. The few rich kids got
brand new cars or new wardrobes. Just having my family there
was enough for me. But after the graduation, my dad said, 'I have
your graduation gift.' He extended his hand toward me – a nickel!
'Buy a newspaper with that,' he said. 'Read every word of it, page
one to the last page. Then turn to the classified section and get
yourself a job. Get into the world. It's all yours now.'
I laughed. 'A nickel! Thanks a lot,' I said as I forced a smile.
I always thought that was a great joke my father played on me until
a couple of years later as I sat in a foxhole in the Army thinking
about my family and my life. It was then that I realized that my
friends had gotten *only* cars, *only* clothes or *only* tuition from their
parents. My father had given me the whole world! I think the day
I realized this was the day I became a man."
~ Bits and Pieces

Recall a lesson you learned from an adult. Why is that lesson still
a part of you today?

*The world is not to be put in order; the world is order, incarnate.
It is for us to harmonize with this order.* ~ Henry Miller

August 17

UNITY is marital oneness

In this same way, husbands ought to love their wives as their own bodies. He who loves his wife loves himself. After all, no one ever hated his own body, but he heeds and cares for it, just as Christ does the church… ~ Ephesians 5:28-29

Husband, take positives steps to meet your partner's emotional needs. Your wife longs to be encouraged, built up, and praised. She wants to feel close to you emotionally. This will come as you love her in the way the Bible describes. A husband can always meet his wife's deepest needs by loving her as Christ loves us. A husband's love has been compared to a warm coat he wraps around his wife. As long as she feels encircled and sheltered in his love, she can give herself completely to him. In this safety, she can accept herself as a woman and value her femininity.
We husbands may not be able to fully appreciate the deep longings that influence our wives, but if we love them with the sheltering love described in Ephesians 5:28-29 we will be rewarded. Our wives reflect the love or lack of love we have provided.
~ Ed Wheat, adapted from *Love Life for Every Married Couple*

The husband must fulfill his duty to his wife, and likewise also the wife to her husband. ~ 1 Corinthians 7:3

Are you tending to the needs of your Lady? Do you tap into the spiritual dimension of your marriage by praying together?

Let family worship be short, savory, simple, plain, tender, heavenly. ~ Richard Cecil

August 18

FRATERNITY is giving the first pancake to your brother

Should anyone press you into service for one mile, go with him for two miles. Give to the one who asks of you, and do not turn your back on one who wants to borrow. ~ Matthew 5:41-42

A mother was preparing breakfast for her sons, Christian, 6, Douglas, 4.

The boys began to argue over who would get the first pancake. Their mother saw the opportunity for a moral lesson.

"If Jesus were sitting here, He would say, 'Let my brother have the first pancake. I can wait.'"

Christian turned to his little brother and said, "Doug, you be Jesus!" ~ Melissa Flores, adapted

When you read the above Scripture, who in your life do you think of?

You will never be saved by works; but let us tell you most solemnly that you never will be saved without works.
~ T.L. Cuyler

August 19

CHARITY is a top Pop

The righteous man leads a blameless life; blessed are his children after him. ~ Proverbs 20:7

Some years ago a newspaper ran an interesting contest in which children were to write essays on "My Pop's Tops." Here is a young son's top entry:

"We have so much fun with my dad that I wisht [sic] I had known him sooner. He is a farmer. He smells like a cow, and when I smell that cow in the house, I know Pop is home and I am glad. My pop's tops because every time I ast [sic] for a knickel [sic] he will start preeching [sic] that when he was a boy he had to earn his knickels [sic], and at the same time he is putting his hand in his pocket and pulls out a knickel [sic] for me. My pop's tops because he was a brave soldier. He didn't see me till I was three years old, yet he is just as good to me as if he knew me all my life."

It's evident this little guy was judging his dad by the common everyday things. A smell, a nickel, the feeling inside. Does anything matter more than living so our children could say, *"We have so much fun with my dad, I wisht I had known him sooner."*
~ Charlie Shedd, adapted from *A Dad Is for Spending Time With*

What will your children remember about you?

We are never more like Jesus than when we are selflessly, lovingly, reaching out to meet somebody else's needs.
~ Author unknown

August 20

UNITY is hanging it out to dry

Let patience have her perfect work. ~ James 1:4

The carpenter hired to restore an old farmhouse had just finished a
rough first day on the job. A flat tire made him lose an hour of
work, his electric saw quit and now his old pickup truck refused to
start. While I drove him home, he sat in stony silence.
Upon arriving, he invited me to meet his family. As we walked
toward the front door, he paused briefly at a small tree, touching
the tips of the branches with both hands. When opening the door,
he underwent an amazing transformation.
His tanned face was wreathed in smiles and he hugged his two
small children and gave his wife a kiss. Afterward he walked me to
the car. We passed the tree and my curiosity got the better of me.
I asked him about what I had seen him do earlier.
"Oh, that's my trouble tree," he replied. "I know I can't help
having troubles on the job but one thing for sure, troubles don't
belong in the house with my wife and children. So I just hang
them up on the tree every night when I come home. Then in the
morning I pick them up again.
"Funny thing is," he smiled, "when I come out in the morning to
pick them up, there aren't nearly as many as I remember hanging
up the night before." ~ Author unknown

In your family, who does everyone lean on in hard times?

In your patience ye are strong.
~ E.B. Browning

FRATERNITY is sharing the fruit of the Spirit

*But the fruit of the Spirit is love, joy, peace, patience, kindness,
goodness, faithfulness, gentleness and self-control...*
~ Galatians 5:22-23

There was a little boy with a bad temper. His father gave him a
bag of nails and told him that every time he lost his temper, to
hammer a nail in the back fence.
The first day the boy had driven thirty-seven nails into the fence.
Then it gradually dwindled down. He discovered it was easier to
hold his temper than to drive those nails into the fence.
Finally the day came when the boy didn't lose his temper at all. He
told his father about it and the father suggested that the boy now
pull out one nail for each day that he was able to hold his temper.
The days passed and the young boy was finally able to tell his father
that all the nails were gone. The father then led him to the fence.
He said, "You have done well, my son, but look at the holes in the
fence.
The fence will never be the same. When you say things in anger,
they leave a scar just like this one. You can put a knife in a man
and draw it out. It won't matter how many times you say I'm
sorry, the wound is still there. A verbal wound is as bad as a
physical one." ~ Author unknown

Which spiritual fruits (see above verse) are blossoming in your
life? Which are still in the bud?

*Patience is something you admire in the driver behind you, but
not in one ahead.* ~ Bill Mcglashen

PATRIOTISM is taking care of our own

If any one does not provide for his relatives, and especially for his own family, he has disowned the faith and is worse than an unbeliever. ~ 1 Timothy 5:8

Christian faith has always been measured (in the Catholic tradition) not by miracles or wonders, but by love. Miracles alone do not a saint make. After all, Balaam's Donkey performed the wonder of speaking, but the Church never got around to canonizing it. Likewise, Caiaphas, the man who desired the execution of Christ, made the true prophecy that it was better for one man to die than for a whole nation to perish, but this hardly guaranteed his sanctity. No, the way the Church has always determined the measure of a person is by the love they demonstrate. Such love, as always, begins at home. We crawl before we walk or run. And so, before we try to save the world or be Mother Teresa, we begin by loving the people God has surrounded us with: our mother, father, brother, sister, son, daughter, uncle, aunt. Often, just loving these people is challenge enough for a lifetime. But caring for them is the bare minimum, the basic training ground, the place we begin. Learn our lesson well there, and we shall be able to move on to the higher lessons of love in the Kingdom.
~ Dr. Scott Hahn and Jeff Cavins

Today, make a special gesture of love for your family.

The wisest keeps something of the vision of a child. Though he may understand a thousand things that a child could not understand, he is always a beginner, close to the original meaning of life.
~ John Macy

August 23

CHARITY is doing what we say

As the body without the spirit is dead, so faith without deeds is dead. ~ James 2:26

I'll never forget the day I saw my boy trudging home in the driving rain. Mark's clothing was drenched and his hair was plastered against his head. I opened the door and he looked up at me with a little smile, his face red from the cold.

"Hi, Dad!" he said. "You're home early."

"Mark, you know, if you'd ride your bike you'd get home faster."

He looked at me rather sheepishly, "I know, Dad."

I was puzzled. "Well, Son, if you *know*, why didn't you do it?" Then he hung his head, and I felt like crawling under a table. He had told me several times before that his bike had a flat tire. He could have said that *someone* promised to help him but never did. But he didn't. What he did say remains printed indelibly on this dad's heart. "I know how busy you are, and – I just didn't want to bother you with it again."

I wasn't too busy; just too selfish. A bike tire was just one more addition to a long "to-do" list. But for Mark, it meant more than a long walk home in the rain. It meant trusting his father to meet his every need. I'm sure glad my heavenly Father doesn't forget. He knows about my flat tires. He knows about the things that matter most to me. ~ Ron Mehl, adapted from *God Works the Night Shift*

Do you unwittingly brush aside the wants and needs of your wife and children?

We are reaping the bitter fruit of decades of pathetic tolerance for all that is wrong in ourselves and others. ~ L. Bowles

UNITY is a handful of prayers

The prayer of a righteous man is powerful and effective.
~ James 5:16
The Five Finger Prayer

1. Your thumb is nearest to you. So begin your prayers by praying for those closest to you. To pray for our loved ones is, as C.S. Lewis once said, a "sweet duty."
2. The next finger is the pointing finger. Pray for those who teach, instruct and heal. This includes priests, doctors, teachers and coaches. They need God's guidance.
3. 3. The next finger is the tallest finger. It reminds us of those people who shape our nation and guide public opinion. They need God's wisdom.
4. The fourth finger is our ring finger. This is our weakest finger; as any piano teacher will testify. Pray for those who are weak, in trouble or in pain. You cannot pray too much for them.
5. 5. And lastly comes our little finger; the smallest finger of all. Which is where we should place ourselves in relation to God and others. As the Bible says, "the least shall be the greatest among you." By the time you have prayed for the other four groups, your own needs will be put into proper perspective and you will be able to pray for yourself more effectively.
   ~ Author unknown

When have you come the closest to wandering from the faith? What or who helped bring you back?

Prayer is the mortar that holds our house together.
~ Saint Teresa of Avila

FRATERNITY is sacrificing His life for us

The Son of man... [came] to give his life to redeem many people.
~ Matthew 20:28

Little Jason was returning home later and later each afternoon from school. His father lectured him on punctuality, but it made little impact on the boy.
Finally, he told Jason, "The next time you come home late, you can expect bread and water for supper."
Sure enough, the next night Jason was late. When he sat down to supper, he was stunned. On his plate was a single slice of bread. Jason saw that his father meant business.
When the punishment had sunk in fully, Jason's father gave him his own full plate and took Jason's single slice of bread. That was all Jason's father ate that night.
Years later, Jason said that what his father did that night taught him in the most eloquent way what Jesus did for the human race 2,000 years ago. ~ Author unknown

Today, what are you doing in return for what Jesus did 2,000 years ago? Do you have a favorite memory of a lesson in life that your father taught you?

Yet it was our infirmities that he bore, our sufferings that he endured. ~ Isaiah 53:4

CHARITY is adhering to a new commandment

A new commandment I give you: love one another. As I have loved you, so you must love one another. ~ John 13:34

Jesus' disciples were arguing about which of them would be the greatest in the kingdom. They were on an ego trip: they were being selfish, self-centered, self-indulgent, and insensitive to Jesus and the pain and sin He was about to bear. Finally, Jesus did what they wouldn't do for each other. He washed their filthy feet. Then He said, "A new commandment I give you, that you love one another, even as I have loved you." By washing their feet, he showed that where there is a need, love acts, sacrificially. This is the husband's role in marriage.

Paul says true love "does not seek its own (1 Corinthians 13:5)." As long as a man is looking for what can be personally gained from marriage he will never know what it is to love his wife as Christ loves the Church, and he can never experience the richness of self-giving and its amazing dividends.

The world teaches us to "be the macho man, the big shot. Don't let anyone step on your territory, fight back, grab all that you can because you deserve it." But the Bible simply says, "Set yourself aside." ~ John MacArthur, Jr.

When was the last time you made a sacrifice for your wife? When was the last time you changed your own carefully laid plans to accommodate her wishes?

If you are to love that woman in your house like Christ loves the Church, you will have to see the death of your own selfish desires. ~ John MacArthur, Jr.

UNITY is a council of super heroes

In a large house there are articles not only of gold and silver, but also of wood and clay; some are for noble purposes and some for ignoble. If a man cleanses himself from the latter, he will be an instrument for noble purposes, made holy, useful to the Master and prepared to do any good work. Flee the evil desires of youth, and pursue righteousness, faith, love and peace, along with those who call on the LORD out of a pure heart. ~ 2 Timothy 2:20-22

The world doesn't need supermen, but super-*natural* men. Men who will turn the *self* out of their lives and let divine power work through them. We can let inspiration take the place of aspiration. We can seek to grow spiritually, rather than to acquire fame and riches. Our chief ambition can be to be used by God. The divine force is sufficient for all the spiritual work in the world. God only needs the instruments for God's use. God's instruments can remake the world. ~ Fr. Pat Umberger

Pray that we may be an instrument of the divine power. Pray that we may do our share in remaking the world.

What do you need to turn from? What do you need to pursue?

What good will it be for a man if he gains the whole world, yet forfeits his soul? ~ Matthew 16:26 NIV

August 28

FRATERNITY is looking beyond ourselves

When the face is sad the heart grows wiser. ~ Ecclesiastes 7:3

One of the ways my students have surprised me is that they find
God in failure more than in success or beauty.
The death of a parent or relative, the breakup of a love affair, the
loss of a game or a job are for them windows of discovery.
They realize that they are not self-sufficient, not in control of life, so
they look beyond themselves.
They learn a lot from failure. It is one of the paradoxical secrets of
Christian life.
~ Francis Buckley, *Growing in the Church: From Birth to Death*

Throughout the fraternal year, our council struggles with adversity
in its mission to serve our parish, our community and our country.
How have these trials and tribulations brought us closer together and
closer to God?

Not until each loom is silent
And the shuttles cease to fly,
Will God unroll the pattern
And explain the reason why.
The dark threads are as needful
In the weaver's skillful hand
As the threads of gold and silver
for the pattern which is planned.
~ *The Loom of Time*

PATRIOTISM is doing things unpopular with others

Amen, I say to you, among those born of women there has been none greater than John the Baptist... ~ Matthew 11:11

John is the last prophet before the Birth of Christ. He was actively "preparing the way of the LORD." His message was directed to the poor and weak, and the rich and powerful. He dressed in camel's hair and ate locusts and wild honey, yet people were drawn to his message of repentance and forgiveness, and flocked to him to be baptized. Christ Himself came to John to be baptized, to mark the beginning of His public ministry. Humble, John tried to refuse but did baptize Jesus, and we see here the first "Theophany" - the Father, Son, and Holy Spirit all present as distinct Persons. John had publicly criticized King Herod for living with his brother's wife. Herod feared John, knowing him to be a holy and upright man.... When he heard him speak he was very much disturbed, yet he felt the attraction of his words. Eventually, he was beheaded, as payment for a dance Salome had given Herod.
~ J.M. Guerin

Responding to God's call may require us to say or do things that are unpopular with others – including people who have authority over us or who possess the ability to harm us. In what specific ways can Sir Knights be like John the Baptist in our parish, our community, our country?

In the beginning of a change, the patriot is a scarce man and brave, hated and scorned. When his cause succeeds however, the timid join him, for then it costs nothing to be a patriot.
~ Mark Twain, 1935

August 30

CHARITY is imitating a good father

Therefore I urge you to imitate me. ~ 1 Corinthians 4:16

If you are one of the 17% of this country's men who, as a Gallup poll suggests, characterizes his relationship with his father as negative, it's likely you are consciously trying hard not to pattern your life after him. His fathering style, you believe, affects you neither one way or the other.

We are witnessing what may be the first generation of Americans in which a substantial number of dads have grown up without fathers in their homes. Two years after a divorce, more than 80% of the noncustodial parents, generally the fathers, have little or no steady pattern of visitation with the children. Men learn best how to be a father by watching and imitating a good one. The most important model is their own dad. Without a good dad to guide them – no matter how strong their desire to do a better job – boys usually grow up into fatherhood with much confusion. So whether good, bad, or indifferent, your father has left his imprint on you. His presence or absence contributed to how you see yourself and how you perform a father's role. Recognizing and dealing with your father's imprint on you, particularly if it has been negative, is a prerequisite to good fatherhood. ~ Paul Lewis

By accentuating the positive in our fathers' relationship with us and processing the negative, all of us can be good fathers. Once we Knights have honed good fathering skills, shouldn't we share them in our Squires Circle?

It doesn't matter who my father was; it matters who I remember he was. ~ A. Sexton

243

August 31

UNITY is making time for our children

I know that there is nothing better for men than to be happy and do good while they live. ~ Ecclesiastes 3:12

Every man lives in two very different worlds: a *positional* world and a *personal* world. Most of the mistakes men make in fathering are due to a lack of balance between the two. In the *positional* world, men develop clout. They flex their authority, title, or buying power and crave respect. Most men thrive in the *positional* arena – it's what they're wired for, and they typically enjoy the game. That's why they get up early for work and put in overtime at the office. The *personal* world is where a man has the potential to become an adored husband, and a hero to his kids. But unlike the *positional* world, the *personal* world doesn't come naturally. It all comes down to this: The *positional* world doesn't ultimately matter; the *personal* world is what really counts. Lee Iacocca once said, "No one on their death bed wishes they spent more time at the office." ~ David Moore, adapted from *Five Lies of the Century*

Are we sensitive to our children's *personal* world? Are we failing to develop *personal* skills?

A man without ambition is dead. A man with ambition but no love is dead. A man with ambition and love for his blessings here on earth is ever so alive. Having been alive, it won't be so hard in the end to lay down and rest. ~ P. Bailey

September 1

FRATERNITY is celebrating the risen Christ

He changes times and seasons;
he removes kings and sets up kings;
he gives wisdom to the wise
and knowledge to those who have understanding. ~ Daniel 2:21

Periodically, somebody stops to wonder why Christians celebrate their Sabbath on Sunday when Judaism celebrates it on Saturday. The answer is hinted at in today's verse. God changes times and seasons. Sunday is a "little Easter." Every Sunday is a feast day in honor of the great Marriage Feast of the Lamb that goes on perpetually in heaven and into which we enter at every Mass. The Church celebrates this final and greatest rest into which God entered after he conquered death on the mystical Eighth Day of Creation. Let Sunday be a sacrament of the mystery that goes on eternally outside of time: the Day on which Christ gave us his wisdom and knowledge, overthrew the King of Death, and was crowned the LORD of lords. ~ Dr. Scott Hahn and Jeff Cavins

Do you believe the consecrated bread is indeed the Body of Christ?

So we, who are many,
are one body in Christ,
and individually members one of another.
~ Romans 12:5

September 2

CHARITY is applying business lessons from the Master

The LORD does not look at the things man looks at. Man looks at the outward appearance, but the LORD looks at the heart.
~ 1 Samuel 16:7

Jesus is an excellent model for the business leader, and it is possible to apply His approach to the workweek. In three years, He demonstrated a radical form of servant leadership that created spectacular results with otherwise ordinary people, thereby transforming the course of human history. Jesus launched His vision with twelve followers. Now, 1.9 billion people worldwide consider Him their leader.

As a leader, Jesus served. He told His disciples, "Whoever wants to become great among you must be your servant, and whoever wants to be first must be slave of all (Mark 10:43-44)." Therefore, serve others by thinking carefully about customers and employees when you're making a decision. Some actions that might seem to improve the bottom line might harm people and morale along the way. Beware. Listen to employees and customers and follow-up on their feedback. Above all, be accountable for your actions.
~ A. Reynolds Alexander, excerpted

Jesus' message is not just for the mind, it is directed at the heart. Is it possible to climb the corporate ladder without compromising the high ideals of Knighthood?

The secret of my success? It is simple. It is found in the Bible, "In all thy ways acknowledge Him and He shall direct thy paths."
~ George Washington Carver

September 3

UNITY is compassion for the trials of others

As God's chosen ones, holy and beloved, clothe yourselves with compassion, kindness, humility, meekness, and patience. Bear with one another and, if anyone has a complaint against another, forgive each other; just as the LORD has forgiven you, so you also must forgive. Above all, clothe yourselves with love, which binds everything together in perfect harmony. And let the peace of Christ rule in your hearts, to which indeed you were called in the one body. ~ Colossians 3:12-15

Having compassion for all who are in temptation, a condition which we are sometimes in, we have a responsibility toward them. Compassion always includes responsibility. Pity is useless because it does not have a remedy for the need. But wherever our sympathy goes, our responsibility goes as well. When we are moved with compassion, we can go to the one in need and bind up that person's wounds as best we can. ~ Fr. Pat Umberger

Pray that we may have compassion for those in temptation. Pray that we may have concern for the trials of others, and the willingness to offer our help.

With what piece of Christ's wardrobe (see above verse) do you need to clothe yourself with, in relation to your Lady, your children, your Brother Knights, your siblings, your parents, your neighbor, your employer or employees?

A human life is a single letter in the alphabet. It can be rendered meaningless, or it can be part of a great meaning.
~ *New York Herald Tribune*, "Who Takes Delight in Life"

247

September 4

The Grunt Padre

I have fought a good fight, I have finished my course,
I have kept the faith. ~ 2 Timothy 4:7

On this date in 1967, Father Vincent Capodanno was doing what he had done since the beginning of his tour in Vietnam, he was ministering to his men. Capodanno was the Battalion Chaplain for the 1st Marine Division. In response to reports that a platoon was being overrun by enemy forces, Capodanno disregarded intense fire and moved about the battlefield administering last rites to the dying and giving medical aid to the wounded. When an exploding mortar round inflicted multiple wounds to his arms and legs, severing a portion of his right hand, he steadfastly refused all medical aid. Instead, with calm vigor, he provided encouragement by voice and example to his valiant Marines. Upon encountering a corpsman in the line of fire, Capodanno rushed forward to aid the mortally wounded Marine. At that instant, he was struck down by a burst of machine gun fire.

For his heroic conduct on the battlefield, Father Capodanno was posthumously awarded our nation's highest award for valor, the Congressional Medal of Honor. ~ selected from the government citation of Father Capodanno's valorous service

How may Father Capodanno's conduct serve as an inspiring example to our council and assembly?

Any personal sacrifice I may have to make will be compensated for by the fact that I am serving God. ~ Father Vincent R. Capodanno, 1LT, 3d Battalion, 5th Marines, 1st Marine Division (Rein) FMF, Congressional Medal of Honor Recipient

September 5

PATRIOTISM is freedom of worship

He said to them, "Go into the whole world and proclaim the gospel to every creature. Whoever believes and is baptized will be saved; whoever does not believe will be condemned. ~ Mark 16:15

Penn State University's D. J. Dozier knelt and prayed after scoring in the 1987 Fiesta Bowl. Dozier's action touched-off instant criticism.

Coming to Dozier's defense, R. D. Lashar, placekicker for the state champion Plano HS Wildcats, said, "Before and after each place kick, I kneel and pray. The day someone tells me I can't pray is the day I don't play! It's a free country."

Mark Roberts wrote, "Personally, I find it refreshing to see someone do something besides a silly dance and parading around, flaunting an oversized ego." ~ Mark Link, S.J.

How we witness to the Gospel is one thing; that we *must* witness to it is another. How do we, as Knights, witness to the Gospel?

I'd rather see a sermon than hear one. ~ Edgar A. Guest

September 6

CHARITY is paying in full

If you then, who are wicked, know how to give good gifts to your children, how much more will your heavenly Father give good things to those who ask him. ~ Matthew 7:11

A young man was graduating from college. He had been admiring a sports car, and knowing his father could well afford it, he told him that was all he wanted.

Just before graduation, his father told him how proud he was of his son, and how much he loved him. Then he handed him a box. Curious, but somewhat disappointed, the young man opened it and found a handsome, leather-bound Bible, with the young man's name embossed in gold. Angrily, he raised his voice to his father and said, "Thanks a lot!" Then he stormed out of the house, leaving the gift behind.

Many years passed before the young man received news that his father had passed away and had willed all of his possessions to him. He was searching through his father's papers when he found the Bible, just as he had left it years ago. He turned the pages. His father had carefully underlined a verse (*see above*). He then noticed a lump in the back of the Bible. It was the keys to the]sports car he had coveted, still tagged with the date of his graduation, and the words, PAID IN FULL. ~ Author unknown

How many times do we miss God's blessings because they are not packaged as we expected?

By the time a man realizes that maybe his father was right, he usually has a son who thinks he's wrong. ~ Charles Wadworth

September 7

UNITY is turning to God for strength

*My flesh and my heart may fail, but God is the strength of my heart
and my portion forever. Those who are far from you will perish;
you destroy all who are unfaithful to you. But as for me, it is good
to be near God. I have made the Sovereign LORD my refuge.*
~ Psalm 73:26-28

We can pray for faith as a thirsty person prays for water in a desert.
Do we know what it means to feel sure that God will never fail us?
Are we sure of this as the air that we breathe? We can pray daily
and most diligently that we may appreciate and use the faith we
have been given. There is nothing lacking in our lives because,
really, all we need is ours, only we sometimes find it difficult to see
it. ~ Fr. Pat Umberger

Pray for the realization that God has everything we need. Pray that
we may know that God's power is always available.

What unifying activity does our council have planned this month?

*Beware of despairing about yourself: you are commanded to put
your trust in God, and not in yourself.*
~ Saint Augustine

FRATERNITY is a legion of Knights behind Mary

The angel said to her, "Do not be afraid, Mary; for you have found favor with God." ~ Luke 1:30

The Church has celebrated Mary's birth since at least the sixth century. The September 8th date helped determine the feast of the Immaculate Conception on December 8th (nine months earlier). Scripture does not give an account of Mary's birth. However, the apocryphal *Protoevangelium of James* fills in the gap. According to this account, Anna and Joachim receive the promise of a child that will advance God's plan of salvation for the world. Such a story (like many biblical counterparts) stresses the special presence of God in Mary's life from the beginning.
St. Augustine connects Mary's birth with Jesus' saving work. He tells the earth to rejoice and shine forth in the light of her birth. "She is the flower of the field from whom bloomed the precious lily of the valley. Through her birth the nature inherited from our first parents is changed." The opening prayer at Mass speaks of the birth of Mary's Son as the dawn of our salvation and asks for an increase of peace. ~ *American Catholic*

What should a Knight carry at all times, as instructed when we were inducted into the fraternity? (Hint: The _____ is the Bible translated into prayer)

Mary is our best guide to her Son, Jesus Christ. How has our council increased our devotion to Mary this year?

Mother of our Savior, pray for us.
~ Litany of Our Lady (selected)

252

September 9

CHARITY is declaring trumps

Love your enemies, do good to those who hate you... and pray for those who mistreat you... If you love only the people who love you, why should you receive a blessing? Even sinners love those who love them! ~ Luke 6:27–28, 32

When we hate our enemies, we give them power over us – power over our sleep, our appetite and our happiness. They would dance with joy if they knew how much they were worrying us. Our hate is not hurting them at all, but it is turning our own days and nights into hellish turmoil.
~ Dale Carnegie, *How to Stop Worrying and Start Living*

How does the above verse challenge you? How can this be a model for relating to someone you find difficult? Have you ever shown love to an enemy?

In this death and life game of high stakes God has already, as it were, declared what are trumps. They are not clubs (sheer blind force), diamonds (the power of wealth), or even spades (dogged hard work), but hearts.
~ R.C. Walls

September 10

UNITY is a mission of conciliation

Peace I leave with you; my peace I give to you. I do not give to you as the world gives. Do not let your hearts be troubled, and do not let them be afraid. ~ John 14:27

We need not allow ourselves to become encumbered by petty annoyances.
We need not respond to emotional upsets by emotional upset. We can try to keep calm in all circumstances. We need not try to fight back. We can call on the grace of God to calm us when we feel like retaliating. We can look to God for the inner strength to drop those resentments that drag us down. If we are burdened by annoyances, we can lose our inward peace and the spirit of God can be shut out. We can try to keep peaceful within.
~ Fr. Pat Umberger

Pray that we may do the things that make for peace. Pray that we may have a mission of conciliation.

In the above verse, what is the difference between how *Jesus* gives peace and how the *world* does?

All men desire peace, but very few desire those things that make for peace. ~ Thomas á Kempis

September 11

PATRIOTISM is virtuous bravery in the face of the Adversary

The Lord has said to me in the strongest terms: "Do not think like everyone else does. Do not be afraid that some plan conceived behind closed doors will be the end of you. Do not fear anything except the Lord Almighty. He alone is the Holy One.
If you fear him, you need fear nothing else. He will keep you safe." ~ Isaiah 8:11-14

In the best of times, our days are numbered anyway. And so it would be a crime against nature for any generation to take the world crises so solemnly that it put off enjoying those things for which we were designed in the first place - the opportunity to do good work, to fall in love, to enjoy friends, to hit a ball, and to bounce a baby. ~ Alistair Cooke

During tragic events, such as the terrorist attack that occurred on American soil on this date in 2001, confused thought breeds confused action. How do we, as Sir Knights - patriotic Catholic gentlemen of our Order's highest degree, respond in a positive way to serve our country?

... Let us summon one more time the better angels of our nature. Let us comfort the injured and grieving in every way that mercy and ingenuity can devise. Let us give our money, our sweat, our blood, whatever the moment requires. Let us... work as one nation to rebuild the great city at the mouth of the Hudson... Let us show the world how a free, brave and united nation behaves in the face of calamity and of evil.
~ The Philadelphia Inquirer, September 12, 2001

September 12

PATRIOTISM is a path made straight by John

[People began asking John, "Who are you?" He said,] "I am 'the voice of someone shouting... Make a straight path for the LORD to travel!'" ~ John 1:23

General Charles Gordon was admired by all who knew him. When England proposed to honor him with money and titles, he refused. He did agree, however, to accept a lone gold medal with a brief inscription etched on it.

After Gordon's death in 1885, the medal could not be found anywhere. It was later learned that Gordon had melted the medal down, sold the gold, and given the cash to the poor.

On the date of the gift, his diary reads:

"The last earthly thing I had in this world that I valued, I have \given to the LORD." ~ Mark Link, S.J.

How is Gordon's action a perfect response to what John had in mind when he preached, "Make a straight path for the LORD"? What is one concrete action our assembly might take in response to John's message?

It is not for him to pride himself who loveth his own country, but rather for him who loveth the whole world. The earth is but one country and mankind its citizens. ~ Baha'u'llah

September 13

CHARITY is using our gifts from God to help others

*Give to others, and God will give to you... The measure you use
for others is the one that God will use for you.* ~ Luke 6:38

John D. Rockefeller's obituary read: "He died this morning [May
23, 1937] missing the century mark by little more than two years.
The richest man in the world was also the greatest giver."
~ Chronicles of the 20th Century
But that was not always the case. Beginning with little formal
education and less capital, Rockefeller got into the oil business.
At the age of 53, he was incredibly rich and world famous. He was
also troubled and disillusioned. Success hadn't brought happiness.
Then came a life-changing decision. After deep soul-searching, he
resolved to use his wealth to help others. He established a
foundation and dedicated it to fighting disease and ignorance.
~ Mark Link, S.J.

What keeps you from giving more than you do? How has our
council used its coffers, however small or large, to help our parish
and community?

*The true meaning of life is to plant trees, under whose shade you
do not expect to sit.* ~ Nelson Henderson

September 14

UNITY is being part of the cure

Do not be overcome by evil, but overcome evil with good.
~ Romans 12:21

The spiritual and moral will eventually overcome the material and immoral. That is the purpose and destiny of the human race. Gradually the spiritual is overcoming the material in our minds. Gradually the moral is overcoming the immoral. Faith, fellowship, and service are cures for most of the ills of the world. There is nothing in the field of personal relationships that they cannot do.
~ Fr. Pat Umberger

Pray that we may do our share in making a better world. Pray that we may be part of the cure for the ills of the world.

What ills of the world are our council planning to confront?

Service is the rent we pay for our room on earth.
~ Author unknown

September 15

FRATERNITY is being strong and of good courage

*Be strong and of good courage, do not fear or be in dread of them:
for it is the LORD your God who goes with you; he will not fail
you or forsake you.* ~ Deuteronomy 31:6

Henry David Thoreau once remarked that the mass of people live
lives of quiet desperation. That is why the above verse is as
applicable now as it was to the people of Moses' day. We may not
be faced with the task of conquering the Holy Land after spending
generations in slavery and then wandering around the desert for
forty years, but we do have the job of trudging off to work, of
trying make sense of a world that fights against our hopes at every
turn, and of trying to ward off the boredom, sadness, bustle, vanity
and tedium that so many voices in our culture try to palm off on us
as "real life." Remember that in a spiritual war, God's promise in
the above verse is made to you as much as to ancient Israel. He
will not fail you or forsake you. So be strong and of good courage!
~ Dr. Scott Hahn and Jeff Cavins

For what today does our council need strength and courage?
How should we go about finding it?

Never swap horses when crossing a stream.
~ American Proverb

259

September 16

CHARITY is an ark of salvation

Then the LORD said to Noah, "Go into the ark, you and your whole family, because I have found you righteous in this generation. ~ Genesis 7:1

May I, without irreverence, venture to recast a Bible story? If the account of Noah and the flood went something like this, what would you think of it? Suppose that after the ark was completed God said unto Noah, "Now, get eight great spikes of iron and drive them into the side of the ark. Then come thou and all thy house and hang on to these spikes. If you hang on till the deluge is over you will be saved!" Can you imagine Noah and his wife, and their three sons and their wives each hanging on with straining muscles as the water rose?

But oh, how different is this simple story. "And the LORD said unto Noah, Come thou and all thy house into the ark." That is a very different message than holding on! Inside the ark they were safe.

Look away then from all self-effort and trust Him alone. Rest in the ark and rejoice in God's great salvation. Remember that it is Christ who holds you, not you who hold Him. He said, "I will never leave thee, nor forsake thee." He who died for you now lives at God's right hand to keep you, and the Father sees you in Him. "He hath made us accepted in the beloved." Could anything be more sure? ~ Harry Ironside, adapted from *Full Assurance*

Do we sometimes forget to "give it to Christ"?

There is not greatness where there is not simplicity, goodness and truth. ~ Leo Tolstoy, *War and Peace*

September 17

UNITY is knowing Jesus is the answer

... And all the people shall answer and say, 'Amen!'
~ Deuteronomy 27:15

A pastor was addressing the children during Mass. On this
particular Sunday, he was using squirrels for an object lesson on
industry and preparation.
He started out by saying, "I'm going to describe something, and I
want you to raise your hand when you know what it is." The children nodded eagerly.
"This thing lives in trees (pause) and eats nuts (pause)..." No hands
went up.
"And it is gray (pause) and has a long bushy tail (pause)..."
The children were looking at each other, but still no hands raised.
"And it jumps from branch to branch (pause) and chatters and flips
its tail when it's excited (pause)..."
Finally one little boy tentatively raised his hand. The pastor
breathed a sigh of relief and called on him.
"Well..." said the boy, "I know the answer must be Jesus... but it
sure sounds like a squirrel to me!" ~ Author unknown

Do you know that Jesus is the answer or do you sometimes forget
during the course of a busy day?

*The only important decision we have to make is to live with God;
He will make all the rest.* ~ Author unknown

September 18

FRATERNITY is sailing down the middle

Jesus said to him, "I am the way, and the truth, and the life; no one comes to the Father, but by me." ~ John 14:6

In Greek mythology, there were two terrible rocks in the sea near the world's end called Scylla and Charybdis. In avoiding the one, sailors usually smashed into the other. The trick was to sail between them. The devil, as C.S. Lewis says, is fond of sending his lies into the world in pairs too, so that in avoiding one lie, we might embrace the opposite lie. In the past, Christians have embraced a lie that twists the meaning of today's verse: namely, the notion that only those who are consciously aware of the name of Jesus and have "asked him into their hearts as their personal LORD and Savior" are going to go to heaven. Then, in reaction to this, other people have rejected the idea that Jesus matters for our salvation at all. Between these twin lies – these theological Scylla and Charybdis – the Ship of Peter sails, teaching that the only way to God is Jesus. Abraham, for instance, never heard Jesus' name. But he was faithful to the light Jesus gave him and followed it all the way to heaven. Let us as Catholics be thankful for the light Jesus has given us. Let us neither pass judgment on our neighbor, nor ignore our responsibility to bear witness to Jesus. That way, we can sail on through to heaven and bring a few folks with us as we go! ~ Dr. Scott Hahn and Jeff Cavins

If Jesus is the Way, is our council on a bumpy side street, or on a four-lane highway?

Rather than love, than money, than fame, give me truth.
~ Henry David Thoreau

September 19

PATRIOTISM is a nation united behind a common cause

God made . . . the moon to rule the night. ~ Genesis 1:16

Millions of people on earth watched on TV as the moon module,
Eagle, descended slowly toward the surface of the moon.
Cheers rang out when Armstrong announced, "Houston, the *Eagle*
has landed."
The time was July 20, 1969, 4:17 pm, EDT, Physicist Robert
Hofstadler spoke for many when he said, "In a thousand years
there will be few things remembered, but this will be one of them."
What journalist William F. Buckley said after the spacecraft's
liftoff from Florida, applies now. A reporter asked him, "If you
were asked to describe what you just saw, how would you do it?"
Buckley said, "With silence!" ~ Mark Link, S.J.

If you could ask God one question, what would it be?

*[The moon landing] symbolized man's wondrous capacity for
questing... It was also a reminder of something else... Man
inhabits a smallish planet... that occupies the tiniest corner of a
universe that is beyond comprehension.* ~ Time

CHARITY is all that matters in the end

I may have all knowledge and understand all secrets... but if I have no love, this does me no good. ~ 1 Corinthians 13:2-3

As a physician who has been privileged to share the most profound moments of people's lives, including their final moments, let me tell you a secret. People facing death don't think about what degrees they have earned, what positions they have held or how much wealth they have accumulated.
At the end, what really matters – and is a good measure of a past life – is who you loved and who loved you. The circle of love is everything. ~ Mark Link, S.J.

How do you presently measure your life, and, in the end, will your measurement really matter?

Each one has a mission to fulfill, a mission of love. At the hour of death when we come face to face with God, we are going to be judged on love, not how much we have done, but how much love we have put in the doing. ~ Mother Teresa of Calcutta

September 21

UNITY is sharing the cup with one another

Then Jesus took the cup, gave thanks to God, and said, "Take this and share it." ~ Luke 22:17

Jesus introduced the Passover meal with the pre-meal cup of red wine. Sharing the same "cup" dramatizes the unity of all present; red wine recalls both the blood-marked doors in Egypt and the covenant blood at Mount Sinai.
The meal begins with the eating of bitter herbs, which recall Israel's years of bitter slavery in Egypt.
Clay-colored sauce recalls making clay bricks under the hot sun.
Unleavened bread recalls Israel's swift exit from Egypt—not even waiting for the next day's bread to rise.
The lamb recalls both the sacrificial blood that the Hebrews smeared on their doorposts to save them from the "angel of death" and the sacrificial flesh that nourished them as they set out on their journey to freedom. ~ Mark Link, S.J.

How could you incorporate the submissive, sacrificial lifestyle of the Lamb of God into your own life? Of the titles for Jesus (the Word, the Light, the Messiah, the Son of God, the Lamb of God) which means the most to you?

The Baptist said, "There is the Lamb of God, who takes away the sin of the world!... He is the Son of God."
~ John 1:29, 34

September 22

FRATERNITY is a cord of three strands

Though one may be overpowered, two can defend themselves. A cord of three strands is not quickly broken. ~ Ecclesiastes 4:12

What do you do to render a man worthless? Unrecognizable? A thin shadow of his glorious potential?
Nothing. Nothing at all. Just leave him alone. Don't let him rub shoulders with another man. Don't let him come into regular contact with other growing, capable men.
It is not good that man be alone. Period. We weren't made for it. And left to it, we die. Perhaps that's why solitary confinement is considered "cruel and unusual" punishment by some. Ask any POW and he'll tell you the roughest part is the aloneness.
Somewhere along the line there developed the myth of "The Man Alone." We were taught that true men were to be "rugged individualists." John Wayne usually rode alone. So did Clint Eastwood. And it's *killing* us. When men stumble toward isolation, when men lose touch with each other and the home, that's when men, marriages, families, and an entire culture begin to die. ~ Stu Weber, adapted from *Locking Arms*

Are you a member of the fraternity of Knights in name only? What would it take to get you involved in council activities? When was the last time you attended a council meeting? What should our council do to bring our band of brothers closer together?

Let us not give up meeting together, as some are in the habit of doing, but let us encourage one another – and all the more as you see the Day approaching. ~ Hebrews 10:25

September 23

CHARITY is supporting family members in God's call

Whoever loves father or mother more than me is not worthy of me, and whoever loves son or daughter more than me is not worthy of me; and whoever does not take up his cross and follow after me is not worthy of me. ~ Matthew 10:37-38

The first canonized saint of the Western Hemisphere was St. Rose of Lima (1586-1617). At an early age, Rose was attracted by the spirituality and mysticism of St. Catherine of Siena – but her attempts to imitate her brought only opposition from her family and friends. Rose's parents wanted her to marry, and for ten years they tried in vain to arrange this. Rose refused; her parents in turn refused to let her enter a convent, so she became a member of the Third Order of St. Dominic and lived at home, continuing her life of solitude and penance.

A few years before her death, Rose used a room in the family home to care for the elderly, the homeless, and the sick (particularly Indians and slaves). After years of poor health and violent temptations by Satan, St. Rose of Lima died at the age of thirty-one; most of the city's inhabitants attended her funeral, with prominent men taking turns carrying her casket. ~ J.M. Guerin

Family members and friends do not always understand or support our efforts to respond to God's call. If your son or daughter informed you that they wanted to become a priest or a nun, how would you react? Do you actively encourage your children to explore these vocations?

If you seek perfection, go, sell your possessions, and give to the poor... Afterward, come back and follow me. ~ Matthew 19:21

September 24

UNITY is walking with Christ throughout the day

Make my joy complete by being of the same mind, maintaining the same love, united in spirit, intent on one purpose.
~ Philippians 2:2

A Daily Prayer:

I want to thank you, LORD,
for being close to me so far this day.
With Your help,
I haven't been impatient,
lost my temper,
been grumpy,
judgmental,
or envious of anyone.
But I will be getting out of bed in a minute,
and I think I will really need your help then.

Amen.
~ Dean Alan Jones, Church of the Risen Christ, Denver, Colorado

Read Paul's plea for unity in Philippians 2. What is the closest you have come to being in a fellowship that cared for one another as Paul describes. Your high school sports team? Your buddies in war? Your council brothers?

In union there is strength.
~ Aesop

September 25

FRATERNITY is taking the whole armor of God

Therefore take the whole armor of God, that you may be able to
withstand in the evil day, and having done all, to stand.
~ Ephesians 6:13

The ancient king Pyrrhus fought a tremendous and ultimately
successful battle with the foe, but with such catastrophic loss to his
army that he lamented, "Another such victory and I am undone."
Some Christians tend to achieve Pyrrhic victories too, while
catastrophically neglecting their marriage, children, or commitment
to God. It is one thing to "withstand in the evil day." It is another
thing entirely to "stand" when all the dust has settled. That's why
God provides us with his spiritual armor: the helmet of salvation,
breastplate of righteousness, belt of truth, feet shod with the
readiness that comes from the gospel of peace, sword of the Spirit
and shield of faith. All these are forged for us in the Eucharist and
all these are put on by us when we faithfully participate in the
sacraments and life of Holy Church. Today, take the whole armor
of God and soldier through to the end.
~ Dr. Scott Hahn and Jeff Cavins

Are you achieving Pyrrhic victories in your life?

He that loves not his wife and children
feeds a lioness at home,
and broods a nest of sorrows.
~ Jeremy Taylor

September 26

PATRIOTISM is jumping with an archangel

Then war broke out in heaven; Michael and his angels battled against the dragon. The dragon and its angels fought back, but they did not prevail and there was no longer any place for them in heaven. ~ Revelation 12:7-8

Each time a paratrooper walks out the door of an aircraft, an overwhelming feeling of mortality usually strikes as he plummets to the drop zone.

All troopers wear a jumpmaster-inspected parachute to reach the ground safely. Since the birth of the airborne community, Michael the archangel watches over paratroopers of every Christian nation. Troopers wear the patron saint's medallion as a reminder and a comfort. The medallion portrays Michael slaying Lucifer, and in the background, paratroopers are falling from the sky with fully-developed canopies and twist-free risers. The portrayal is surrounded by the words, "Patron of Paratroopers Protect us." Yet, it's not a good-luck charm. It won't keep your feet and knees together and it won't keep you from breaking bones, as many troopers can attest. It simply reminds you that there is a God and that God watches over all of us.
~ SPC Jeanine Dubnicka, 82nd ABN

What encouraging reminders do you carry with you that help you endure another day?

But Michael the archangel, when he disputed with the devil and argued about the body of Moses, did not dare pronounce against him a railing judgment, but said, "The LORD rebuke you!"
~ Jude 1:9

September 27

CHARITY is God's shadow in our universe

Those who love me will obey my teaching. My Father will love them, and my Father and I will come to them and live with them. Those who do not love me do not obey my teaching.
~ John 14:23-24

The Taj Mahal is located on the Junna River, southeast of Dehli, India. It was built in the 17th century by Emperor Shah Hahan as a symbol of his love for his wife, Mumtaz Maha, who died in childbirth.
Shifts of 22,000 men and women worked 24 hours a day for 22 years to complete the project. Twenty-eight gems adorn the white marble structure. Magnificent solid silver doors and a solid gold balustrade enclosed the tomb (later stolen by an enemy army). This monument of the Shah's love for his wife is but a faint glimmer of the Father's love for us. ~ Mark Link, S.J.

How do you account for the Father's incredible love for the human family? How have we Knights expressed love for our Ladies recently?

To love another person is to touch the face of God.
~ Finale of the musical, *Les Miserables*

September 28

UNITY is juggling all five balls in your life

Teach us to number our days aright, that we may gain a heart of wisdom. ~ Psalm 90:12

In a university commencement address several years ago, Brian Dyson, CEO of Coca Cola Enterprises, spoke of the relation of work to one's other commitments:

"Imagine life as a game in which you are juggling some five balls in the air. You name them – work, family, health, friends and spirit – and you're keeping all of these in the air. You will soon understand that work is a rubber ball. If you drop it, it will bounce back.
But the other four balls – family, health, friends and spirit – are made of glass. If you drop one of these, they will be irrevocably scuffed, marked, nicked, damaged or even shattered. They will never be the same. You must understand that and strive for balance in your life."

How do you count your days (see above verse) – one day at a time, make each one count, on a scale of 1 to 10, as a win or loss… lost count?

The end of life is to be like God, and the soul following God will be like Him. ~ Socrates

September 29

FRATERNITY is angels here on earth

What are angels, then? They are spirits who serve God and are sent by him to help those who are to receive salvation.
~ Hebrews 1:4

The word angel means "messenger." The Bible portrays angels as being God's messengers to his people. Ancient artists depicted angels as having wings. But you can no more depict an angel than you can the wind.
It was an angel who told Mary she was to be the mother of Jesus. It was an angel who told Joseph that Mary had conceived by the Holy Spirit. It was an angel who told Joseph to flee Egypt with Jesus and Mary. ~ Author unknown

How deeply do we believe in God's personal concern for us, as manifested by angels in biblical times? Is it possible for Knights to serve as angels here on earth? Does our council serve as guardian angels for our Squires?

You will see angels of God ascending and descending on the Son of Man. ~ John 1:51

September 30

CHARITY is offering our everyday lives to God

Nathaniel answered him, "Rabbi, you are the Son of God; you are the King of Israel." ~ John 1:49

St. Bartholomew is included among the Twelve Apostles, but aside from this, there's no mention of him in the New Testament. Many scholars feel he is the same man as Nathaniel, whom Jesus describes as "an Israelite in whom there is no guile (John 1:45)." Bartholomew initially doubted the possibility of the Messiah coming from Nazareth, but upon meeting Jesus he immediately declared Him to be the Son of God. Bartholomew preached the Gospel in India and Armenia, where he supposedly suffered martyrdom by being flayed alive.

St. Bartholomew is the "unknown apostle," so he can serve as a patron saint for almost all of us. We may never become famous or important in the eyes of the world, but this matters little; all of us are infinitely important in the eyes of God. The simple, everyday lives we lead can, if we offer them to God, become ways of helping bring about His Kingdom. ~ J.M. Guerin

Jesus is not offended by our doubts, but He asks us to rise above them through our personal relationship with Him; the closer we come to the LORD, the more willing we should be to serve Him – even if we don't always fully comprehend His will. Each Knight within our council is his own man, how can we ensure that collectively we are doing God's will?

But if any of you lacks wisdom, let him ask of God, who gives to all generously and without reproach, and it will be given to him. ~ James 1:5

October 1 *Respect Life Month*

UNITY is setting aside the judgment of the world

Have nothing to do with profane myths and old wives' tales. Train yourself in godliness, for, while physical training is of some value, godliness is valuable in every way, holding promise for both the present life and the life to come. ~ 1 Timothy 4:7-8

We can seek to set aside the valuations of the world which seem wrong and try to judge only by those valuations which seem right to us. We need not seek the praise of the world. We can be one of those who, though sometimes scoffed at, have a serenity and peace of mind which the scoffers never know. We can feel God's presence in the world, though God be often rejected because He cannot be seen. ~ Fr. Pat Umberger

Pray that we may not heed too much the judgment of the world. Pray that we may test things by what seems right, and what would reflect God's values.

Today marks the beginning of Respect Life Month. Though the Church's stand on Life issues is unpopular in today's society, we as Knights must remain steadfast to our core values. How is our council calling attention to Life issues within our ranks, our parish, our community and our nation?

All that is necessary for the forces of evil to win the world is for enough good men to do nothing.
~ Edmund Burke

FRATERNITY is a foe to our foes

See, I am sending an angel before you, to guard you on the way and bring you to the place I have prepared. Be attentive to him and heed his voice. Do not rebel against him, for he will not forgive your sin. My authority resides in him. If you heed his voice and carry out all I tell you, I will be an enemy to your enemies and a foe to your foes. ~ Exodus 23:20-23

Some people are surprised to learn that the Church has never taught as a matter of strict faith that every person has a personal guardian angel.

Nevertheless, the idea of a guardian angel enjoys a long tradition in the Church. And many Christians will testify that they have experienced a special protection at times in their lives.

The idea of a guardian angel underscores one of the most important truths of our faith: God exercises a special love and concern over each one of us. Speaking of this, Jesus said to his disciples: "Not one sparrow is forgotten by God… So do not be afraid; you are worth much more than many sparrows (Luke 12:6-7)."
~ Author unknown

How can Knights be the "guardian angels" of babies who are under threat of being murdered?

And who so shall receive one little child in my name receiveth me.
~ Matthew 18:5

October 3 *Respect Life Month*

PATRIOTISM is convincing our nation to respect creation

When my bones were being formed, carefully put together in my mother's womb... you knew that I was there – you saw me before I was born. ~ Psalm 139:15-16

A poster on the wall of a post office in Tulsa informed citizens that it was a violation of federal law to kill an eagle. Moreover, the law extended its protection to eagle eggs – that is, to unborn eagles.

The poster triggered this thought in author Michael Staton: "Isn't it ironic that we pass laws to protect unborn birds, but refuse to pass laws to protect unborn humans?" ~ Mark Link, S.J.

How comfortable are you with our nation's attitude toward human life? As Catholic gentlemen, are we to just sit on the sidelines as spectators to this injustice?

All human life – from the moment of conception and through all subsequent stages – is sacred, because human life is created in the image and likeness of God. Nothing surpasses the greatness or dignity of a human person.
~ Pope John Paul II

CHARITY is a merciful Saviour

"I am the Alpha and the Omega," says the Lord God, "who is, and who was, and who is to come, the Almighty." ~ Revelation 1:8

You are holy, LORD, the only God, and your deeds are wonderful.

You are strong. You are great. You are the Most High, You are almighty. You, holy Father, are King of heaven and earth.

You are Three and One, Lord God, all good. You are Good, all Good, supreme Good, Lord God, living and true.

You are love, You are wisdom. You are humility, You are endurance. You are rest, You are peace. You are joy and gladness. You are justice and moderation. You are all our riches,
And you suffice for us.

You are beauty. You are gentleness. You are our protector, You are our guardian and defender. You are courage. You are our haven and our hope.

You are our faith, Our great consolation. You are our eternal life, Great and wonderful LORD, God almighty, Merciful Saviour.
~ St. Francis of Assisi, Patron Saint of the State of Colorado

Leave me, brother, to rejoice in the LORD, for... I can well be merry in the Most High.
~ St. Francis of Assisi, on his deathbed, when reproved for singing

UNITY is bearing our share of hardship

So do not be ashamed of your testimony to our LORD, nor of me, a prisoner for his sake; but bear your share of hardship for the gospel with the strength that comes from God. ~ 2 Timothy 1:8

Pastor Martin Niemoller condemned the Nazis during World War II and was sent to a concentration camp.
After the war, he was heckled and jeered by 1,200 students for telling a Jew in public, "I acknowledge my guilt and beg you to forgive me and my people for this sin."
Rev. Neimoller did not let the heckling and jeering silence him. He showed the kind of courage Paul showed in his own imprisonment. It is the courage to stand up for what we think is right, which every Christian should have. ~ Mark Link, S.J.

Rev. Niemoller courageously stood up for the lives of the Jews. How courageous has our council been in standing up for the unborn, the weak, the sick and the old?
If you struggle to come up with specific examples across the board, how might our council strategy be changed to mobilize Knights for Life?

He who has saved a single life it is though he has saved the entire world. ~ The Talmud

FRATERNITY is witnessing His glory everywhere

When I look at the sky which you have made, at the moon and the stars which you have set in their places – what are human beings, that you think of them; mere mortals that you care for them?
~ Psalm 8:3-4

Has not everyone, at one time in life,
climbed a hill and gazed at the sky above
and the fields below – and asked,
"Whence all of this? Who put it here?"
Why the newborn calf staggering alongside
its mother grazing in the meadow?
Why the thousands of daisies
dancing daintily along the fence row?
Why the summer sun
ripening these groves of fruit trees?
Why these acres clothed in beauty?
Why this world of birth, growing, and dying?
Does it speak to the secret
of my own graced existence?
~ Mark Link, S.J.

When our society chooses to terminate human life, aren't we offending the Author of all life? Knights, this month at least, let us not be silent.

Scattering a thousand graces, he passed through these groves in haste, and looking upon them as he went, left them by his glance alone, clothed in beauty. ~ Saint John of the Cross

October 7 *Respect Life Month*

CHARITY is a servant of the rest

If one of you wants to be great, you must be the servant of the rest... For even the Son of Man did not come to be served.
~ Mark 10:43, 45

Henry Drummond said: "There is no happiness in having or getting, but only in giving. [Happiness] consists in giving and serving others." ~ Mark Link, S.J.

The best thing to give an enemy is forgiveness;
to an opponent, tolerance;
to a friend, your heart;
to your child, a good example;
to your father, deference;
to your mother, conduct that will make her proud of you;
to yourself, respect;
to all, charity. ~ Francis M. Balfour

How will you enthusiastically serve another life today?

... Christ founded the Church to "teach all nations all that I have commanded you (Matthew 28:20)." No other institution can claim the moral authority to speak in regard to life than that authority which Christ himself endowed the Catholic Church... Therefore, we show ourselves to be most fully in touch with Christ... when we too proclaim and defend human life from conception until natural death no matter the circumstances in which it comes into being and no matter the actions of any single individual.
~ Monsignor Edward L. Buelt, Our Lady of Loreto Parish

UNITY is praying for one another

*For where two or three are gathered together in my name,
there am I in the midst of them.* ~ Matthew 18:20

I was taking my usual morning walk when a garbage truck pulled
up beside me.
I thought the driver was going to ask for directions. Instead, he
showed me a picture of a cute little five-year-old boy.
"This is my grandson, Jeremiah," he said. "He's on a life-support
system at a Phoenix hospital."
Thinking he would next ask for a contribution to his hospital bills,
I was about to reach for my wallet. But he wanted something more
than money. He said, "I'm asking everybody I can to say a prayer
for him. Would you say one for him, please?"
I did. And my problems didn't seem like much that day.
~ Author unknown

Has our council underestimated the power of prayer when
confronting those who disrespect Life?

*Let everyone try and find that as a result of daily prayer he adds
something new to his life, something with which nothing can be
compared.* ~ Mahatma Gandhi

FRATERNITY is a desire to change the world

I planted, Apollos watered, but God gave the growth. So neither he who plants nor he who waters is anything, but only God who gives the growth. ~ 1 Corinthians 3:6-7

As the people of God we naturally have a desire to change the world. We must remember however, that our cries to change the world must be spoken with a note of humility. For if we are going to change the world, we must start with the most difficult of battles and that is changing our own hearts. We know after much struggle and disappointment that only God can really transform our hearts as we cooperate with him. In the same way may our evangelistic efforts focus on the power of Christ, for only Christ can change the world. ~ Dr. Scott Hahn and Jeff Cavins

What does Jesus want to change in your life? How can this change in your heart change the world? What Life projects can our council point to that prove we Knights are a dwelling place for God's Spirit?

Woe to you if you do not succeed in defending life.
~ Pope John Paul II, World Youth Day 1993, Denver, Colorado

PATRIOTISM is citizens with a moral compass

The LORD is near all who call upon Him in truth. ~ Psalm 145:18

The Washington Post carried a six-panel cartoon strip.
Panel one shows the head of a sleeping unborn infant, his head on
his arms. The words were: "It was a big day for the little one! He
was just minutes away from being America's newest citizen!"
In panel two, the baby's eyes are open: "The time had come!"
The baby's head and shoulders have moved toward the bottom of
panel three: "He was being pushed through a small place!"
Only the head remains in panel four: "He felt air touch his body
for the first time! His hands were free!"
In Panel five: "Then he felt a sharp pain at the base of his skull!
He jerked violently! And then... it was over…"
The sixth panel shows the facade of the Supreme Court: "And the
Supreme Court, in its wisdom, asks, 'So, what's the problem!?'
Here's the problem: Five more seconds and he'd go to the cradle,
instead of the grave. Partial birth abortion. Does this seem right to
anyone?" ~ A Sir Knight, adapted

*A patriot must always be ready to defend his country against his
government.* ~ Edward Abbey

Is our assembly committed to changing public opinion on these
atrocities? In the meantime, how many more babies have been
murdered while you have been reading this meditation?

*When bad men combine, the good must associate, else they will fall
one by one, an unpitied sacrifice in a contemptible struggle.*
~ Edmund Burke

CHARITY is the fine craftsmanship of fatherhood

Let us not become weary in doing good, for at the proper time we will reap a harvest if we do not give up. ~ Galatians 6:9

In a moment of great love and affection, you conceived a human being, a child. What an incredible feat in and of itself! Here is flesh of your flesh, bone of your bone: a son or daughter. A miracle. A living, breathing human being who will grow up and think thoughts, and cry tears, and shake hands, and tell jokes, and fall in love, and battle the odds. But however incredible that may be, we have to admit that any male graduate of puberty can father a child; but it takes a man to be a father.

In a newborn child, you have raw material that's beautiful, but capable of so much more. Fathers need to shape that life and mold it. Anyone can hammer a nail into a board, but only a craftsman can build a home. Be that craftsman! Be skilled in your fathering! Produce in your family a thing of quality and usefulness.

In order to become skilled craftsmen, we must begin as apprentices. We need to turn to other men and ask, "Show me how to do this and do it well. What are your tricks of the trade?
~ Ken Canfield, *The Seven Secrets of Effective Fathers*

Fathers, how are you honing your craft?
Knights, are you sharing your secrets with your brothers?
With the above verse in mind, would not our council *and* country reap a fine harvest if we were to teach our Squires to defend human life from conception to natural death?

It is a wise father that knows his own child.
~ William Shakespeare

Columbus set sail for Him

They that go down to the sea in ships, that do business in great waters; these see the works of the LORD, and his wonders in the deep. ~ Psalm 107:23-24

The following are the musings of a strongly devout man and his efforts to find a shortcut to the Indies:

At a very early age I began to sail upon the ocean. I prayed to the most merciful LORD about my heart's great desire, and He gave me the spirit and the intelligence for the task.
It was the LORD who put into my mind the fact that it would be possible to sail from here to the Indies. All who heard of my project rejected it with laughter, ridiculing me.
But no one should fear to undertake any task in the name of our Savior, if it is just and if the intention is purely for His holy service… Oh what a gracious LORD… Day and night, moment by moment, everyone should express to Him their devoted gratitude. ~ Christopher Columbus, *Book of Prophecies*

Because Columbus was a devout Catholic and a great explorer of the Americas, Father McGivney chose to name our Order after him. In recent years, the legacy of Columbus has come under increasing fire. How can we as Knights of Columbus restore his rightful place in history?

Columbus brought America to the attention of the scientific civilizations of Western Europe. The result, ultimately, was the United States of America.
~ adapted from Michael S. Berliner, Ph.D.

October 13 *Respect Life Month*

FRATERNITY is being glad when trials come

I do have faith, but not enough. Help me have more! ~ Mark 9:24

Saint Augustine was walking along a beach. He was lost in meditation on the central mystery of Christianity, the Holy Trinity: "How could God be three and one at the same time?"
Suddenly, his attention was drawn to a little girl carrying a small container of water from the sea to a hole she had dug on the beach. What are you doing?" he asked her.
With childlike simplicity, she replied: "I'm emptying the sea into this hole."
Then he stopped dead and thought: "I am trying to do what that little girl is doing – trying to crowd the infinite Creator into the finite creation of my little mind." ~ Mark Link, S.J.

Jesus said (Mark 9:23), "everything is possible to one who has faith." Why can't the Knights be the ones who have faith? What council activity can we engage in that would save just one life?

[Be glad when trials come.]
Their purpose is to prove that your faith is genuine.
Even gold, which can be destroyed, is tried by fire;
and so your faith, which is much more precious than gold,
must be tested, so that it may endure.
~ 1 Peter 1:6-9

October 14 *Respect Life Month*

CHARITY is the blind leading the blind

Be still and know that I am God. ~ Psalm 46:10

Disillusioned by life with good reason to frown,
I thought the world was intent on dragging me down.
And if that weren't enough to ruin my day,
A young boy out of breath approached me, all tired from play.
He stood right before me with his head tilted down
And said with great excitement, "Look what I found!"
Wanting him to take his dead flower and go off to play,
I faked a small smile and then shifted away.
He declared, "It sure smells pretty and it's beautiful, too.
That's why I picked it; here, it's for you."
But instead of placing the flower in my hand,
He held it mid-air without reason or plan.
It was then that I noticed for the very first time
That weed-toting boy could not see: he was blind.
I heard my voice quiver; tears shone in the sun
As I thanked him for picking the very best one.
"You're welcome," he smiled, and then ran off to play,
Unaware of the impact he'd had on my day.
How did he know of my self-indulged plight?
Perhaps from his heart, he'd been blessed with true sight.
~ Author unknown

Recall a trouble in your life and then read Psalm 46:10 (above) in response.

Let your intellect, your judgment, your reason, rest in God.
~ James Hamilton

UNITY is letting your light shine forth

You are like light for the whole world. ~ Matthew 5:14

Dr. Robert Healy wrote a letter to *Psychology Today* about a young man who had entered therapy after near-suicide. The man was driving to a bridge, intending to leap off it.

Routinely, he stopped at a traffic light and looked toward the sidewalk.

There on the curb stood an elderly lady, who gave him the warmest, most beautiful smile he could ever remember receiving.

It was as if she knew that he needed it.

The light changed and he drove on. But her smile drove away with him.

He said later that he had no idea who she was; nor did he see her again. He only knows he owes his life to her, and to what her smile said to him at the most critical moment of his life.
~ Mark Link, S.J.

Can you recall receiving a seemingly small kindness just when you needed it most?

Small drops wear down big stones.
~ Russian Proverb

FRATERNITY is experiencing God's presence

Unless you change and become like children, you will never enter the Kingdom of heaven. ~ Matthew 18:3

After reading a magazine article about how people find God, Jean Shea asked her grade-school students where they readily find God. One of the students, Allison Janik wrote:
"I find God in babies because they express love, kindness, and gentleness. Babies symbolize God because babies are gentle and kind, and can always make you smile... If you talk to babies and they don't talk back, you still know they love you. I think that's how it is with God." ~ James Martin

With Matthew 18:3 in mind, what Life issue can our council undertake in conjunction with our Squires Circle?

Every child comes with the message that God is not discouraged with us. ~ Rabindranath Tagore

October 17 *Respect Life Month*

PATRIOTISM is serving the people with righteousness

In all your ways be mindful of him, and he will make straight your paths. ~ Proverbs 3:6

When Joe Wright was asked to open the new session of the Kansas Senate, everyone was expecting the usual politically correct generalities. But in 1996, they heard instead a stirring prayer, excerpted below. The response was immediate – with a number of legislators walking out during the prayer.

Heavenly Father, we ask Your forgiveness and seek Your guidance. We know Your Word says, "Woe onto those who call evil good," but that's exactly what we have done. We have lost our spiritual equilibrium and inverted our values. We confess that:

We have endorsed perversion and called it an alternative lifestyle;
We have neglected the needy and called it self-preservation;
We have rewarded laziness and called it welfare;
We have killed our unborn and called it choice;
We have abused power and called it political savvy;
We have ridiculed the time-honored values of our forefathers and called it enlightenment.

Guide and bless these men and women who have been sent here by the people of Kansas, and who have been ordained by You, to govern this great state. Grant them Your wisdom to rule and may their decisions direct us to the center of Your will. Amen.

Does this prayer challenge us to make straight our paths?

*My great concern is not whether God is on my side;
my concern is to be on God's side.*
~ Abraham Lincoln

291

October 18 *Respect Life Month*

CHARITY is choosing life

I set before you life and death... Choose life then, that you and your
descendants may live. ~ Deuteronomy 30:19

Would you respect human life in the following situations?

1. A preacher and his wife are very, very poor. They already
    have 14 kids. Now she finds out she's pregnant with the 15th
    child. They are living in severe poverty.
2. The father is ailing, the mother has tuberculosis. The eldest
    child is blind, the second died, the third is deaf, and the
    youngest also has TB. The mother learns she's pregnant again.
3. A white man raped a 13 year-old black girl and now she's
    pregnant.
4. Another teenage girl is pregnant. She's not married. Her fiancé
    is not the father of the baby, and he's very upset.

If you thought ending an innocent life was the best solution under
these circumstances – In the first case, you have just killed John
Wesley before he could become the famed evangelist from
England. In the second case, you aborted Beethoven and deprived
the world of some of our greatest musical compositions. In the
third case, you gave up on Ethel Waters, the renowned black
gospel singer.
In the fourth case, the teenage girl is the Blessed Virgin Mary, and
you have just declared the murder of our Savior, Jesus Christ.
~ Author unknown

No law can give me the right to do what is wrong.
~ Abraham Lincoln

UNITY is loving your wife and turning your house into a home

When Joseph awoke, he did as the angel of the LORD had
commanded him and took his wife into his home. ~ Matthew 1:24

Mothers are the ones who carry children for nine months. They are
the ones who learn to sleep on their backs… They are the ones who
sweat, push, and cry out in pain in the labor room.
Dads pass out cigars.
Mothers are the ones who spend hours spooning out jars of strained
apricots… and picking up half-eaten cookies from the floor…
Dads lunch at the Racquet Club.
~ D. L. Stewart, *Dallas Morning News*

Joseph never passed out cigars nor lunched at the Nazareth Racquet
Club, but you can be sure he appreciated what Mary went through.
It takes a lot of living – and even more loving – for spouses to turn
a house into a home.

How deeply do we appreciate wives and mothers and what they go
through?

The way to plan the family is natural family planning, not contra-
ception.
~ Mother Teresa of Calcutta

October 20 *Respect Life Month*

FRATERNITY is full communion with Our Father's will

Our Father... May your will be done on earth as it is in heaven.
~ Matthew 6:9–10

One night a young man was home alone. He began thinking about his life. Suddenly, he saw himself as being selfish and self-centered. He was shocked!
Next, he turned his thoughts from himself to all the suffering people in the world. He began feeling compassion for them. Then, he did something that surprised even himself. He knelt down and told his heavenly Father that he wanted to change his life.
The next morning when he awoke, he had a sudden illumination. He wrote:
"I knew that love and service of mankind was the will of God... We are to serve God by serving his purpose... My whole outlook on life changed... It was as if all my life I had been in a darkened room and then I had suddenly walked out into the sunlight."
~ Alister Hardy, *The Spiritual Nature of Man*

In terms of all Life issues – abortion, euthanasia, care for the sick and elderly, human embryonic stem cell research, cloning, et al – what is Our Father's will?
How can Knights be an instrument for His will to be done?

Our Constitution was made only for a moral and religious people. It is wholly inadequate to the government of any other.
~ John Adams

CHARITY is a mother's protective pinions

[He] will shelter you with his feathers, and under his wings you will find refuge... ~ Psalm 91:4

An article in *National Geographic* several years ago provided a penetrating picture of God's wings...
After a forest fire in Yellowstone National Park, rangers began their trek up a mountain to assess the inferno's damage. One ranger found a bird literally petrified in ashes, perched statuesquely on the ground at the base of a tree. Somewhat sickened by the eerie sight, he knocked over the bird with a stick. Three tiny chicks scurried from under their dead mother's wings. The loving mother, keenly aware of impending disaster, had carried her offspring to the base of the tree and had gathered them under her wings, instinctively knowing that the toxic smoke would rise.
She could have flown to safety but had refused to abandon her babies. When the blaze had arrived and the heat had scorched her small body, the mother had remained steadfast. Because she had been willing to die, those under the cover of her wings would live.

Being loved this much can make a difference in our lives. Think about all the potential for harm in your life. Could angels be guarding you?
Recall an instance when you are delivered or protected against all odds. What did you learn from the experience?

When you say that a situation or a person is hopeless, you are slamming the door on the face of God.
~ John Churton Collins

UNITY is our spirit in harmony with God's spirit

Do you not know that you are God's temple and that God's Spirit dwells in you? ~ 1 Corinthians 3:16

We can gently breathe in God's spirit, that spirit which, if not barred out by selfishness, will enable us to do good works. This means rather that God can be enabled to do good works through us. We can become a channel for God's spirit to flow through us and into the lives of others. The works that we can do will only be limited by our spiritual development. We can let our spirits be in harmony with God's spirit and there is no limit to what we can do In the realm of human relationships. ~ Fr. Pat Umberger

Pray that we may become a channel for God's spirit. Pray that God's spirit may flow through me into the lives of others.

Are you a channel for God's good works? What council Life activities have you participated in this month?

The Church is a workshop, not a dormitory; and every Christian is bound to help in the common cause.
~ Alexander Maclaren

FRATERNITY is being third

Our love should not be just words and talk; it must be true love, which shows itself in action. ~ 1 John 3:18

Gale Sayers, who played for the Chicago Bears, was one of the greatest running backs of all time. Around his neck he wore a gold medal. On it were inscribed three words: "I am Third."
Those words became the title of his best-selling autobiography.
The book explains the meaning behind the words:
"The LORD is first; my friends are second; and I am third."
Sayers is the first to admit that he doesn't always live up to the motto. But wearing it around his neck keeps him from straying too far from it. ~ Mark Link, S.J.

If our society dealt with issues concerning Life by placing ourselves "third", wouldn't we respect Life in every instance?

Always put justice above the law, and when the law is unjust, challenge it directly. ~ William Penn

October 24 *Respect Life Month*

PATRIOTISM is welcoming our veterans back home

A man's spirit sustains him in infirmity – but a broken spirit who can bear? ~ Proverbs 17:14

A soldier who was finally coming home after having fought in Vietnam. He called his parents.
"Mom and Dad, I'm coming home, but I've a favor to ask. I have a friend I'd like to bring home with me."
"Sure," they replied, "we'd love to meet him."
"There's something you should know." the son continued, "He was hurt pretty badly in the fighting. He stepped on a land mine and lost an arm and a leg. He has nowhere else to go, and I want him to come live with us."
"I'm sorry to hear that, son. Maybe we can help him find somewhere to live."
"No, I want him to live with us."
"Son," said the father, "you don't know what you're asking. He would be a terrible burden. He'll find a way to live on his own."
Their son hung up the phone. They heard nothing more from him until they received word that he had died after falling from a building – suicide. The grief-stricken parents were taken to identify the body. They recognized him, but to their horror they also discovered something they didn't know – their son had only one arm and one leg. ~ Author unknown

What difference would 'listening before speaking' make in your personal relationships? With Veterans Day approaching, how is our assembly planning to salute our patriots?

This only is charity – to do all that we can. ~ John Donne

October 25 *Respect Life Month*

CHARITY is submitting to His will

Mary said, "Behold, I am the handmaid of the LORD. May it be done to me according to your word." Then the angel departed from her. ~ Luke 1:38

Today I saw a water lily growing in a pond. It had the freshest yellow color I'd ever seen. The lily – a precious treasure – was unconcerned about whether anyone noticed its astounding beauty. As I sat there, watching it unfold its petals noiselessly, I thought of Mary pregnant with Jesus. She, too, was a precious treasure. She, too, was unconcerned about whether anyone noticed her astounding beauty.
But to those who did, she shared a secret. Her beauty came not from herself, but from the Jesus life within her, unfolding its petals noiselessly.
~ A meditation on Mary composed by a college student

Hail Mary... gentle woman... peaceful dove...
teach us wisdom, teach us love.
~ Carey Landry

What role does Mary play in our own spiritual life?
Would our council consider starting a tradition of regularly reciting the rosary at an abortion clinic? Ask for Mary's intervention in ending the carnage of innocent children.

Every abortion clinic should have a sign over the door that says, 'OPEN BY PERMISSION OF THE CHURCHES IN THIS AREA.'
~ F. Schaeffer

October 26 *Respect Life Month*

UNITY is remembering that all lives are significant

And what does the LORD require of you? To act justly and to love mercy and to walk humbly with your God. ~ Micah 6:8 NIV

When I was in medical school, our professor gave us a pop quiz.
I was a conscientious student and had breezed through the questions, until I read the last one: "What is the first name of the woman who cleans our school?"
Surely this was some kind of joke. I had seen the cleaning woman almost every day. She was tall, dark-haired and in her 50s, but how would I know her name?
I handed in my paper, leaving the last question blank.
Before class ended, one student asked if the last question would count toward our quiz grade.
"Absolutely," said the professor. "In your careers you will meet many people. All are significant. They deserve your attention and care, even if all you do is smile and say 'hello'."
I've never forgotten that lesson. I also learned her name was Dorothy. ~ Author unknown

Knowing that God loves you and hates your sin (see above verse), how will you be weighed in the balance? Do we have a tendency to forget those who may seem least among us?

Be that Good News to your own people first. And find out about your next door neighbors. ~ Mother Teresa of Calcutta

FRATERNITY is one body in Christ

... there should be no division in the body, but that its parts should have equal concern for each other. If one part suffers, every part suffers with it; if one part is honored, every part rejoices with it.
~ 1 Corinthians 12:25-26

I tremble to make the analogy between cancer in the physical body and mutiny in the spiritual body of Christ. But I must. In His warnings to the church, Jesus showed no concern about the shocks and bruises His Body would meet from external forces. "The gates of hell shall not prevail against my church (Matthew 16:18)."
I must concentrate on how I, as an individual cell, should respond to the crying needs of the Body of Christ in other parts of the world… From the perspective of spending eighteen years in one of the poorest countries on earth, the contrasts in resources are astonishingly large. We treated leprosy patients on three dollars per patient per year. Then we came to America where some churches were heatedly discussing their million-dollar gymnasiums and a new steeple. I could easily point to examples of hoarding in every society I've seen: in the cruel Iks of Africa, in Soviet Russia, in the disparity within the Christian community in India. My only message is the caution of a doctor: the body will have health only if each cell regards the needs of the whole body.
~ Paul Brand and Philip Yancey

How can our council respond in some way to the crying needs of the Body of Christ in other parts of the world?

Instead of destroying LIFE, let us seek to destroy the conditions which make LIFE intolerable. ~ Eunice Kennedy Shriver

CHARITY is compassion for a life lost

*When Jesus saw his mother and the disciple there whom he loved,
he said to his mother, "Woman, behold, your son." Then he said to
the disciple, "Behold, your mother." And from that hour the
disciple took her into his home.* ~ John 19:26-27

American servicemen came home from the Pacific with all kinds of
remembrances. Cyril O'Brien treasures one, especially. It is a
small holy picture of Our Lady.
One day, on the island of Guam, his patrol encountered three
Japanese soldiers. A volley of gunfire followed. Routinely, the
patrol checked the dead soldiers for grenades and possible
intelligence material. O'Brien put his hand into the pocket of one
of the Japanese solders. It contained a picture of Mary. It was the
pocket over the soldier's heart.

"At the cross her station keeping,
Stood the mournful Mother weeping,
Close to Jesus to the last.

Through her heart, his sorrow sharing,
All his bitter anguish bearing,
Now at length the sword had passed." ~ Stabat Mater

What are some of the modern sorrows of Mary?

*If a man loses reverence for any part of life, he will lose his
reverence for all of life.*
~ Albert Schweitzer

October 29 *Respect Life Month*

UNITY is every person taking a stand

Then I heard the voice of the LORD saying,
"Whom shall I send? Who will go for us?"
"Here I am;" I said; "send me!" ~ Isaiah 6:8

One of God's people said to God, "LORD, there is so much pain
and suffering in Your world. Why don't You send help?"

God said, "I did send help, I sent you!"
~ Two Seekers in No Jesus, *No Peace, Know Jesus, Know Peace*

God's holiness and universal reign awed Isaiah. Why has God sent
you to your world?

Respect Life Month is drawing to a close, what has our council
accomplished during this time?

Will our efforts now cease and move on to less burdensome
endeavors?

Once or twice a century an issue arises... so far-reaching in its
consequences, and so deep in its foundations, that it calls every
person to take a stand.
~ John T. Noonan

FRATERNITY is a brotherhood of men defending the truth

I have chosen the way of truth; I have set my heart on your laws.
~ Psalm 119:30

Seek the truth
Teach the truth
Love the truth
Abide by the truth
And defend the truth
Unto death. ~ John Hus, selected

As a Knight, have you taken the time to educate yourself on the
Church's stand on *all* Life issues from the moment of conception
until natural death?
How have you defended the truth in your everyday life when
confronted with a particular Life issue?
Why does the Church teach that married couples are to remain
open to the transmission of new life?
Why is the dignity of the human person seriously threatened by
genetic manipulation and fetal experimentation?
How do we affirm the right to life of the elderly and the terminally
ill against the satanic seductions of euthanasia and assisted suicide?
Where does Christ, Himself executed as a capital criminal,
command us to stand on the issue of capital punishment?
How is our council preparing each of its Brothers to abide by the
truth in any Life situation?

*The hottest places in hell are reserved for those who in a period of
moral crisis maintain their neutrality.* ~ Dante Alighieri

October 31 *Respect Life Month*

PATRIOTISM is a government that respects human life

Someone asked Jesus,
"Good Teacher, what must I do to receive eternal life?"...
[Jesus answered]
"You know the commandments... Do not commit murder."
~ Luke 18:18-20

Thomas Jefferson was the author of the Declaration of Independence and the 3rd president of the United States. He once said:

"The care of human life and happiness, and not their destruction, is the first and only object of good government."

Yet, today, thousands of 'legalized' abortions destroy human life each day in the country that Jefferson helped to found. Meanwhile, several million U.S. couples are on agency lists, waiting to adopt a child. ~ Mark Link, S.J.

How do you explain the drift from the thinking of our founding fathers to the practice of modern citizens?

The basis of effective government is public confidence, and that confidence is endangered when ethical standards falter or appear to falter. ~ Sir Knight John F. Kennedy

November 1 - All Saints' Day

*Blessed are the pure in heart, for they shall see God: blessed are the
peacemakers, for they shall be called the children of God: blessed
are they that are persecuted for righteousness' sake, for theirs is the
kingdom of heaven.* ~Matt. 5: 8-10

All Saints' Day is for all the known and unknown saints who have
died and gone before us and who are at rest with Christ. Simply put,
to be a saint is to do God's will each day throughout one's life to the
best of one's ability. This is God's call for each of us who have been
brought into His Body, the Church, through Baptism. The origin of
this feast day can be traced back to the 4th century. Ephrem of Syria
and John Chrysostom, both Eastern Church Fathers, called this day
the feast of martyrs of the whole world. Pope Gregory IV (827-844)
made November 1st as the feast day for all the Saints.
~Catholic Encyclopedia

How does our council remember our deceased brothers? Are you a
Knight who each day lives his faith the best that he can?

*God, you allow us to honour all Your Saints in one common festival.
Through the prayers of so many intercessors grant us an abundance
of Your merciful favours which we so greatly desire. Amen.*
~ *www.Domestic-Church.com*

November 2 *All Souls*

UNITY is climbing into a neighbor's lap

*Amen, amen, I say to you, the hour is coming and is now here
when the dead will hear the voice of the Son of God, and those who
hear will live.* ~ John 5:25

Author and lecturer, Leo Buscaglia, once talked about a contest he
was asked to judge. The purpose of the contest was to find the most
caring child.
The winner was a four year old child whose next door neighbor was
an elderly gentleman who had recently lost his wife.
Upon seeing the man cry, the little boy went into the old gentleman's yard, climbed onto his lap, and just sat there.
When his mother asked him what he had said to the neighbor, the
little boy said, "Nothing... I just helped him cry."
~ Fr. Pat Umberger

Remember our Order's admonition, "Time flies, remember
death"…

How do you honor those who have died? What do your actions
say about your belief in the resurrection of the dead
(see 2 Maccabees 12)? What has our council done to remember
fallen Knights?

It is a good and holy deed to pray for the dead.
~ 2 Maccabees 12:44-45 (paraphrased)

*Never let anything so fill you with sorrow as to make you forget for
one moment the joy of Christ risen.*
~ Mother Teresa

November 3

FRATERNITY is seeking the LORD

Seek the LORD while he may be found, call upon him while he is near. ~ Isaiah 55:6

God is near in every good thing. He is nearer still in the creature called man and woman. He comes even closer in good men and women, closer still in his saints, closer still in the greatest saint, Mary, and closest of all in the person of the God-Man Jesus Christ. Draw near to these (and especially to Jesus, who is present in all His saints and most especially in the Holy Eucharist) and He will draw near to you. ~ Dr. Scott Hahn and Jeff Cavins

What does it mean to "seek the LORD"? What hopeful promise is associated with doing so? Have you been seeking Him or hiding from Him?

An open mind, like an open window, should be screened to keep the bugs out. ~ V. Hutchinson

November 4

CHARITY is a healing presence

People would take their sick to the marketplaces and beg Jesus to let the sick at least touch the edge of his cloak. And all who touched it were made well. ~ Mark 6:56

England was involved in the Crimean War in Russia from 1845 to 1856. The wounded were laid side by side in makeshift hospitals that were dirty, overcrowded, and understaffed. The wind blew the stench from open sewers, making breathing difficult. Rats ran wild. Into this incredible, hopeless situation came Florence Nightingale and 38 nurses she had trained in England. Sometimes she spent 20 hours straight on her feet, directing sanitation efforts and bandaging the wounded. The bedridden soldiers worshiped her and would "kiss her shadow as it fell across their pillows."
If the sick and the needy are to experience Jesus' healing presence today, it must be through loving, caring people. ~ Mark Link, S.J.

How is our council striving to be a healing presence of Jesus in today's world?

Blessed is the influence of one, true, loving human soul on another. ~ George Eliot

November 5

UNITY is doing all we can for each other

Each man should give what he has decided in his heart to give, not reluctantly or under compulsion, for God loves a cheerful giver. And God is able to make all grace abound to you, so that in all things at all times, having all that you need, you will abound in every good work. ~ 2 Corinthians 9:7-8

We can share our love, our joy, our happiness, our time, our food, our money gladly with all. We can give out all the love we can with a glad, free heart and hand. We can do all we can for others and back will come countless stores of blessings. Sharing can draw others to us. We can take all who come as sent by God and give them a royal welcome. We may never see the results of our sharing. Today they may not need us, but tomorrow may bring results from the sharing we did today. ~ Fr. Pat Umberger

I pray that I may make each visitor desire to return. I pray that I may never make anyone feel repulsed or unwanted.

What have you reaped by being generous to others? How can God's promise in the above verse enable you to be more generous? To persevere in your work? How do generosity, financial planning and responsibility fit together?

A man's true wealth is the good he does in this world.
~ Bendixline

November 6

FRATERNITY is building spiritual muscles

We ought always to thank God for you, brothers, and rightly so,
because your faith is growing more and more, and the love every
one of you has for each other is increasing. ~ 2 Thessalonians 1:3

Living in the spiritual realm is much like preparing for a race in the
physical realm. At one point I'm working on speed, then
endurance, then on muscle tone. When not actually running I'm
conscious of diet, of rest, and other factors. There are strategies
and goals to be considered.
Spiritual growth progresses according to much the same pattern.
Every incident I face throughout the day is intended to "train" my
spiritual muscles of patience or kindness or reliance on the LORD.
The difficulties and trials I continue to encounter teach me
endurance in much the same way a ten-mile run every morning
does for my body.
Once my competitive running days were behind me, I continued to
train, but in a different way. My goal became modeling myself
after Jesus – ridding myself of old attitudes, letting Christ put in
His way of thinking and acting.
And that is the essence of growth, the essence of life itself. That is
where the abundant and fulfilling life originates – by living
according to the example of Jesus. It is a life outside of one's self,
a life founded in a loving and intimate relationship with God the
Father. ~ Jim Ryun, *In Quest of God*

How will our council exercise faith this month in a specific way?

Honor lies in honest toil. ~ Grover Cleveland

PATRIOTISM is exercising the power to vote

A nation will be strong and endure when it has intelligent, sensible leaders. ~ Proverbs 28:2

Susan B. Anthony was arrested in 1892 for demanding to vote in the presidential election in Rochester, New York. She knew the value of one vote. In 1649, one vote caused King Charles of England to be executed. In 1876, one electoral vote elected Rutherford Hayes president. In 1875, one vote changed France from a monarch to a republic. In 1886, one vote kept Andrew Johnson from being impeached as president of the United States.
~ Mark Link, S.J.

Pray that the LORD may flood a superabundance of grace into the hearts of American voters so that their choice will reflect Your Will for the United States and a profound respect for human life.

Should the Knights take a more aggressive stance to inform the electorate on critical issues, especially those pertaining to justice, human rights, and peace?

Vote not as other men dictate, but rather like men with the interest of your country at heart. Vote according to the dictates of your own consciences. ~ Father Michael J. McGivney, Founder of the Knights of Columbus

When I consider what tremendous consequences come from little things... I am tempted to think... there are no little things.
~ Bruce Barton

November 8

CHARITY is seeing with the heart

Whatever you did for one of the least important of these followers of mine, you did it for me! ~ Matthew 25:40

An editorial began: "A priest we know recently described his experience of being confronted by a beggar while eating at a fast-food restaurant. The beggar said he was hungry, and the priest, intimidated and nervous, could only say, 'I'm sorry,' and look the other way.

Later, as the priest recounted the story, he was praying Psalm 80, 'LORD, let me see your face,' when the image of the beggar came to mind.

How many times have you seen the LORD and not recognized him?...

Christ simply appears before us: hungry, cold and ill.
Once He was a condemned prisoner led to the slaughter for the sins of others. Now He approaches us in McDonald's smelling badly... Do we see His face?" ~ *Our Sunday Visitor*

What keeps us from seeing Jesus' face in the people around us?

Beware of the man whose God is in the skies.
~ George Bernard Shaw

November 9

UNITY is one simple nut

Behold, how good and how pleasant it is for brothers to dwell together in unity! ~ Psalm 133:1-2

Mike Moran was flying Navy helicopters in 1982. One day at lunch, he was explaining to his parents the mechanics of his "chopper."

"As complex and sophisticated as those machines are," he said enthusiastically, "those whirling rotors are actually held in place by one simple hexagonal nut."

Then turning to his mother, Mike said, "Guess what that nut is called, the one that holds it all together…"

She shrugged unknowingly.

"It's called a 'Jesus Nut'."
~ Mark Link, S.J.

Do we, as a united council, truly believe that it's Jesus who "holds it all together" in our lives?

Christ is not valued at all, unless he is valued above all.
~ Saint Augustine

November 10

FRATERNITY knowing a friend would come

Greater love has no one than this, that he lay down his life for his friends. ~ John 15:13

A platoon of U.S. troops was driven back and one of their infantrymen was wounded by gunfire. As he lay on the battlefield, a friend asked his sergeant in the foxhole, "Can I go get 'im?"
"There's no use. He's probably dead," the sergeant answered.
"And even if he isn't dead, you'd never make it back alive. But if you want to…"
Those last few words were all the friend needed to hear. Crawling on elbows and knees he reached the bleeding infantryman, hoisted him to his shoulders, and hobbled back. As he neared the foxhole, the heroic friend was hit in the chest with a bullet and the two friends collapsed in a heap. The sergeant tried to find the pulse of the infantryman and there was none. Dead.
Then he told the soldier, "I told you it would be senseless. Your friend is dead, and now you've been shot."
Fighting for air, the friend painfully explained, "No, I have no regrets. You see, when I first got to him, he was alive. He recognized me and said, "'Thanks, Jack. I knew you'd come.'"
With those words the soldier friend died.
That is friendship. Friendship says, "I knew if I needed you, you'd be there for me. I knew I could count on you."
~ Fred Hartley, adapted

Have you ever been able to count on a Brother Knight to be there?

If God is thy father, man is thy brother.
~ Alphonse de Lamartine

November 11 *Veterans Day*

PATRIOTISM is kneeling in the mud

The LORD is my shepherd… Even if I go through the deepest darkness, I will not be afraid. ~ Psalm 23:1, 4

Father Joseph Hogan was a chaplain in Europe with the U.S. Third Army. One Sunday, he felt the presence of God in a way that touched him deeply. He wrote:
"I was saying Mass on top of a jeep. The men were standing there with their guns slung over their backs and their helmets on. The ack-ack was pecking at the planes upstairs. There was a torrent of rain coming down and a sea of mud to wallow in. So I said, 'Don't bother to kneel down.' And they didn't, until the Consecration. Then every man went down on his knees… When they sloshed up to receive Holy Communion, they again knelt in mud puddles."
~ Joseph F. Hogan, *A Do-It-Yourself Retreat*

In what way have you sensed God's presence at Mass?

God has been profoundly real to me in recent years. In the midst of outer dangers, I have felt an inner calm. In the midst of lonely days and dreary nights, I have heard an inner voice saying, "Lo, I will be with you."
~ Dr. Martin Luther King, Jr., *Strength to Love*, 1963

November 12

UNITY is standing firm together

He who stands firm to the end will be saved. ~ Matthew 24:13

How many of the world's prayers have gone unanswered because those who prayed did not endure to the end? They thought it was too late, that they must act for themselves, that God was not going to guide them. Can I endure to the very end? If so, we shall be saved. We should try to endure with courage. Then God will unlock those secret spiritual treasures which are hidden from those who give up too soon. ~ Fr. Pat Umberger

Pray that we may follow God's guidance, so that spiritual success shall be ours. Pray that we may never doubt the power of God and so take things into our own hands.

What principles or matters must Knights stand firm on to the end?

Prayers travel more strongly when said in unison.
~ Petronius

November 13

FRATERNITY is a sure foundation

So this is what the Sovereign LORD says: See, I lay a stone in Zion, a tested stone, a precious cornerstone for a sure foundation; the one who trusts will never be dismayed. ~ Isaiah 28:16

I live in earthquake country, astride the Hayward fault, itself connected to the gigantic San Andreas fault. I have often thought of the Golden Gate Bridge in San Francisco as our city's boldest structure in that its great south pier rests directly upon the fault zone of the San Andreas.

That bridge is an amazing structure of both flexibility and strength. It is built to sway some twenty feet at the center of its one-mile suspension span. The secret to its durability is its flexibility, which enables this sway. By design, every part of the bridge – its concrete roadway, its steel railings, its cross beams – is inevitably related from one welded joint to the other, up through the vast cable system to two great towers and two great land anchor piers. The towers bear most of the weight, and they are deeply imbedded into the rock foundation beneath the sea.

In other words, the bridge is totally preoccupied with its foundation. This is its secret! Flexibility and foundation.

In the Christian life, it is the forgiveness of the gospel that grants us our flexibility; and it is the LORD of the gospel who is our foundation. There is no other. ~ Earl Palmer

If Jesus is the foundation stone of our lives, how will you demonstrate that in a practical way this week?

Hear my voice, O God, in my prayer; preserve my life from fear of the enemy. ~ Psalm 64:1

November 14

PATRIOTISM is concern for our fighting men

I have fought a good fight, I have finished my course, I have kept the faith. ~ 2 Timothy 4:7

The following inscription was reportedly discovered on an old stone sentry box on the island of Gibraltar.

God and the soldier
All men adore
In time of trouble,
And no more;
For when war is over
And all things righted,
God is neglected –
The old soldier slighted.

Nations last when citizens remember the important things in times of difficulty *and* in times of ease. How does our assembly minister to homeless veterans?

There is nothing more soulless than a religion without good works unless it be a patriotism which does not concern itself with the welfare and dignity of the individual.
~ Brigadier General S. L. A. Marshall

November 15

CHARITY is giving His only Son to the world

God loved the world so much that he gave his only Son, so that everyone who believes in him may... have eternal life.
~ John 3:16

The LORD says, "My thoughts... and my ways are different from yours. As high as the heavens are above the earth, so high my thoughts and ways are above yours (Isaiah 55:8-9)."

Consider one example of God's ways:

"When God wants a great job done in the world or a great wrong righted, He goes about it in a very unusual way.

He doesn't stir up His earthquakes or send forth His thunderbolts.

Instead, He has a helpless baby born, perhaps in a simple home... [to] some obscure mother. And then God puts the idea into the mother's heart, and she puts it into the baby's mind.

And then God waits." ~ E.T. Sullivan

Why did God choose this way of bringing his only son into the world?

The mother's love is like God's love. God loves not because we are lovable, but because it is God's nature to love. And because we are his children. ~ Earl Riney

November 16

UNITY is setting our minds on the Spirit

*Those who live according to the flesh set their minds on the things
of the flesh, but those who live according to the Spirit set their
minds on the things of the Spirit.
To set the mind on the flesh is death, but to set the mind on the
Spirit is life and peace.* ~ Romans 8:5-6

We can try to see the life of the spirit as a calm place, shut away
from the turmoil of the world. We can think of our spiritual home
as a place full of peace, serenity and contentment. We can go to
this quiet, meditative place for the strength to carry us through
today's duties and problems. We can keep coming back here for
refreshment when we are wary of the hubbub of the outside world.
From this quietness and communion comes our strength.
~ Fr. Pat Umberger

Pray that we may keep this resting place where we can commune
with God. Pray that we may find refreshment in meditation on the
Eternal.

Where must the battle for control of your life be fought?
How does God's spirit help us fight our battle?

*It is not the fact that a man has riches which keeps him from
heaven, but the fact that riches have him.*
~ J. Caird

November 17

FRATERNITY is walking together toward the Father

My soul clings fast to you; your right hand upholds me.
~ Psalm 63:9

Sir Winston Churchill once remarked that it was dangerous to "always [be] feeling one's pulse and taking one's temperature." His words were addressed to those who looked at the wildly fluctuating fortunes of battle to determine England's success or failure in World War II.

His words are apropos as well for the Christian who constantly gauges his relationship with Christ based on feelings. Emotions are unreliable barometers, and if you attach your faith to them, you are in for an upsetting experience. The prescription to a steady, progressive walk of faith is focusing on God's love for you. Imagine your hand and God's clasped together. Your grip loosens during a season of temptation, sin, doubt or apathy. But rather than concentrating on your slackness, look to the hand of God. His grip of love is solid. "For I am the LORD, your God, who takes hold of your right hand (Isaiah 41:13)." You can cease, as Churchill said, from the paralysis of morbid introspection.

The favorable winds of God's love for you blow continuously. Move forward in that truth, and the turbulence of gusty emotions will not blow you off your course of growing in the grace and knowledge of Jesus Christ. ~ excerpted from Charles Stanley

St. John Chrysostom advised reading Psalm 63 in its entirety every day. Commit to this for a week and share any impact with a Brother Knight.

Smooth seas do not make skillful sailors. ~ African Proverb

November 18

CHARITY is helping the least of us

*Whenever you refused to help one of these least important ones,
you refused to help me.* ~ Matthew 25:45

Malcolm Kushner tells about a chairman of a hospital fund drive
who learned that the richest tycoon in town hadn't yet made a
contribution.
Calling on him, he said, "Our records show you've not yet donated
to our drive.
The tycoon said, "And do your records show my mother died
penniless? Do they show that my brother is disabled? Do they
show that my sister was abandoned and left to support four kids?"
The chairman felt ashamed of his approach. He apologized, "No,
they don't. I'm sorry."
"Well," said the tycoon, "if I didn't help my own family, why
should I help you?"
~ *The Light Touch: How to Use Humor for Business Success*

Is this story a true picture of our society's attitude toward the needy
of our human family?
When have you been challenged to put your faith to the test in a
major way?

*Suppose there are brothers or sisters who need clothes and don't
have enough to eat. What good is there in your saying to them,
"God bless you! Keep warm and eat well!" – if you don't give
them the necessities of life?* ~ James 2:15–16

November 19

UNITY is "No Fear"

Even though I walk through the darkest valley, I fear no evil for you are with me; your rod and your staff give me courage.
~ Psalm 23:4

We need fear no evil, because the power of God can conquer evil. Evil has power to seriously hurt only those who do not place themselves under God's protection. This is not a question of feeling, it is an assured fact of our experience. We can say to ourselves with assurance that whatever it is, no evil can seriously harm us as long as we depend on God. We can be sure of the protection of God's grace. ~ Fr. Pat Umberger

Pray that fear of evil will not discourage us. Pray that we may try to place ourselves under the protection of God's grace.

What dark valley to you walk now? Have you turned to your Brother Knights for support?
Recall Psalm 23 in its entirety, what "green pastures and safe waters" has God brought your way?

Behind an able man there are always other able men.
~ Chinese Proverb

November 20

FRATERNITY is reaching out to a brother in need

Jonathan said to David, "Whatever you want me to do, I'll do it for you." ~ 1 Samuel 20:4

One of the great values of the Knights of Columbus are that it promotes relationships with other men who are truthful and real. Many men carry deep, deep hurts that need to be healed and men need to build trustful relationships to begin to address those hurts. When events occur in a man's life that threaten his self-concept and he is so overwhelmed with events he finds difficult to deal with; he may not be able to bring himself to get out of bed in the morning. Sometimes the pain goes deeper and into the past.

In all of these situations, men need to be ministered to by other men by praying together, working together and playing together. It may mean listening to a man who has never revealed the brutal details of his darkest combat days in Vietnam.

Men are afraid that other men will reject them if they show any weakness, so they keep their emotions to themselves. The community of Knights and Christian men can help men heal from the wounds in their hearts – old wounds as well as new. It can help them grow more fully into Christian manhood, and help put into action what Christ planted in their hearts when they became Christians. ~ A Sir Knight

How hard is it for you to trust your Brother Knights with the heavy stuff in your life? What could help?

Join the company of lions rather than assume the lead among foxes. ~ The Talmud

November 21

PATRIOTISM is having a grateful heart

Give thanks to the LORD. ~ Psalm 107:1

Peter Marshall spoke this prayer before the Senate of the United States:

"Our Father in heaven, if ever we had cause to offer unto Thee our thanks, surely it is now, on the eve of our Thanksgiving Day, when we the people of this nation are comfortable, well-fed, well-clad, and blessed with good things beyond our deserving.
May gratitude, the rarest of all virtues, be the spirit of our observance… May our glorious heritage, remind us of the God who led our fathers every step of the way by which they advanced to the character of an independent nation.
For if we do not have the grace to thank Thee for all that we have and enjoy, how can we have the effrontery to seek Thy further blessings? God, give us grateful hearts. For Jesus' sake. Amen."

What are you most grateful for and why?

*O God, who has given us so much, give us one thing more:
a grateful heart.* ~ George Herbert (slightly adapted)

November 22

CHARITY is His love through us

When the Son of Man comes as King, and all the angels with him,... he will say to those on his left... "Whenever you refused to help one of these least important ones, you refused to help me."
~ Matthew 25:31, 41, 45

After graduating from Georgetown University, Anne Donahue volunteered a year at New York's Covenant House, a refuge for kids who wanted to quit the streets. Every night she put hot chocolate and sandwiches into a van and toured the city's juvenile prostitution areas.

Anne said, "We're out there because many kids haven't tried Covenant House yet. We show the kids that somebody cares – somebody not interested in exploiting them.

At first, I was very depressed. What kind of God would let kids suffer so much? Finally it hit me.

God's not going to come down and show us his love. We have to let God's love shine through us." ~ Mark Link, S.J.

What is one way this month that we have let God's love shine through our council?

Yours are the only hands with which God can do his work...
Yours are the only eyes through which God's compassion can shine upon a troubled world.
~ Saint Teresa of Avila

November 23

UNITY is living in harmony

Live in harmony with one another; do not be haughty, but associate with the lowly; do not claim to be wiser than you are. Do not repay anyone evil for evil, but take thought for what is noble in the sight of all. If it is possible, so far as it depends on you, live peaceably with all. ~ Romans 12:16-18

We can spread peace, not discord, wherever we go. We can try to be part of the cure of every situation, not part of the problem. We can work patiently to make things better. We can always try to build up, never to tear down. We can show others by our example that happiness comes from living the right way. The power of our example is greater than the power of what we say.
~ Fr. Pat Umberger

Pray that we may try to bring something good into every situation today. Pray that we may be constructive in the way we think and speak and act today.

Of the commands listed in the verse above, which are the easiest for you to keep? Which are the most difficult?

We cannot do evil to others without doing it to ourselves.
~ Joseph Francois Eduard Desmahis

November 24

FRATERNITY is doing for others

Do nothing out of selfish ambition or vain conceit, but in humility consider others better than yourselves. ~ Philippians 2:3

As head football coach of the Colorado Buffaloes, I have an intense desire to beat our arch-rival, Nebraska. Unfortunately, when we were facing them in 1991, we had not won when we played in Lincoln for *twenty-three years*. So, before the game, I brought the team together and explained that we spend 80 percent of our time thinking about *ourselves* and 14 percent thinking about *others*. I said, "Men, we're going to put the final score of the game on sixty footballs, and send them to each person you've designated in advance. I'm requiring any player who wants to get on that airplane to Nebraska to dedicate this game to somebody other than himself. I want you to tell that person that they ought to watch you on every play. Tell them you are going to play with all your heart, and that you're playing this game for them. Then, I want you to demonstrate that love on Saturday."

Do you remember what happened? Colorado broke a twenty-three year losing streak in Lincoln and won the game 27-12. Christian men all over our nation are suffering because they feel they are on a losing streak and they can't break the pattern. The Adversary has us where he wants us – feeling defeated. It need not be that way.
~ Bill McCartney, excerpted from *What Makes a Man?*

Has our council fallen into any bad habits or losing streaks?
How can we fraternally overcome them?

Take back the nation for Christ.
~ Bill McCartney

November 25

CHARITY is thanks for all Thy goodness

Give thanks to God the Father always and for everything in the name of Our Lord Jesus Christ. ~ Ephesians 5:20

Almighty God, Father of all mercies,
We, thine unworthy servants, do give thee most humble and hearty thanks for all thy goodness and loving-kindness to us, and to all men.
We bless thee for our creation, preservation, and all the blessings of this life; but above all, for thine inestimable love in the redemption of the world by our Lord Jesus Christ; for the means of grace, and for the hope of glory. And, we beseech thee, give us that due sense of all thy mercies, that our hearts may be unfeignedly thankful; and that we show forth thy praise, not only with our lips, but in our lives, by holiness and righteousness all our days; through Jesus Christ our LORD, to whom, with thee and the Holy Ghost, be all honor and glory, world without end.
Amen. ~ Book of Prayers

As you look back over your life and give thanks, what kind of spiritual growth have you experienced? In what areas have you seen the greatest change – in your motives and desires, your values, in the way you treat others?

What thanks can we give to God for all the joy we feel in His presence? ~ 1 Thessalonians 3:9

November 26

UNITY is thanking God by living a better life

*Let the word of Christ dwell in you richly; teach and admonish one
another in all wisdom; and with gratitude in your hearts sing
psalms, hymns, and spiritual songs to God. And whatever you do,
in word or deed, do everything in the name of the Lord Jesus,
giving thanks to God the Father through him.*
~ Colossians 3:16-17

We need never forget to say thank you to God, even on the grayest
days. Our attitude can be one of humility and gratitude. Saying
thank you to God is a daily practice that is absolutely necessary.
If a day is not one of thankfulness, the practice has to be repeated
until it becomes so. Gratitude is a necessity for those who seek to
live a better life. ~ Fr. Pat Umberger

Pray that gratitude will bring humility. Pray that humility will
bring us to live a better life.

In what ways are letting "the word of Christ dwell in [us] richly"?

*Count your blessings, name them one by one;
Count your blessings, see what God hath done.*
~ J. Oatman, Jr.

November 27

FRATERNITY is meditating on our heavenly Father

O LORD . . .
When I look at the sky, which you have made,
at the moon and the stars, which you have set in their places –
what are human beings, that you think of them...
that you care for them? ~ Psalm 8:1, 3-4

I have been a night walker for years; I love to contemplate the
stars. Their vastness evokes constant wonder... Some people tell
me they feel small when they look at the stars and they don't like
the feeling. I feel small, too, but I find it comforting...
I want creation to be a lot bigger than me, in part because I want
the Creator to be a whole lot bigger than me. I need a God whose
ability to forgive, to love, to heal are much greater than mine.
~ Edward S. Gleason, *Forward Day by Day*

How do you feel when you look at the stars?

The world will never starve for wonders; but only for the want
of wonder. ~ Gilbert K. Chesterton

November 28

PATRIOTISM is a revelation in the midst of a mission

I know a certain Christian man who... was snatched up to the highest heaven... and there he heard things which cannot be put into words. ~ 2 Corinthians 12:2-4

Astronaut James Irwin says that when he, Scott, and Worden, blasted off on Apollo 15 to the moon, he thought it was merely "to get rocks and take some pictures." What happened, however, changed his life. He wrote in his book *To Rule the Night*:

"I wish I had been a writer or a poet so that I could convey more adequately the feeling of this flight. It has been sort of a slow-breaking revelation for me. The ultimate effect has been to deepen and strengthen all the religious insight I ever had. It has remade my faith."

Later, he said in a public lecture:
"God became closer and closer to us as we ventured deeper and deeper into space... I felt the power of God as I never felt it before." ~ Mark Link, S.J.

When was the last time God made his presence known at a Knights gathering?

On the moon the total picture of the power of God and His Son Jesus Christ became abundantly clear to me.
~ James Irwin

November 29

CHARITY is the faith of a centurion

When the centurion who stood facing him saw how he breathed his last he said, "Truly this man was the Son of God!" ~ Mark 15:39

Beneath the cross at Golgotha there stood a soldier to whom history and legend have given the name Longinus. It was he who, witnessing all the tragic events of the Crucifixion, said of Jesus: "Clearly this man was the son of God."
Legend says that Longinus was cured of partial blindness by the blood of Christ that fell on him and that he left soldiering to become a Christian. He reportedly went on to lead a monastic life and, by his words and example, to win many souls for Christ. Some stories have him arrested for his faith and brought before a judge. After Longinus refused to renounce his faith, according to those stories, the judge ordered his teeth to be knocked out and his tongue cut off. Picking up an ax and still able to speak, Longinus broke the idols into pieces crying out, "Now we shall see whether they are gods." ~ J.M. Guerin

What is significant about Longinus' confirmation of Jesus' death? When did the Crucifixion begin to make a difference in your life?

Faith is not belief without proof, but trust without reservation.
~ Elton Trueblood

November 30

UNITY is turning to God as our refuge

God is our refuge and strength, a very present help in trouble.
Therefore we will not fear, though the earth should change, though
the mountains shake in the heart of the sea; though its waters roar
and foam, though the mountains tremble with its tumult.
~ Psalm 46:1-3

God is a sanctuary, a refuge from the cares of life. We can get
away from the misunderstandings of others by retiring into our own
place of meditation. But from ourselves, from our own sense of
failure, our weakness, our shortcomings, where can we flee? Only
to the eternal God, our refuge, until the immensity of God's spirit
envelopes our spirit and it loses its smallness and weakness and
comes into harmony again with God's. ~ Fr. Pat Umberger

Pray that we may lose our limitations in the immensity of God's
love. Pray that our spirit may be in harmony with God's spirit.

What difference does it make to know Jesus is LORD over all
chaotic events? Where do you feel a need for his special
protection right now?

I have been driven many times to my knees by the overwhelming
conviction that I had nowhere else to go.
~ Abraham Lincoln

December 1

FRATERNITY is ordinary men with the right stuff

When they saw the courage of Peter and John and realized that they were unschooled, ordinary men, they were astonished and they took note that these men had been with Jesus. ~ Acts 4:13

The Disciples were a band of illiterates, utterly devoid of social consequence, not likely to be chosen by one having supreme regard to prudential considerations. Why would Jesus choose such men? The truth is that Jesus was obliged to be content with fishermen, publicans, and quondam zealots. Those who deemed themselves better were too proud to become disciples. A few of good position were sincere sympathizers, but they were not eligible for apostles. Nicodemus was barely able to speak a timid apologetic word in Christ's behalf, and Joseph of Arimathea was a disciple "secretly," for fear of the Jews. These were hardly the men to send forth as missionaries of the cross – men so fettered by social ties and so enslaved by the fear of man. And so Jesus was obliged to fall back on rustic, but simple and energetic men. And He was quite content with His choice, and thanked His Father for giving Him even such as they. Rank, wealth, refinement – freely given up to His service – He would not have despised; but He preferred devoted men who had none of these advantages to undevoted men who had them all. ~ A.B. Bruce

Ideally, a Knight would give of himself to His service. Do you qualify yourself as a devoted man of God?

The LORD doesn't ask about your ability, only your availability; and, if you prove your dependability, the LORD will increase your capability. ~ Unknown

December 2

CHARITY is the Good Shepherd

I am the good shepherd, who is willing to die for the sheep. As the Father knows me and I know the Father, in the same way I know my sheep and they know me. ~ John 10:1, 14–15

Jesus went on to say, "There are other sheep which belong to me that are not in this sheep pen. I must bring them, too; they will listen to my voice and they will become one flock with one shepherd. The Father loves me because I am willing to give up my life... that I may receive it back again. No one takes my life away from me. I give it up of my own free will... This is what my Father has commanded me to do (John 10:1, 14-18)."
~ Author unknown

Who are the "other sheep" who listen to the shepherd's voice? Besides listening to it in Scripture, where else might they listen for it?

God talks to us at a level in ourselves that we cannot reach... an inner dimension that we didn't know we possessed until He declared Himself in it. ~ Louis Evely

December 3

UNITY is journeying to Christ anyway

Make my joy complete by being of the same mind, maintaining the same love, united in spirit, intent on one purpose.
~ Philippians 2:2

People are often unreasonable, illogical, and self-centered;
Forgive them anyway.
If you are kind, People may accuse you of selfish, ulterior motives;
Be kind anyway.
If you are successful, you will win some false friends and some true enemies;
Succeed anyway.
If you are honest and frank, people may cheat you;
Be honest and frank anyway.
What you spend years building, someone could destroy overnight;
Build anyway.
The good you do today, people will often forget tomorrow;
Do good anyway.
Give the world the best you have, and it may never be enough;
Give the world the best you've got anyway.
You see, in the final analysis, it is between you and God;
It was never between you and them anyway. ~ Mother Teresa

What was at one time discouraging to you until you read Mother Teresa's words? Are you emboldened to overcome the obstacle now?

In essential things, unity; in doubtful things, liberty; in all things, charity. ~ St. Augustine

December 4

FRATERNITY is calling a brother to fellowship

Call to me, and I will answer you; I will tell to you things great beyond reach of your knowledge. ~ Jeremiah 33:3

One day, Jerry was approached by his older brother, Jim, to join the Knights of Columbus. Jerry was just twenty-two years old at the time and cruising along in life, so his response was "Why?"

His brother replied, *"For the greater honor and glory of God."*

That exchange between brothers may have seemed insignificant at first. After all, many men are invited into the fraternity, but soon after they join, they lose their way again. But in other instances, it is a wake-up call for a man, because he finds spiritual nourishment and Catholic brotherhood. Sometimes, this leads to untold influences on families, parishes and communities. This is what happened to Jerry. His thirty-eight years with the Knights were capped by his election as State Deputy of Colorado. With his administration's theme of *"For the greater honor and glory of God!"*, Jerry harkened back to the guidance he had received from his brother. He seemed to have come full circle, but his journey to Christ and his leadership of men continues to this day.
~ A Sir Knight

Is there a hidden call for you to be an example for other men in the Knights? Are you helping others to heed the call by inviting them to become part of our fraternity?

If God can work through me, he can work through anyone.
~ Saint Francis of Assisi

December 5

PATRIOTISM is Duty, Honor, Country

Blessed is the nation whose God is the LORD, the people chosen as his very own. ~ Psalm 33:12

These words were excerpted from a speech General Douglas MacArthur delivered at West Point on May 12th, 1962. Every cadet entering the military academy receives a copy of the General's address in its entirety.

Duty. Honor. Country. Those three hallowed words reverently dictate what you ought to be, what you can be, what you will be. They are your rallying points, to build courage when courage seems to fail, to regain faith when there seems to be little cause for faith, to create hope when hope becomes forlorn…
They mold you for future roles as the custodians of the nation's defense. They teach you to be proud and unbending in honest failure, but humble and gentle in success; not to substitute words for actions, not to seek the path of comfort, but to face the stress and spur of difficulty and challenge… They teach you to be modest so that you will remember the simplicity of true greatness, the open mind of true wisdom, the meekness of true strength… They teach you in this way to be an officer and a gentleman.

These are great words for every soldier. Are they great words for every Knight? Are you the kind of Knight that would have made Father McGivney proud?

Patriotism means to stand by the country. It does not mean to stand by the president or any public official, save exactly to the degree he himself stands by the country. ~ Theodore Roosevelt

340

December 6

CHARITY is not doubting, but believing

Then Jesus said to Thomas... "Stop your doubting and believe."
~ John 20:27

Once, twins were conceived in a womb. Together they explored it
saying, "How great is our mother's love that she shares with us her
very life."
Weeks passed; the twins began to change.
The first said to the second, "This means our life in the womb is
coming to an end."
The second replied, "I don't want it to end. I want to stay here
forever."
The first said, "But maybe there is life after birth."
The second replied, "How can there be? We'll shed our mother's
cord, and how is life possible without it?"
The twins fell into doubt. "If life in the womb ends in death," they
said, "What's its purpose?"
And so the last days in the womb were filled with confusion and
fear. Finally, the moment of birth came. When the twins opened
their eyes, they cried for joy. For what they saw exceeded their
wildest dreams.
~ Mark Link, S.J.

What is the point of this parable?

*What no one ever saw or heard, what no one ever thought could
happen, is the very thing God prepared for those who love him.*
~ 1 Corinthians 2:9

December 7

UNITY is peace centered in God

For the sake of my brothers, I say, ""May peace be within you.''
~ Psalm 122:8

Sometimes TV reporters ask insensitive questions of people who have just suffered a tragedy. For example, John Cogan, a cancer victim, was asked how he felt about dying.

He stunned the reporter saying, "There's a joy deep down inside me that I can't express.
I feel perfectly free . . . . I want to reach out and embrace the whole universe."

Tragedy had set before John Cogan the choice of life and death in the ultimate sense of the word. He chose life – eternal life.
~ Mark Link, S.J.

How can we accept unfortunate circumstances of our life? How can we help brother knights and their families when they face the imminent reality of death and help them see eternal life? How will you know when you've achieved true peace in your heart?

I am the resurrection and the life; whoever believes in me, even if he dies, will live, and everyone who lives and believes in me will never die. ~ John 11:25-26

December 8

FRATERNITY is a few good men

And the angel of the LORD appeared unto Gideon, and said unto him, "The LORD is with thee, thou mighty man of valor."
~ Judges 6:12

The Midianites had been preying on the Israelites and their land. Gideon had lost all of his brothers in battle, but God put a thought in his heart to save his people. He sent messengers throughout the land to form a band of fighting men. At first, an army of 32,000 men was formed. But many were not sure the LORD would lead them to victory. So God told Gideon to send home all those who were afraid to fight. Gideon saw that a small army of brave men would be better than a multitude of cowards, so he told anyone that was afraid to fight to go home. He was down to 10,000 men. But God said that he needed only the best and bravest men, so he told Gideon to send his men to the water and He would show him which men to keep. At the river, almost every man laid down his weapon and quenched their thirst. God told Gideon to send these men home. But a few men merely caught a handful of water and remained en garde. God said to Gideon that these were the men who would set Israel free. They numbered only 300 strong.
~ adapted from the book of Judges

Should our council leadership concern itself with membership quotas just to increase our numbers? Or should we build a small corps of men who acknowledge a deep-seated hunger for spiritual nourishment and Catholic fellowship – men who will actively come together to make a difference?

Man to man shall be friend and brother. ~ Gerald Massey

December 9

CHARITY is sowing to the Spirit

*Do not be deceived; God is not mocked, for whatever a man sows,
that he will also reap. For he who sows to his own flesh will from
the flesh reap corruption; but he who sows to the Spirit will from
the Spirit reap eternal life.* ~ Galatians 6:7-8

In this verse, we have encapsulated the entire Catholic teaching
concerning the idea of "merit." Many people think that when the
Church speaks of "merit" she means "extra good deeds you do to
make up for Jesus' inadequate efforts at atonement for sin." But
this completely misunderstands the Church's teaching. In reality,
everything that we do that contributes to our salvation is the result
of the grace of Christ, not a supplement to or a cause of grace.
Sowing to the Spirit (seeking God consistently in prayer, or doing
works of mercy, or faithfully approaching the sacraments) is not a
thing we do to put God in our debt. We do this because God is at
work in us already and inspiring us to obey him. When we do
obey him we mysteriously discover that we have gotten "bigger
inside" and have a greater capacity for his grace. And so the
process continues throughout our lives, growing in grace,
responding to grace, receiving more grace till we are fully
conformed to the image of Christ. Today, sow to the Spirit.
You will reap eternal life. ~ Dr. Scott Hahn and Jeff Cavins

As you reflect on what you have sown this year, what harvest are
you expecting – weeds? A bumper crop?

*Acts of penance are not a payback that evens the score, but a way of
recalling that we are constantly in God's debt.*
~ *Practicing Catholic*

December 10

UNITY is heeding the counsel of loved ones

Arrogance causes nothing but trouble. It is wiser to ask for advice.
~ Proverbs 13:10

It's hard to imagine a Christmas program without *Rudolph the Red-Nosed Reindeer* being on the music menu. The story behind the hit goes back 50 years. After his previous year's blockbuster hit, *Here Comes Santa Claus*, Gene Autry was looking for a follow-up for the current year. One day the mail brought a recording of *Rudolph the Red-Nosed Reindeer*. It was the work of a young songwriter named Johnny Marks. Autry listened to it, but he was not keen on it.
His wife, however, counseled otherwise. She felt kids would go for it. They did! Today, more than 400 artists have recorded it, and over 100 million copies of the song have been sold.
~ Mark Link, S.J.

The counsel of others often brings matters into perspective. How readily do you seek the counsel of your Brother Knights? How do you decide whose counsel to follow?

You should be careful to observe the way toward which your heart draws you; then choose this way with all your strength.
~ Martin Buber

December 11

FRATERNITY is an umbrella on a rainy day

The storm makes my heart beat wildly… God sends lightning across the sky… and torrents of drenching rain. He brings our work to a stop. ~ Job 37:1-2, 6-7

As a boy, Frederick Buechner loved the rain. He loved the feel of it on his face and legs. Above all, he wrote:
"I loved the sound of it on trees and roofs and window panes… I loved the hiss of rubber tires on rainy streets and the flip-flop of windshield wipers. I loved the smell of wet grass and raincoats and shaggy coats of dogs. A rainy day was a special day… a day when the ordinariness of things was suspended… and even people transformed… as the rain drew them closer."
~ Frederick Buechner, *The Sacred Journey*

Why do rainy days draw us closer?
Why does this hold true for "figurative" rainy days as well?

How beautiful is the rain!
After the dust and heat,
In the broad and fiery street,
In the narrow lane,
How beautiful is the rain.
~ Henry Wadsworth Longfellow

December 12 Our Lady of Guadalupe

PATRIOTISM is following the Patroness of the Americas

Who is this that comes forth like the dawn, as beautiful as the moon, as resplendent as the sun...? ~ Song of Songs 6:10

In 1531, Mexican Aztecs had a death wish. Their entire civilization had been destroyed by the Spaniards and many were forced to choose between baptism or death. A poor Indian named Juan Diego was walking to Mass when he heard his name called. He saw the Virgin Mary dressed in clothing symbolic to the Aztecs, including a brown rope tied around her waist, which symbolized pregnancy. Her skin was dark like his own and she spoke his language. She comforted Diego and asked him to visit the Bishop of Mexico. He was to tell the bishop her name was Santa Maria de Coatlallope and that she wanted a church built on the mountain. The bishop didn't believe Diego, but Our Lady appeared to Diego again and sent him back to the bishop with a sign. Diego gathered roses from the mountain, Tepeyac, although the ground was dry and frozen. When he spilled the roses in front of the bishop, the image of the Holy Mother of God appeared on the cloth. Within six years, six million Mexicans had converted to Catholicism. Since then Our Lady of Guadalupe has had special significance for Catholics of Mexican decent. ~ Catholic Encyclopedia

God chose Mary to lead us to Jesus. She appeared to Juan Diego not as a European madonna but as a beautiful Aztec princess speaking to him in his native dialect. What does Mary teach us about understanding and appreciating other cultures?

I am a nobody, a small rope, a tiny ladder, the tail end, a leaf. ~ Juan Diego, in humility to the Blessed Virgin Mary

December 13

CHARITY is what goes around and comes around

Give, and it will be given to you. A good measure, pressed down, shaken together and running over, will be poured into your lap.
~ Luke 6:38 NIV

He said, "Why don't you wait in the car where it's warm? By the way, my name is Bryan." Well, all she had was a flat tire, but for an old lady, that was bad enough. She asked him how much she owed him. This was helping someone in need, and God knows there were plenty who had given him a hand in the past. He told her that if she really wanted to pay him back, she could take care of the next person who needed help and "think of me." A few miles down the road the lady saw a small cafe. Her waitress came over with a sweet smile. She was eight months pregnant, but she never let the strain and aches change her attitude. Then the lady remembered Bryan. After she finished her meal, she left the waitress five $100 bills and a note – "You don't owe me anything, I have been there too. If you really want to pay me back, here is what you do: Do not let this chain of love end with you."
That night when she climbed into bed, she wondered how the lady could have known – with the baby due soon, it was going to be hard. She knew how worried her husband was, and as he lay sleeping next to her, she gave him a soft kiss and whispered, "I love you, Bryan." ~ Author unknown

During the last storm to hit your life, what did you learn about your life's foundation?

What a joy it is to find just the right words for the right occasion.
~ Proverbs 15:23

December 14

UNITY is striving for greater works

*Very truly, I tell you, the one who believes in me will also do the
works that I do and, in fact, will do greater works than these.*
~ John 14:12

We can do greater works when we have more experience of the
new way of life. We can have all the power we need from God.
We can have God's grace, God's spirit, to make us effective as we
go along each day. Opportunities for a better world are all around
us. Greater works can we do. But we do not work alone. The
power of God is behind all our good works.
~ Fr. Pat Umberger

Pray that we may find a rightful place in the world. Pray that our
work may be made more effective by the grace of God.

In the above verse, does Jesus mean the Church will do works
greater in *power*? Greater in *scope*? How could this be?

When there is no wind, row.
~ Chinese Proverb

December 15

FRATERNITY is manhood to the highest degree

We do not want you to become lazy, but to imitate those who through faith and patience inherit what has been promised.
~ Hebrews 6:12

It is the highest stage of manhood to have no wish, no thought, no desire, but Christ – to feel that to die were bliss, if it were for Christ – that to live in penury, and woe, and scorn, and contempt, and misery, were sweet for Christ – to feel that it matters nothing what becomes of one's self, so that our Master is but exalted – to feel that though, like a mere leaf, we are blown in the blast, we are quite careless whither we are going, so long as we feel that the Master's hand is guiding us according to His will; or, rather, to feel that though, like the diamond, we must be exercised with sharp tools, yet we care not how sharply we may be cut; so that we may be made fit brilliants to adorn his crown…
I do think that one of the worst sins a man can be guilty of in this world is to be idle. I can almost forgive a drunkard, but a lazy man I do think there is very little pardon for. I think a man who is idle has as good a reason to be a penitent before God as David had when he was an adulterer, for the most abominable thing in the world is for a man to let the grass grow up to his ankles and do nothing. ~ Charles Haddon Spurgeon

When have you been lazy? What motivates you to move forward again?

Whoever is careless with the truth in small matters cannot be trusted with important matters. ~ Albert Einstein

350

December 16

CHARITY is remembering that Baby Jesus was homeless

Mary gave birth to her firstborn son and wrapped him in bands of cloth, and laid him in a manger, because there was no place for them in the inn. ~ Luke 2:7

On this date, Mexican Catholics begin the beautiful celebration of *Posadas* ("shelter"). During this period, Mexican children dress up and reenact the Holy Family's search to find a place where Mary can give birth to the Savior of the world. Every night for the next nine nights, the children knock on doors asking for shelter.
The celebration of *Posadas* takes on special significance in these times, when so many homeless people walk the streets and alleys of so many major cities. ~ Mark Link, S.J.

How has our council ministered to the needs of the homeless this year? How is our assembly reaching out to homeless military veterans this Christmas season?

I was a stranger but you did not welcome me into your homes. ~ Matthew 25:43

December 17

UNITY is malice toward none

He is before all things, and in him all things hold together.
~ Colossians 1:17

The Civil War was a very sad and tragic chapter in the history of the United States. In no other struggle of this country have so many died and suffered tragically. It was nearing its end when Abraham Lincoln gave his second inaugural address on March 4, 1865. The concluding paragraph of his address set the tone for recovery from the war:

"With malice toward none, with charity for all, with firmness in the right as God gives us to see the right, let us strive on to finish the work we are in, to bind up the nation's wounds, to care for him who shall have borne the battle and for his widow and his orphan, to do all which may achieve and cherish a just and lasting peace among ourselves and with all nations."

Are there disagreements within your council? Will you strive to reconcile once a decision on a difficult issue is reached?

Commit your way to the LORD; trust in him and he will do this: He will make your righteousness shine like the dawn, the justice of your cause like the noonday sun. ~ Psalm 37:5-6

December 18

FRATERNITY is His life in us

I have been crucified with Christ and I no longer live, but Christ lives in me. The life I live in the body, I live by faith in the Son of God, who loved me and gave himself for me. ~ Galatians 2:20

We sometimes think we do things *for* Christ. But today's scripture quote suggests that Christ's life should be in and through us. It's like putting a tea bag in a cup of hot water. The water is us. The tea bag is the life of Christ. The water is not the tea and the tea is not the water. The tea bag is *for* the water, but that by itself doesn't change the water. However when the tea bag is placed in the water, something does indeed change. The water becomes indwelt by a new and dominant nature: the tea. The tea is in the water, and the water is in the tea – just as we are "in Christ", Christ is "in us." The tea has changed the nature of the water, so you would not say "would you like a cup of colored, flavored water?" Instead you would say: "Here is a cup of tea." The tea bag in the water transforms the water into something else. Now people will see Christ in us. We become more like Christ and less like we had been. ~ Jack Taylor, *The Key to Triumphant Living*

Applying the spiritual concept of the above verse, who is "alive" in your life right now – "I" or "Christ in me"?

Whatever is your best time in the day, give that to communion with God. ~ Hudson Taylor

353

December 19

PATRIOTISM is an Airborne Paratrooper

*Whoever wishes to become great among you shall be your servant;
and whoever wishes to be first among you shall be slave of all.*
~ Mark 10:43-44

They come from the day and night sky by parachute, glider and
helicopter. They put their lives on the line to keep our nation free
and many pay the ultimate price for that dedication to duty and
country.

From the Troop Carrier Pilots, Glider Pilots and Helicopter Pilots
who must deliver their cargo of airborne soldiers safely to the Drop
Zone or Landing Zone, to the paratroopers, glider troops, and air
assault troopers plunging into battle, airborne soldiers have always
shared a common bond of brotherhood.

For fifty years, the United States Armed Forces have relied upon
elite airborne units to lead the way in difficult, dangerous and vital
missions. The courageous men who have earned the "silver badges
of courage" of the airborne forces have fought and died so their
fellow Americans might live in freedom.
~ History of the Screaming Eagles , The 101st Airborne Division
Association

Knights, do you lead the way in your family, parish and community
through selfless service?

*All must admit that the reception of the teachings of Christ results in
the purest patriotism, in the most scrupulous fidelity to public trust,
and in the best type of citizenship.* ~ Grover Cleveland

December 20

CHARITY is a miraculous rescue

*The LORD who created you says, "Do not be afraid – I will save you... I have called you by name – you are mine." * ~ Isaiah 42:1

On Christmas Eve 1983, Tim Anderson and two college roommates were driving from Connecticut to Chicago. The car radio warned against going outside, because a wind chill of 80-below had hit the Midwest.
The boys dropped off one roommate in Fort Wayne and took off by a rural route to the Indiana tollway. Miles from nowhere, their car choked, sputtered, and died. No lights could be seen anywhere.
As the frigid cold invaded their car, the desperate boys began to pray for help.
Suddenly, lights appeared out of nowhere – a tow truck. It took them back to their friend's house in Fort Wayne. Tim ran inside to get money for the tow fee.
When Tim returned, he stopped dead. No tow truck was in sight – and only one set of tire tracks was in the snow: their car's.
~ digested from Joan Webster Anderson's *Where Angels Walk*

How firmly do you believe that God can and does hear our prayers?

If I don't pray with confidence, how can I hope to receive that for which I pray? ~ Anonymous

December 21

UNITY is keeping our eyes on the prize

Brothers, I do not consider myself yet to have taken hold of it. But one thing I do: Forgetting what is behind and straining toward what is ahead, I press on toward the goal to win the prize for which God has called me heavenward in Christ Jesus.
~ Philippians 3:13-14

In a race, it is when the goal is in sight that the heart and nerves and muscles and courage are strained almost to the breaking point. So it is with us. The goal of the spiritual life is in sight. All we need is the final effort. The saddest records are made by people who ran with brave, stout hearts, with the goal in sight, and then some weakness or self-indulgence held them back. They never knew how near they were to victory. ~ Fr. Pat Umberger

Pray that we may press on until the goal is reached. Pray that we may not give up in the final stretch.

What prize (see above verse) are Knights after?
How are we going to reach it?

All men dream: but not equally. Those who dream by night in the dusty recesses of their minds wake in the day to find that it was vanity. But the dreamers of the day are dangerous men, for they may act on their dream with open eyes, to make it possible.
~ T.E. Lawrence

December 22

FRATERNITY is invading a battleground

"Do not come any closer," God said, "Take off your sandals, for the place where you are standing is holy ground." ~ Exodus 3:5

Christian service means invading a battleground, not a playground; and you and I are the weapons God uses to attack and defeat the enemy. When God used Moses' rod, He needed Moses' hand to lift it. When God used David's sling, He needed David's hand to swing it. When God builds a ministry, He needs somebody's surrendered body to get the job done. You are important to the LORD, so keep your life pure. There is no substitute for Christian character. No matter how much talent and training we may have, if we don't have character, we don't have anything… The person who cultivates integrity realizes that there can be no division between "secular and sacred" in the Christian life; everything must be done to the glory of God (1 Corinthians 10:31). God reminded two of his greatest leaders, Moses (Exodus 3:5) and Joshua (Joshua 5:15), that the servant of the LORD is *always* standing on holy ground and had better behave accordingly. If anybody else is watching, God is; and He will be our judge. ~ Warren Wiersbe

Do you lead a dual everyday life between "secular and sacred" or are *all* of your actions for the greater honor and glory of God? Does our council emphasize character and integrity as hallmarks of our knighthood?

For we are God's workmanship, created in Christ Jesus to do good works, which God prepared in advance for us to do.
~ Ephesians 2:10

December 23

CHARITY is maximizing today's deposits

You also must be ready, because the Son of Man will come at an hour when you do not expect him. ~ Luke 12:40

Imagine there is a bank that credits your account each morning with $86,400. It carries over no balance from day to day. Every evening deletes whatever part of the balance you failed to use during the day. What would you do? Draw out every cent, of course!

Each of us has such a bank – it's *TIME*. Every morning it credits us with 86,400 seconds. Every night it writes off, as lost, whatever we have failed to invest to good purpose. It carries over no balance. It allows no overdraft. Each day it opens a new account for us. Each night it burns the remains of the day. If we fail to use the day's deposits, the loss is ours. There is no going back. There is no drawing against the "tomorrow". ~ Author unknown

We must live in the present on today's deposits. Invest it to gain the utmost in CHARITY, UNITY, FRATERNITY and PATRIOTISM! The clock is running…

Has our council and assembly made the most of the year – have we drawn out every cent? In terms of CHARITY, UNITY, FRATERNITY and PATRIOTISM, where can we improve in the coming year?

Even a clock that is not going is right twice a day.
~ Polish Proverb

December 24

UNITY is remembering your faith even in your darkest hour

*So Joseph also went up from the town of Nazareth in Galilee to
Judea, to Bethlehem the town of David, because he belonged to the
house and line of David. He went there to register with Mary, who
was pledged to be married to him and was expecting a child.
While they were there, the time came for the baby to be born, and
she gave birth to her firstborn, a son. She wrapped him in cloths
and placed him in a manger, because there was no room for them
in the inn.* ~ Luke 2:4-7

I'll never forget that first Christmas Eve in captivity. It was terribly
cold, and though I knew of one other American nearby, I was still
alone. My body ached, and my wounds were only beginning to
heal. In my ice-cold misery, I heard a Christmas carol. It was an
incredible surprise. For a moment I thought my mind was playing
treacherous tricks – "Silent Night, Holy Night." The fidelity was
awful, but it was the first song I had heard since bailing out more
than a month ago. Scratches and all, that carol was beautiful
beyond describing. Then the carol ended, and the voice of Hanoi
Hanna came on with a barrage of propaganda. "Radio Stateside"
may have been a tool to break us down, but the snatches of
American music, especially that carol on Christmas Eve, was like
discovering hidden treasure, and I reveled in it.
~ Howard E. Rutledge, *In the Presence of Mine Enemies*

Has God ever revealed His everlasting love for you in times of
trial?

*Call upon Me in the day of trouble; I shall rescue you,
and you will honor Me.* ~ Psalm 50:15

Christmas

But the angel said to them, "Do not be afraid, I bring you good news of great joy that will be for all the people. Today in the town of David a Savior has been born to you; he is Christ the LORD."
~ Luke 2:10-11

Strange is our situation here on earth, each of us comes for a short visit, not knowing why, yet sometimes seeming to divine a purpose. From the standpoint of daily life, however, there is one thing we know:

That Man is here for the sake of other Men.
Above all for those upon whose smile and well-being our own happiness depends, and also for the countless unknown souls with whose fate we are connected by a bond of sympathy.
Many times a day I realize how much my own outer and inner life is built upon the labors of my fellow men, both living and dead, and how earnestly I must exert myself in order to give in return as much as I have received. ~ Albert Einstein

Brother to Brother, family to family, we celebrate as Knights the birth of our Saviour, the Son of God, and that in our faith we may have life in His name.

How can we make the spirit of Christmas last for more than just one day?

Happiness will never be ours, if we do not recognize to some degree that God's blessings were given us for the well-being of all.
~ Anonymous

December 26

PATRIOTISM is a blameless walk

Better a poor man whose walk is blameless than a rich man whose ways are perverse. ~ Proverbs 28:6

A man is called to a manhood defined by the life of Jesus Christ. Exciting but shallow pleasures, the kind that do not require us to worry about some deep call to manhood, may disguise themselves as true happiness. Power, money, status, connections, achievement, success, possessions, food, sex, recreation: lots of things, many of them good in their place, get defined as the source of happiness. But none of these characterized the life of Christ. While these false pleasures make us feel good, they do not produce a contentment that survives loss, a joy that deepens through suffering, a humble confidence that persists through failure and setback. By going after these sources of pleasure, we reduce ourselves to puppets, supported by strings that, if cut, leave us in a heap on the ground.

No man can be happy without living out the call to make visible that which is hard to see about God. Happiness comes for a man when he shows, by his life modeled after Christ, that God is always moving, is never stopped by darkness, and is continually up to something good, no matter how bad things may appear.
~ Larry Crabb

In what way is it "better" to be poor (see above verse)? In what way can one be rich and blameless, or rich and unpunished?

The burden is equal to the horse's strength. ~ The Talmud

December 27

CHARITY is listening to the inner voice

Encourage the timid, help the weak, be patient with everyone.
~ 1 Thessalonians 5:14

Dan Begley settled into his plane seat in Seattle, hoping to get a lot of work done before arriving in Dallas.
Just then a mother and three kids got on. The mother and a four-year-old sat behind him; the two older kids, next to him.
Once airborne, they began turning around every ten minutes to ask their mother, "Where are we now?"
Dan's irritation rose to the "danger" level. Suddenly an "inner voice" told him, "Be patient! Love these kids. They need it."
He put away his work, took the in-flight magazine, turned to the flight map, and showed the kids the route to Dallas. He divided the route into 15-minute lengths so that they could see exactly where they were at any moment. Then he explained a lot of things about planes to them.
As the plane touched down in Dallas, Dan asked if their father would be waiting. A short silence ensued.
Then one of the kids said softly, "No, we buried him in Seattle."
~ Mark Link, S.J.

How patient am I, especially with children?
Of all the places you live (at home, work, school, community), where do you feel the need for more faith, more hope or more love?

Patience is bitter, but its fruit is sweet.
~ Jean Jacques Rousseau

December 28

UNITY is proletarian service to God

His master said, 'Well done, good and faithful servant! You have been faithful with a few things; I will put you in charge of many things. Come and share your master's happiness!'
~ Matthew 25:23-24

These words are for many ordinary people whom the world may pass by, unrecognizing. Not to the world-famed, the proud, the wealthy, are these words spoken, but to the quiet followers who serve God unobtrusively yet faithfully, who bear their crosses bravely and put a smiling face to the world. "Enter into the joy of your LORD." Pass into that fuller spiritual life, which is a life of joy and peace. ~ Fr. Pat Umberger

We pray that we may not desire for the world's applause. We pray that we may not seek rewards for doing what we believe is right.

The Son of Man did not come to be served, but to serve, and to give His life as a ransom for many. Have we Knights maximized service to our parish and our community this past year?

This service that you perform is not only supplying the needs of God's people but is also overflowing in many expressions of thanks to God. ~ 2 Corinthians 9:12 NIV

December 29

From here to FRATERNITY

How good and pleasant it is when brothers live together in unity!
~ Psalm 133:1

When I was in college, I joined a "crew" in an eight-man shell with coxswain. When we first learned to row together it was extremely awkward, with the oars slapping from side to side and the boat rocking. But after months of practice, we were able to row with great speed through the water.

Even though each of the individual men was rowing with extremely violent force, the timing and cooperation was so perfect that there would be no side movement in the boat. When rowing reached racing speed, the hull would rise slightly out of the water. There is poetic beauty in the intuitive sense of teamwork and unity among men. The slightest wrong move by any of the oarsmen can ruin a race. Not only was it a joy to compete well, but the privilege to experience that perfection of teamwork was a spiritual reward in itself.

Serving should have the sweet spiritual reward of being a team member. There is a joy of fraternity and kinship in working together. ~ Keith Intrater, *Covenant Relationships*

Do we have widespread espirit de corps in our council? If not, what is hindering it? What activities can we plan that would build it? How are you personally helping to build kinship in our fraternity?

Great achievements in war and peace can only result if men form an indissoluble band of brothers.
~ Paul von Hindenburg

December 30

CHARITY is the great commandment

Thou shalt love the LORD thy God with all thy heart,
and with all thy soul,
and with all thy mind.
This is the first and great commandment.
And the second is like unto it;
Thou shalt love thy neighbor as thyself.
On these two commandments hang all the law and the prophets.
~ Matthew 22:37-40

How is loving God related to loving your neighbor?
In what way
do you want to grow in love right now:
Toward God?
Toward your family?
Toward your Brother Knights?
Toward the needy?
Toward yourself?

Love is the verb of which God is the object.
~ Lycurgus M. Starkey, Jr.

December 31

Knights in UNITY

*I pray... that all of them may be one, Father, just as you are in me
and I am in you. May they also be in us so that the world may
believe that you have sent me.* ~ John 17:21

Rise up, O men of God,
Have done with lesser things,
Give heart and soul and mind and strength
To serve the King of kings.
Bring in the day of brotherhood
And end the night of wrong.
The Church for you doth wait,
Her strength unequal to her task;
Rise up, and make her great.
Lift high the cross of Christ,
Tread where His feet have trod;
As brothers of the Son of man,
Rise up, O men of God. ~ William P. Merrill

Brother Knights, what are your new year's resolutions for the
greater honor and glory of God?

*Finally, brothers,
whatever is true, whatever is noble, whatever is just, whatever is
pure, whatever is lovely, whatever is admirable – if there is any
excellence and if there is anything worthy of praise – think about
such things. Keep on doing what you have learned and received
and heard and seen in me. Then the God of peace will be with you.*
~ Philippians 4:8-9

Ask of us the same high standards of strength and sacrifice which we ask of you. With a good conscience our only sure reward, with history the final judge of our deeds, let us go forth to lead the land we love, asking His blessing and His help, but knowing that here on earth God's work must truly be our own.

~Sir Knight John F. Kennedy, January 1961

A practical Catholic gentleman _____

Those who love Thy law have great peace, and nothing causes them to stumble. ~ Psalm 119:165

The Order of the Knights of Columbus is a brotherhood that is shaped by virtues of faith, integrity, fidelity, hard work and generous concern for others. A practical Catholic gentleman is one who lives up to the Commandments of God and the Precepts of the Church.

The Greatest Commandment is (Matthew 22:37-39):

You shall love the LORD your God with all your heart, and with all your soul, and with all your mind. This is the great and foremost commandment. The second is like it: You shall love your neighbor as yourself.

The Commandments of God are (Exodus 20:2-17; Deuteronomy 5:6-21):

I. I am the Lord thy God; thou shalt not have strange gods before me.
II. Thou shalt not take the name of the LORD thy God in vain.
III. Remember to keep holy the LORD's day.
IV. Honor thy father and thy mother.
V. Thou shalt not kill.
VI. Thou shalt not commit adultery.
VII. Thou shalt not steal.
VIII. Thou shalt not bear false witness against thy neighbor.
IX. Thou shalt not covet thy neighbor's wife.
X. Thou shalt not covet thy neighbor's goods.

The Precepts of the Church are (*Catechism of the Catholic Church*, 2041-2043):

☐ To assist at Mass on all Sundays and holy days of obligation.

☐ To fast and abstain on the days appointed.

☐ To confess our sins at least once a year.

☐ To receive Holy Communion during the Easter time.

☐ To contribute to the support of the Church.

☐ To observe the laws of the Church concerning marriage.

Other basic truths of the Faith so dear to all Knights:

☐ The Apostles' Creed - A formula containing the fundamental tenets of Christian belief.

☐ The rosary – A prayer centered on the mysteries or events in the life of Jesus. Also known as the Bible translated into prayer. The mysteries are:

    ○ Joyful – Annunciation; Visitation; Birth of Jesus; Presentation of Jesus; Finding of the Child Jesus in the Temple.

    ○ Sorrowful – Agony in the Garden; Scourging at the pillar; Crowning with thorns; Carrying of the Cross; Crucifixion.

    ○ Glorious – Resurrection; Ascension; Descent of the Holy Spirit; Assumption of Mary; Crowning of Mary.

    ○ Luminous (Mysteries of Light) – Baptism in the Jordan; Wedding of Cana; Proclamation of the Kingdom; Transfiguration; Institution of the Eucharist

- ❑ The seven sacraments – Baptism, Penance, Holy Eucharist, Confirmation, Matrimony, Holy Orders and the Anointing of the Sick.

- ❑ Grace – *Sanctifying grace* makes us holy and pleasing to God. *Actual grace* helps us to do good and avoid evil.

- ❑ The seven gifts of the Holy Spirit – wisdom, understanding, counsel, fortitude, knowledge, piety and fear of the LORD.

ACKNOWLEDGEMENTS

We wish to acknowledge the contributions of so many men and women identified throughout *Knights to Christ*. We especially wish to recognize three men who have made a number of contributions to this daily reflection book, all of whom are members of the Knights of Columbus:

Fr. Mark Link, S.J.   www.v2000.org/index.htm

Fr. Pat Umberger   www.frpat.com/

Dr. Scott Hahn   www.scotthahn.com/

Meetings start with a *Call to Prayer*. A member lights a candle and
the following prayer is said reverently:

FIRST READER
Jesus said, "I am the light of the world…
Whoever follows me will have the light of life
And will never walk in darkness." ~ John 8:12

SECOND READER
Lord Jesus,
You also said that where two or three come together in your name,
You are there with them.
The light of this candle symbolizes your presence among us.

THIRD READER
And, Lord Jesus,
Where you are,
There too are the Father and the Spirit.
And so we begin our meeting in the presence and name
Of the Father,
The Son,
And the Holy Spirit.

Closing Meetings

All meetings end with a *Call to Mission*: a charge to witness to Jesus in daily life. It consists in reverently praying the following:

FIRST READER
We conclude our meeting by listening to Jesus say to us
What he said to his disciples in his Sermon on the Mount:

SECOND READER
"You are like light for the whole world. A city built on a hill cannot be hid...

No one lights a lamp and puts it under a bowl;
Instead, it is put on a lamp stand,
Where it gives light for everyone in the house.

In the same way
Your light must shine before people,
So that they will see the good things you do
And praise your Father in heaven. ~ Matthew 5:14-16

At this point, a member of the group extinguishes the candle that was lit at the beginning of the meeting. Then the final reader continues:

FINAL READER
The light of this candle is now extinguished.
But the light of Christ in each of us must continue to shine in our lives.
Toward this end, we pray together the LORD's Prayer:
"Our Father..."

Knights

to

Christ

is a daily meditation program
for Knights of Columbus
members seeking Christ

These devotions were compiled by
Knights for Knights. Please send your
comments, testimonials and inquiries to:

K2C@KofC-Colorado.org

To obtain ordering information:

http://www.kofc-colorado.org/K2C/index.html

Or call Toll free: 1-800-796-4166
(24hr voice mail or fax)

Knights

to

Christ

A 365-day devotion program
for Knights of Columbus
members seeking Christ.

These devotions were compiled by
Deacon Tom Fox. Please contact our
webmaster, feedback, and inquiries at:

KofC4th.Colorado.org

To obtain ordering information:

http://www.KofC-colorado.org/K2CBind_x.html

Or call Toll Free 1-800-766-3166
(Leave your name and/or fax)